Dear Reader,

Congratulations on picking up the latest real-life thriller by acclaimed investigative journalist M. William Phelps. You are about to experience a gripping and provocative true story that illuminates the best—and the worst—of human nature in a drama of powerful passions, cold-blooded murder, and ultimate justice.

Fans of M. William Phelps will recognize his uniquely compelling storytelling skills. Those new to his masterful narrative style will be happy to add him to their lists of favorite authors. And I think readers everywhere will be riveted, as I was, upon seeing this shocking story unfold.

Deep in the heart of Pennsylvania's Amish country, Michael Roseboro and his wife seemed to have it all—a beautiful family, a stunning home, and plenty of money. But Jan's murder led to an investigation that exposed the festering lies at the heart of their lives together. A secret life, a mistress, and a cunning plot are just some of the elements in this headline-making case. Now M. William Phelps takes you to the heart of the story for the first time.

If you enjoy reading LOVE HER TO DEATH, we'd love to hear from you at *marketing@kensingtonbooks.com*.

Don't miss M. William Phelps's other acclaimed true-crime thrillers, available from Pinnacle!

Happy reading,

Michaela Hamilton

Michaela Hamilton
Executive Editor, Pinnacle True Crime

"Starts quickly and doesn't slow down. . . . Phelps consistently ratchets up the dramatic tension. His thorough research and interviews give the book a sense of growing complexity, richness of character, and urgency. . . . A great true-crime story."

—Stephen Singular

"Phelps's sharp attention to detail culminates in this meticulous re-creation of a tragic crime. This gripping true story reads like a well-plotted crime novel and proves that truth is not only stranger, but more shocking, than fiction. Riveting."

—Allison Brennan

Murder in the Heartland

"Drawing on interviews with law officers and relatives, the author has done significant research and—demonstrating how modern forensics and the Internet played critical, even unexpected roles in the investigation—his facile writing pulls the reader along."

—*St. Louis Post-Dispatch*

"Phelps expertly reminds us that when the darkest form of evil invades the quiet and safe outposts of rural America, the tragedy is greatly magnified. Get ready for some sleepless nights."

—Carlton Stowers

Sleep in Heavenly Peace

"An exceptional book by an exceptional true-crime writer. Phelps exposes long-hidden secrets and reveals disquieting truths."

—Kathryn Casey

Every Move You Make

"An insightful and fast-paced examination of the inner workings of a good cop and his bad informant, culminating in an unforgettable truth-is-stranger-than-fiction climax."

—Michael M. Baden, M.D.

"M. William Phelps is the rising star of the nonfiction crime genre, and his true tales of murderers and mayhem are scary-as-hell thrill rides into the dark heart of the inhuman condition."

—Douglas Clegg

Lethal Guardian

"An intense roller coaster of a crime story . . . complex, with a plethora of twists and turns worthy of any great detective mystery, and yet so well-laid out, so crisply written with such detail to character and place that it reads more like a novel than your standard nonfiction crime book."

—Steve Jackson

Perfect Poison

"True crime at its best—compelling, gripping, an edge-of-the-seat thriller. Phelps packs wallops of delight with his skillful ability to narrate a suspenseful story and his encyclopedic knowledge of police procedures."

—Harvey Rachlin

"A compelling account of terror . . . the author dedicates himself to unmasking the psychopath with facts, insight and the other proven methods of journalistic legwork."

—Lowell Cauffiel

Also By M. William Phelps

Perfect Poison

Lethal Guardian

Every Move You Make

Sleep in Heavenly Peace

Murder in the Heartland

Because You Loved Me

If Looks Could Kill

I'll Be Watching You

Deadly Secrets

Cruel Death

Death Trap

Kill for Me

Failures of the Presidents (coauthor)

Nathan Hale: The Life and Death of America's First Spy

The Devil's Rooming House: The True Story of America's Deadliest Female Serial Killer

LOVE HER
TO
DEATH

M. WILLIAM
PHELPS

PINNACLE BOOKS
Kensington Publishing Corp.
http://www.kensingtonbooks.com

PINNACLE BOOKS are published by

Kensington Publishing Corp.
119 West 40th Street
New York, NY 10018

This book is dedicated to all victims of crime.

Author's Note

I conducted what are referred to as "deep background" interviews with many of the key players involved in this true story. Somewhere near two hundred interviews in all. Along with e-mail messages, memorandums, telephone records, letters, affidavits, suspect and witness interviews, trial testimony, and various other forms of documentation, I was able to create scenes that reflect the views of my most cooperative, trustworthy, and vociferous sources.

I interviewed lots of sources who knew Michael Roseboro, Jan Roseboro, Angie Funk, and their families, many of whom would like to remain anonymous—along with scores of others connected to these people by various degrees of separation. In the end, those I expected to talk, talked; and those I suspected wouldn't talk, didn't talk. This happens with each book I write.

That all being said, there was so much information available in the public record (and beyond) that this story, literally, told itself.

I hope you—the ever-important reader—agree and enjoy.

BOOK ONE

THE UNDERTAKER AND THE PO-PO

Two Ways there are: one of Life and one of Death, and there is a great difference between the Two Ways.

—*The Didache*

1

She was fighting for her life. That was about all East Cocalico Township Police Department (ECTPD) patrolman Michael "Mike" Firestone knew as he sat behind the wheel of his cruiser, flipped on the lights and siren, and sped off.

It took Firestone five minutes to get to the Roseboro residence in Reinholds, Pennsylvania, from the ECTPD, in nearby Denver, after the call from Lancaster County-Wide Communications (LCWC) had come in. "The reporting person," Firestone was told along the way, meaning the 911 caller, "had woken up and found his wife in a swimming pool on the property."

And that was all Patrolman Firestone knew going into the situation. Yet, that name, *Roseboro* . . . It was synonymous in this part of Lancaster County with wealth, status, good standing. You mention the name Roseboro to any store clerk or Denver native and you'd likely hear, *Don't they own that funeral home?*

Indeed, the Roseboro family had been morticians for over a century.

On that night, July 22, 2008, at nine minutes after eleven, Firestone pulled into the Roseboros' driveway off Creek Road, a half-tarred, half-gravel, slight uphill path heading toward a white garage off to the right. The massive home took up the entire corner lot of West Main Street (Route 897) and Creek Road. The smaller garage Firestone had pulled up in front of faced the east end of the Roseboros' pool, the back of the home itself. This smaller garage stood about twenty to thirty feet in front of a much larger and longer cooplike structure used years ago to house turkeys when the land was a farm. On either side of the smaller garage were walkways, one heading toward the house, the other into the pool area. Looking, Firestone spotted emergency medical technician (EMT) Cory Showalter, who had been called on his pager and had driven from his house a half mile down the road, beating Firestone to the scene. Showalter, a thirty-year volunteer for Reinholds Ambulance, six years with the Adamstown Fire Department, was performing cardiopulmonary resuscitation (CPR) on a middle-aged, white female, with long, flowing blond hair, who was lying on the ground next to the pool. By trade, Showalter was a full-time painter, and he was quite familiar with the layout of the Roseboro house. He knew the Roseboro family personally, having been hired by Michael Roseboro to paint part of a new addition on the house.

"I saw," Showalter later said, "when I got there . . . I saw it was Mike that was—he was kneeling beside Jan."

Jan Roseboro, the forty-five-year-old wife of the undertaker, was on the ground.

Lifeless and unresponsive.

Firestone had an "immediate view" of the back side of the Roseboros' house as he parked and dashed from his car toward the pool deck area. After having trouble getting into the patio through the iron gate, because he could not get the latch to open, Firestone said later that he thought maybe Michael Roseboro had walked over and opened the gate from the inside for him. Either way, when Firestone got close enough to Roseboro, he noted that the husband appeared calm. His breathing was normal. Roseboro didn't appear to be sucking in or gasping for air, as if winded. He wasn't sweating, either. In fact, Roseboro seemed fairly "with it" for a man who had, only moments before, found his wife comatose inside the family swimming pool. Moreover, he "was not dripping wet, if he was wet at all," Firestone remembered. Calling 911 minutes prior, Roseboro said he had just pulled Jan out of the water.

Heading for the victim, Firestone noticed that Showalter was kneeling beside Jan, his hands crossed over her chest, shoulders hoisted upward, chest out, performing CPR. Jan was wearing a sweatshirt and shorts. She was on the ground, a halo of water stain on the concrete surrounding her body.

Because the Roseboros owned such a large corner lot (probably the biggest in the neighborhood), to the south of the pool area, heading toward the turkey house, was a wide open space, a grassy knoll fenced in by a line of trees and thorny pricker bushes and a swamplike ravine. Beyond that were three additional homes (all facing Creek Road), their backyards edging that wooded area, which was actually part of the Roseboros' property.

As Firestone came upon Showalter, he nodded to the EMT, who was working arduously to get Jan's motionless body to show any signs of life. Sirens were going off around them. The fire department, located on West Main Street, almost diagonally across from the Roseboro home, was but a five-minute walk from where they were.

Around him, Firestone noticed several—he wouldn't know the number until he later counted (six)—tiki torches set around the pool, on the opposite side of where Jan's body was positioned. All of them were burning. What was more, the entire area was well lit by spotlights from the house.

"Once I went through the gate and walked up to the edge of the pool," Firestone later said, ". . . I noticed there were interior pool lights on, as well as that dusk-to-dawn light, which was on the freestanding garage."

Michael Roseboro was dressed in what appeared to be (but no one was certain) red boxer shorts, nothing else. "It was either boxer shorts or a swimsuit," someone on the scene later said.

Roseboro stood nearby, Firestone observed, with no expression on his face.

"It was noticeable how *not* upset he seemed to be," Firestone later remarked.

Perhaps the guy was in such a state of shock, denial, or both, he didn't know what to do with himself. Besides, it was better that the husband of the victim stayed back at this point.

Jan was positioned between the (deep end of the) pool and the main house, her head facing the back of the home, her feet partially in the water, hanging over the pool coping (edge mold). Her body was on a slab of the concrete decking bordering the pool. That sweatshirt and a sports bra she was wearing had been cut off her body.

Showalter had not seen any vomit around Jan. This told the experienced medic that she had not coughed up any water. Coming up on the body and Michael Roseboro moments before Firestone had arrived, Showalter had started CPR immediately, yelling to Roseboro, "Open my bag. . . . Get my airways out!"

Roseboro reacted quickly. He dug in the bag, found the piece of plastic, and then handed Showalter the oral airway, a small half-moon-shaped tube that medics stick in the mouth to keep the tongue down so air can get into the lungs as quickly as possible.

Firestone reacted like the pro he was, kneeling beside Jan, asking Showalter, "Do you need the AED?" The cop had the machine in his hand.

"Yes . . . please," Showalter said breathlessly.

"Get her feet out of the water." Firestone said it would

be impossible to use the automated external defibrillator (AED) if the person's feet were in the water, or the person was wet.

Firestone prepared the AED he had brought from his cruiser. The machine analyzes the rhythm of the heart. It would take a reading of Jan's vital signs and indicate whether to deliver a shock to Jan's heart with the paddles or continue manual CPR. Showalter wasn't getting a pulse. It didn't mean Jan was gone; it told them, perhaps alarmingly, that they needed to get her heart beating again before any major brain damage occurred, or there was no chance of getting a rhythm back. Neither Showalter nor Firestone had any idea how long Jan had been unconscious.

During this critical process of utilizing the AED, which Firestone, like all cops, had been trained to use, Showalter continued working on Jan. As they conducted this procedure together, an ambulance arrived, additional EMTs running toward the pool. Fire trucks pulled up and parked along Creek Road. Roseboro family members were beginning to arrive as well.

After briefly talking to Michael Roseboro, Firestone noticed that Jan's husband had walked off to the side and, smoking a cigarette, was talking on his cell phone.

Once the AED was hooked up to Jan's chest, the apparatus advised them *not* to shock Jan's heart, but to continue CPR, instead.

Was this good news? Did it mean Jan Roseboro was still alive?

Technically, she was. There was no doctor on scene to make a pronouncement of death. By all logical assumptions, however, it seemed Jan Roseboro had breathed her last. She was listless, cold to the touch, not moving. Pale. She had no heart rate or pulse. None of this, of course, was ever mentioned or talked about among those at the scene. To anyone there, watching the events transpire in front of them, it appeared that there was hope for Jan. EMTs were focused on reviving Jan Roseboro and getting her from the ground into the ambulance, then to the nearest hospital emergency room. By all accounts, Jan had only been unconscious and not breathing for minutes.

As Showalter continued CPR and, as Firestone later told it, "people more qualified than me" took over, the patrolman stepped away from Jan, looked around, found Michael Roseboro, and explained to Jan's husband that he needed to ask him a few questions.

You know, procedure. Formalities. For starters, "What happened?"

Roseboro was standing by a patio table, smoking, quietly watching what was going on, cell phone in hand. "I have no idea how long [she has] been in the pool," Roseboro said.

"Okay. But what happened?" Firestone asked again.

"I went to bed at approximately ten o'clock," Jan Roseboro's husband of nineteen years stated, "but Jan stayed outside in the pool area to watch the night sky. I was inside sleeping when I got up to go to the bathroom and noticed that the pool lights and outside torches were still lit." So Roseboro, after finishing up in the bathroom, walked outside to extinguish the tiki lamps and shut off the remaining lights. "When I entered the pool area . . . I noticed my wife in the deep end of the pool, retrieved a telephone, and immediately called 911. The operator advised me how to perform CPR, which I did until [everyone] arrived."

All Firestone had to do was some quick math to realize that Jan could have been in the water anywhere between one and sixty minutes, according to her husband's timeline. Roseboro said he went to bed at ten. The 911 call had been made at 11:02. Either way you added it up, it did not look good for Jan. Yet, Firestone never said any of this to Roseboro.

."Was Jan drinking?" Firestone asked. He was standing closer to Roseboro now and could smell alcohol on his breath.

"No," he said.

"Have *you* been drinking?"

"Yes. . . ."

"Were you swimming earlier tonight, Mr. Roseboro?"

"Yeah."

"Jan was not wearing swimming attire. Had she been swimming, too?"

"No."

A gurney was wheeled toward Jan as EMTs continued working on her. One of the medics put a suction device in Jan's mouth to extract any vomit that might have been lodged in her throat. Showalter later said he believed they were able to suction a small amount of vomit from Jan's mouth.

By now, maybe five minutes since Showalter and Firestone had responded to the scene, it seemed there were people everywhere.

Michael Roseboro—his and Jan's three youngest children inside the house sleeping through all of this—stood by and could only watch as his wife was hoisted onto a gurney and wheeled off toward the driveway and a waiting ambulance.

"His demeanor was sort of flat and calm," Firestone later said, referring to this moment. "Even rote."

One of the officers who had arrived on scene was off to the side calling into the station to get an investigator out there. Another cop regulation. Just a routine matter to check things out. Standard procedure after an incident like this.

Firestone and Roseboro stood together watching the medic wheel Jan away. There was "an uncomfortable lull there," Firestone remembered, "where we were kind of standing and staring at each other."

Breaking that silence, Firestone asked Roseboro, "Hey, is there a pastor or anybody I can call for you?"

"Yes . . . ," Jan's husband said. For some reason, before giving Firestone one of the names, Roseboro felt the need to then explain that he and Jan had separate churches they attended.

Roseboro never approached the ambulance. Nor had he asked Firestone or anyone else which hospital his wife was being taken to, how she was, if she was alive, or if she had died at the scene. Instead, he walked off and put his cell phone to his ear, lit another smoke, and dialed a number.

Firestone assumed Roseboro was calling family and friends. Maybe he was still in shock? Too upset to think or react.

"You can have your suspicions," Firestone commented later, "but you do your best to maintain a neutral and open mind."

Who knew what the guy was going through?

Just then, as the team worked to get Jan secured in back of the ambulance, Firestone noticed two young males walking hurriedly about the scene. They had that what-in-the-world-is-going-on look. One of them, the patrolman learned, was Michael and Jan Roseboro's oldest son, seventeen-year-old Samuel (Sam, they called him).

But where had the boy come from? Why had they shown up at *this* moment?

Then, as Firestone looked around the property for Michael Roseboro, it was as if the guy had vanished.

Michael Roseboro was nowhere to be found.

Maybe he finally got into the ambulance with his wife?

Quite shockingly, as medics got Jan Roseboro's heart beating again—if only mechanically—inside the ambulance as it took off, blood poured out of the back of her head, turning the pillow underneath red as paint, as if a vessel had burst.

There had not been a spot of blood out on the pool deck or inside the water.

Where in the world was all this blood coming from?

2

Someone yelled, "Ephrata Community Hospital."

Michael Roseboro was back outside and heard the comment. He had not gotten into the ambulance. He was also *told* by several professionals on scene where his wife was being taken. Jan was en route to a hospital about fifteen minutes across county. The ambulance attendants would continue CPR all the way to the emergency room (ER), where the mother of four would receive the best medical care available.

There was still a chance. Everyone has heard stories of people being dead fifteen, twenty, or even thirty minutes, only to be brought back to life at the hospital before telling a story about white lights and clouds and people from beyond.

Patrolman Firestone had watched the ambulance prepare to drive off. The vehicle was "very well lit" inside. From where he was standing inside the pool deck area, he'd had a clear view of what was going on and who was there.

Additional family members arrived. Phone records from the night indicate Michael Roseboro called his father, Ralph, at home, and then the family business, the Roseboro Funeral Home, which was closed at this hour, for some reason.

Michael had stayed at the house while Jan was whisked off. Perhaps he wanted to take his own vehicle and follow the ambulance? Or maybe wait for additional family members to show up? Still, there were plenty of people at the house to watch the kids if he wanted to be with Jan.

Why wasn't he leaving?

Firestone took a walk around the pool area. He had an eye and instinct for crime scenes, having worked in the Crime Scene Investigation (CSI) Unit for a time.

"I was looking for any signs of a struggle," Firestone said. "Anything that might stand out as suspicious."

Again, standard procedure. It wasn't that Firestone suspected anything—in fact, quite to the contrary. If nothing else, the Roseboro family, because of who they were and the business they ran, were given the benefit of the doubt more than most others might have been. The problem Firestone encountered from within was that he was trained to think outside the box and search for a reason why this woman—a seemingly healthy adult who had not been drinking—ended up fully clothed and unconscious inside her pool. There was an answer somewhere. Probably an explanation that was going to make a lot of sense as soon as the ECTPD uncovered it.

After a careful walk around, Firestone didn't see anything out of place. Every item—patio furniture, tables and chairs, and anything else associated with the pool area itself—"looked normal." Nothing had been disturbed. In addition, the scene didn't appear to be overly perfect, either, as if someone had gone around and tidied up. The area was well maintained and practical. At least by Firestone's opinion.

More than anything else, Firestone was looking for a sign, he later said, indicating Jan had accidentally stumbled and fallen into the pool. There were only a few scenarios that could have placed Jan in that pool—an accident, right now, at the top of the list. Yet, there should be some indication of what had happened.

"I was looking for blood and hair," Firestone added, "tissue, something of that nature, on the pool edge."

There had to be evidence left behind indicating that Jan had slipped, fallen, and hit her head.

But Firestone found nothing.

Coming around to the deep end of the pool, staring into the water, something caught Firestone's attention.

A cell phone?

The lights inside the pool were on, so it was easy to see to the bottom. As he came around the corner of the deep end, Firestone noticed the item, red in color, on the bottom of the pool.

Yes, a red cell phone was sitting there by a pair of what looked to be reading glasses and "two small brown stones." The stones were similar to those used in the landscaping around that particular section of the pool.

It was near this time that Officer Steve Savage showed up and began combing through the scene with Firestone. Michael Roseboro, who had not gone to the hospital as of yet, was also roaming around, being consoled by family members and friends. Up near the screened-in porch, on the opposite side of the deep end of the pool, where, according to Roseboro, he had found his wife, Firestone and Savage saw a bucket.

They walked over. Took a whiff.

The bucket, filled with a foamy fluid, smelled "heavily of a cleaning solution of some type," Firestone later noted.

Inside the bucket was a "whitish opaque fluid, and there appeared to be a rag floating in it."

A red rag.

3

Mike Texter had been best friends with Jan and Michael Roseboro's oldest child, Sam, for the past year. Mike had graduated just over a month ago from Cocalico High School and was planning to attend classes at Penn State Berks that coming fall, his focus on kinesiology, the science of studying the physical activity, or "movements," of human beings. On July 22, 2008, after he got out of work at 9:00 P.M., Mike headed over to one of his favorite places these days, the Roseboro residence, arriving somewhere near nine-thirty.

"I went there every night," Mike said later, "to hang out with Sam."

Mike parked his car in the gravel section of the driveway near the pool.

Sam met his friend outside. "What's up?"

"Hey," Mike said. After being let in, he walked around the pool toward the screened-in porch. "Hello, Mr. and Mrs. Roseboro," he said to Michael and Jan, who were sitting near each other on the concrete deck, poolside. All the lights were on. The night sky was brilliant. You could still count the stars with your finger. The moon glowed; pending rain clouds not yet visible.

Mike and Samuel headed into the pool house, grabbed

something to eat, watched a little television, and headed back out to the patio after another friend came by and asked if they wanted to go swimming at a fourth friend's house down the road.

As they left, Mike Texter later recalled in court, it was about 10:05 P.M. Michael Roseboro was sitting on the steps inside the pool, his arms out along the edge, half his body underwater, the other half above the waterline, the multicolored pool lights underwater shining on him.

"As far as I can remember," Mike said, ". . . [his] chest would have been exposed out of the water, swimming trunks, legs, would have been in."

Jan was lying on the ground in back of her husband, seemingly content with the wonder of such a glorious night. All the lights were on, Mike said. The tiki lamps, the pool lights, the dawn-to-dusk floodlight out in back of the house hanging off the garage like a kitchen faucet.

"See you later," the kids said to Jan and Michael.

They left.

After swimming for an hour, as they were getting ready to head out to McDonald's for a late-night snack, Mike Texter and Sam Roseboro heard sirens and wondered what was going on in town. Then Sam got word that an ambulance was at his house, so he and Mike took off.

Pulling up, seeing everyone milling about the Roseboros' backyard, Sam wondered what had happened.

One of the first things Mike Texter noticed as he walked up was that Michael Roseboro was wearing those same red swim trunks he had on while sitting in the water a little over an hour earlier. Here was a kid prone to noticing those light shades of human behavior that many of us take for granted.

Asked later what Roseboro was wearing, which would become a key issue in the weeks and months ahead, Mike said, "I believe they were red swim trunks. . . . To my knowledge, the same red swim trunks [he was wearing before] I left."

Realizing that Jan Roseboro was in an ambulance on her way to the hospital, fighting for her life, Sam Roseboro and Mike Texter ran into the house to find out what had happened.

4

Detective Larry Martin had just fallen asleep. That night, a Tuesday, the veteran detective from a liberal Mennonite background had been working in his garden before watching a little television and then heading off to bed to read. It was a few minutes after eleven o'clock when a ringing telephone rustled Martin awake.

The balding white-haired detective, with penetrating blue eyes, had a feeling it wasn't going to be good news— what else could it be at that hour? A call in the middle of the night is never someone expressing gratitude for a favor, or a family member with an invite to a party. In over twenty years of law enforcement experience, Martin had been shuffled out of bed more times than he cared to remember. Yet, inside the boundaries of what had been a simple way of life in rural Lancaster County, Pennsylvania, those calls usually revolved around a deer struck by a car, maybe a brawl at a neighborhood bar that had gotten out of hand, an out-of-towner or couple of punk kids bothering an Amish family who were out minding their own business, trotting along the country roads in a black-as-a-hearse buggy, or perhaps a suicide that, at first glance, didn't look so cut-and-dry. For Detective Larry Martin, the phone ringing when the stars were bright, and his officers knew he was sound asleep, generally meant he was going to have to get himself dressed and head back out the door.

Ugh!

Martin got up and looked at the clock by his bed. It was 11:03 P.M. on the nose, the detective noted to himself. For the next fifty-seven minutes, it was still July 22, 2008, a calm, peaceful night by most standards.

As he listened to the officer explain how he was heading out to a possible adult drowning, with others on the scene already, Martin believed from that first moment this call was not going to be routine. Something was up.

"Look, Sergeant, this lady, Jan Roseboro, was pulled out of her pool," the officer explained. "Doesn't look good. . . . They're giving her CPR right now."

Martin knew the name and said it a few times in his head: *Roseboro.* He had bumped into Jan Roseboro's husband, Michael, on the job from time to time. Michael Roseboro was the local mortician, Martin knew. He and his family had owned and operated Roseboro Funeral Home in Denver, just a five-minute ride from the police department, for well over one hundred years, three generations. Roseboro had often shown up, Martin thought to himself, at death scenes to pick up bodies. An elderly lady would die in her sleep and Roseboro was right there, helping the family, consoling them, telling widows and widowers alike that all would be okay, he'd take care of everything. Roseboro and Martin would chitchat. You know, *How's it going?* Nothing personal. Just men out in the world doing their jobs best they can. Forty-one-year-old Michael Roseboro knew his business; he was well liked and highly respected, in and around Lancaster County. Martin knew this because he had seen it himself on the job.

Boy . . . that's odd, Martin thought as the officer gave him the weak details he had at the time. *Adult people don't normally drown in their own pools.*

The officer explained how he had just gotten to the

scene himself and spoke to a few people, this after
Michael Roseboro called 911.

"Let me ask you," Martin questioned his officer, "do
you know if she was drunk?" Any cop knew, excessive alcohol use and swimming were not a good mix.

"I don't know that," the officer responded. "But
there's no indication."

By now, Jan was long gone from the scene—on her way
to the hospital. The first officers responding, Mike Firestone and Steve Savage, Martin soon found out, had
asked a few people around the Roseboros' home, which
recently had undergone an expansive and expensive
addition, if Jan had been drinking. All indications thus
far were that she had not been. On top of this, there
was no evidence of it. Not an empty glass of wine or a
beer bottle. According to her husband, Jan was a fan of
going out and looking at the stars, sitting by the pool,
contemplating—one could only guess—life.

"I'll be heading out there," Martin told the officer. "I
just want to make sure, and interview some people."

Because it seemed so strange for an adult to end up
drowned in her own pool, Martin wanted to cross every
t and dot every *i*. As a thorough cop, you do that by
speaking to whoever was around the house at the time
of the incident. There would be reports to write, lots and
lots of paperwork. Martin was awake, anyway. Why not
check it out himself?

Martin was no newbie. He understood how things
worked: insurance companies and coroners. It was best
just to take a spin out there and get a firsthand account.
There was probably a sad, but extremely logical, explanation to the entire ordeal. Maybe Jan had fallen and hit
her head? It appeared she was outside by herself. Maybe
she decided on a late-night swim by herself? Martin
knew of warnings about swimming by yourself at night.
Cramp in the leg. Heart attack. Slip and fall. Any number
of things could lead to an adult drowning.

Suicide was always on the table, too.

Martin hung up with the officer. Next, he called Keith Neff, one of two detectives, besides himself, whom Martin had on staff. Kerry Sweigart, Martin's other detective, was on vacation. Thirty-eight-year-old Keith Neff was a vivacious and hyper cop who had never, in his career of more than eleven years, investigated a murder. He was a wiry, skinny guy, who had what his sparring partners might call "cauliflower ears," flaps of skin mushroomed over and bent from all the ground fighting, grappling, and Brazilian jiujitsu that Neff did in his spare time. He was at home, sleeping, his wife by his side, and two kids down the hall.

Martin got no answer on Neff's Nextel, so he left a message.

As Martin got dressed, Neff called to ask what was going on. Burglary and thefts (property crime) were Neff's beat. There had been an explosion of burglaries in and around the Denver/Reinholds area lately.

Had another Turkey Hill convenience store been hit?

"Hey," Martin said, "we have several officers on the scene of what appears to be a reported drowning. Meet me at the station and we'll go up there together."

Groggily, rubbing sleep from his eyes, Neff said, "Okay, Lar (pronounced 'lair'), see you at the station."

5

The Pennsylvania sky looked menacing as Detective Sergeant Larry Martin and Detective Keith Neff met at the ECTPD station house near midnight on July 22. In the starless Lancaster County night, where light pollution is generally at an absolute minimum, the clouds, black as motor oil, swirled like ink in water, no doubt preparing to put on a show. The air was moist, thick, heavy.

By the time Martin and Neff grabbed what they needed and headed out to the Roseboro residence on West Main Street, just on the Denver/Reinholds town line, it was a balmy 72 degrees, just a few minutes after midnight, now July 23. The humidity level had spiked off the charts at a whopping 93 percent; this, mind you, while a composed, subtle haze—which could now be called a slight drizzle—settled down on the region, inspiring the wipers on Neff's white Chevy Impala to pulsate back and forth.

"Odd," Martin said again, thinking out loud, Neff nodding in agreement as he drove, "that an adult could drown in her own pool."

Kids, yeah. Teens fooling around, sure. Those things sometimes happened. But sober adults? Not so much.

And this was certainly not a scenario either of these two cops had ever heard of or encountered before.

Still, Neff and Martin knew better. There is a first for everything. And the only way to be sure was to have a look at the scene, ask a few questions of the family and Michael Roseboro, then hopefully head back home and go back to bed.

"That's what we thought, anyway," Neff said later, "as we headed out there. But, boy, were we wrong."

The ECTPD isn't the type of law enforcement agency brimming with detectives out in the field investigating a laundry list of murder cases, like perhaps in nearby Reading, Allentown, or downtown Lancaster City. In fact, as the summer of 2008 commenced, it had been years since the ECTPD had investigated a single murder case, and over ten since a murder case wasn't actually solved within a few hours.

According to a history of the department, it was 1838 when the Township of Cocalico was divided into Ephrata and East and West Cocalico. Legend has it that Cocalico was a name given by the local Native Americans, back before the Revolutionary War. Translated, *cocalico* means "den of snakes."

The ECTPD was formally organized in the early 1970s. In 1978, according to the department's website, the ECTPD began to provide police service to the Borough of Adamstown under a contractual agreement. It wasn't until 1986 that West Cocalico Township contracted out the department's services. In 1995, the Borough of Denver joined.

That all said, the ECTPD provides law enforcement coverage to an area of approximately fifty square miles and twenty-two thousand people, including the gorgeous rolling hills of the Amish, Mennonite, and Pennsylvania Dutch farming regions housing somewhere just south of ten thousand. The department employs twenty-two full-time officers and two full-time civilian employees, which breaks down into two sergeants, three corporals, fourteen patrolmen, two detectives, and the chief.

Located just outside Denver, a farming community of a little over four thousand, the ECTPD is located in the bottom floor of what looks like an old library, but is actually the Town Services Department. There's a $75,000 crime scene van with all the latest high-tech gadgets parked out back—a gift during the Homeland Security frenzy of bloated government funding—that is rarely ever used, simply because Lancaster County has a team of forensic investigators and crime scene techs at its disposal.

Things are generally slow in the Denver/Reinholds part of the county, and burglary, fueled by an obsession some Americans have with old-school drugs, such as heroin and crack cocaine, is the most popular problem rousting cops from behind their desks.

Or out of bed in the middle of the night.

Keith Neff and Larry Martin considered that Michael Roseboro had to be feeling this pretty darn hard—and was probably frantic and an emotional mess, holding his wife's hand as paramedics and hospital personnel worked on Jan at the hospital. The guy must be going out of his mind. From what Martin and Neff had been told, it appeared that it was Michael Roseboro who had found his wife in the pool, jumped in, and fished her out. Medics had taken Jan away and, theoretically, she was still being worked on.

But things didn't look so good for the mother and wife.

Even though, in his profession, Roseboro had dealt with dead bodies on a daily basis, and had probably been desensitized to death at this point—having been around skin white as chalk, purple fingernails, and cold-as-steel body temperatures for the better part of his life—this was his wife. The mother of his four children.

Things had to be different when it's someone you love. Michael Roseboro himself had talked about how difficult it was working on and being around the body of a family member. E-mailing a friend after his grandfather had died less than a month prior, in June, Roseboro had said he "just got done [with] the embalming" of his eighty-nine-year-old grandpa, E. Louis Roseboro, the patriarch of the Roseboro clan, when "a lot of emotions and thoughts" kicked up and started to burden him. Grandpa Roseboro had lived a long, productive life. But still, preparing a family member's body for burial, seeing him or her lying there on a slab, hoses and needles sticking into the skin, their mouth wired shut, was tough. And now this: Jan, with whom Michael Roseboro was just about to renew his marital vows during an extended vacation to North Carolina in front of a host of friends and family. Jan, the woman everybody adored and loved, was fighting for her life.

How could it be?

Martin and Neff were about to begin looking for that answer.

6

Martin and Neff drove into Reinholds via Hill and Creek Roads. It was probably going to be a quick in and out. At least, that's what they hoped. Speak to a few people, find out what happened to Jan, say a silent prayer, hoping doctors could revive her back at the ER, and then head back home to get some sleep before the sun rose and another day started.

Forty-five-year-old Larry Martin had five kids whom his wife homeschooled. From there, Martin's family tree spread out like roots to three siblings and a whopping twenty-eight cousins. Besides one sister, who had moved to Queens, New York, Martin's Mennonite family had stayed in the confines of Lancaster County—Amish-Mennonite-Pennsylvania Dutch central—for generations.

"As far as I know," Martin said later, "all of my cousins' children live in Lancaster or the neighboring Berks County—which is probably around seventy-five."

In these parts, "family" means *family,* in every sense of the word. It's safe to say Larry Martin knew everybody, and—perhaps more important to how much his professional life was about to be transformed by what at first appeared to be a routine drowning—everybody knew Larry Martin.

Neff parked the Impala in the driveway. The scene was bustling with people, both detectives noticed. Fire trucks and cop cars and medic vehicles lined up and down both streets straddling the Roseboros' corner lot. The backyard was overflowing with friends and family and other people. Neighbors were just now turning on their lights and emerging from their homes, no doubt curious and unnerved by all the commotion.

It was 12:22 A.M. when Neff and Martin started up the driveway and walked into the backyard. As Neff went to unlatch the gate into the pool area, "I had trouble with it," he said later, noting to himself how difficult the thing was to open. Probably for good reason: Michael and Jan Roseboro did not want some curious toddler or teen sneaking into the pool and falling in. Yet, it was so difficult for Neff to open, "I had to actually ask for assistance," he added, "to get in the gate the first time I went in."

ECTPD officers Mike Firestone, Gail Sizer, and Steve Savage briefed Neff and Martin about what was going on as a light rain began to fall a bit steadier now.

The Roseboro house was by far the largest and most contemporary in the neighborhood. In fact, the initial house itself, a World War II-era Cape, was buried—lost and swallowed up—inside the new addition, rendered nearly unnoticeable. If one looked at the house from West Main Street (the front yard), the new addition started from the left side and continued in an L-shaped pattern to nearly the corner of the lot. From the corner, it stretched into the back, ending in a T shape, a court-yard and patio in the middle of it all, leading into the stone deck surrounding the spacious, inkblot-shaped in-ground pool. Think of the house as three separate ranch-style homes connected together, laid out in a horseshoe, with the pool almost inside the open end. A lot of planning and thought had gone into the making of this custom home. As one family friend later put it:

"Jan and Mike hired architects and builders, and Mike supervised *every* aspect of the building process."

It was an addition that had just been completed as the summer of 2008 began.

What Neff and Martin soon learned—a few simple facts that would become important to the case as the night wore on—was that, spread out around the outside of the home, including that dusk-to-dawn light on the peak of the garage roof nearly overlooking the pool, were floodlights and "soft" lights, not to mention that series of tiki torches and underwater pool lights in the deck area. The grounds of the entire Roseboro home were always well lit up, neighbors and friends and family said.

Neff and Martin spoke with Firestone first. There seemed to be a lot of people in the house. Even more family and friends had arrived. Neighbors and onlookers were beginning to emerge and settle around the house.

"Mike Roseboro told me he went to bed at around ten," Firestone explained, looking down at his notes. "Jan, his wife, stayed outside to watch the night sky. He said he got up to use the bathroom and saw that the torch lights were still lit."

It made sense. At that time of the night, it had been clear out; and, arguably, a person could have wanted to go outside, especially out here, where the sky on a clear night is as dark and sparkling as a planetarium. The pool was part of the massive new addition. The tiki torch lamps along the southwest side of the deck were permanent, not the kind you impulsively buy at the local Walmart or supermarket. All of the torches were equally spaced around one side of the pool, the last two of the bunch positioned between the stone walkway into the pool deck area, one on each side. There was a black cast-iron fence, those pointy medieval-like spikes at approximately five feet two inches high all the way around the pool, the only way into the deck area from the yard being through the gate that Neff had had so much trouble unlatching.

"Anything else?" Neff asked.

Martin stood by his side, curious already as to the circumstances. Something just wasn't sitting right with the veteran detective.

"Mr. Roseboro said he went to attend to the torch-lights and saw Jan in the deep end of the pool. He said he pulled her from the pool, retrieved a phone, called 911, and started CPR. I spotted a pair of glasses, some stones, and a cell phone on the bottom of the pool."

Martin was curious. There were people in the yard. Lots of people.

"Yeah," Firestone noted, looking around, "the Rose-boros' son Sam and a friend . . . came home while we were working on her."

"Did you tell Mike Roseboro anything?" Neff wondered.

"Well, I explained to him that based on my experience his wife had probably died. But the ambulance people, I told him, were still working on her and she would get more treatment at the hospital. I explained that a medical doctor would have to make the call whether she died."

Martin stopped him. *"Was* she pronounced?"

"Yeah, at the hospital."

Jan Roseboro was dead. The actual time of death was 11:57 P.M., July 22, 2008. But no one had told Michael Roseboro any of this. He had no idea what was going on, and, surprisingly, had never asked. He had not driven to the hospital or demanded to go in the ambulance. Nor had anyone given him status information on Jan. Yet, everyone walking around was under the assumption (or impression) that Jan Roseboro had died. How in the heck did they know? Did someone call the hospital?

When Martin heard that CPR had been performed from the time police arrived until Jan left in an ambulance, he didn't assume she was going to die, but "my gut told me it was not a good situation. I've heard of them bringing people back."

In any case, with Jan's death came a new set of investigatory problems for the ECTPD. It was going to be a long night. Even accidental drownings can take cops hours upon hours to clear, not to mention all the interviews and paperwork.

Martin found Neff, who had been roaming around, trying to get a feel for the scene. The rain had let up some, yet there was rumbling off in the distance, along with flashes of light. A whopper of a storm was rolling in. You could almost smell it.

"Hey, Keith, she was pronounced," Martin told his detective.

"No kidding," Neff said. He felt bad. By now, they knew that Jan had four children; three of them young kids, the oldest, Sam, just seventeen.

Neff needed to talk with anyone on the scene willing. For Martin, he found it odd that Michael Roseboro was *still* at the house. Watching Roseboro work the crowd around him, Martin thought, *Why is he not at the hospital?*

7

In 1997, Keith Neff transferred from a police force in Reading, which had been in turmoil, a city undergoing a crisis of crime, to the ECTPD. Before that, he had worked part-time for a half year with a police department in Berks County. By the time Neff became a detective in March 2004, just four years before he found himself at Michael Roseboro's house investigating a seemingly uncomplicated and accidental adult drowning, he was experienced in various degrees of police work—with the exception of murder. Murder, if truth be told, was something Neff had never investigated. In the ECTPD there were only two other detectives, including Neff's boss, Larry Martin.

"And I was an add-on," Neff said, "only because there were too many investigations going on for the one detective and Larry."

Neff had not taken the normal path into a career as a police officer, although his stepfather was a state police officer in Pennsylvania for twenty-seven years, and some of that, no doubt, had rubbed off on him. Neff had gone to school for exercise science, physical education, strength and conditioning, with dreams of perhaps one day becoming a trainer for a professional sports team or a local college. He learned quickly after graduation, however, that physical training was not as lucrative or in demand as he might have thought.

"I had trouble paying my bills," Neff explained. He got married. Bought a house. Wanted to start a family (two kids would come later, in 2001 and 2006). And now found himself facing responsibilities. "So I started looking into police work. Possibly maybe getting into the state police and ending up at the academy doing physical conditioning."

The best of both worlds.

Before he became a detective, as a patrol officer for the ECTPD, the shift was "killing me," Neff said. On a good day, he clocked in at 155 pounds. Working the graveyard shift, he added, "I wouldn't eat. Couldn't sleep. I was losing weight. . . ." Ten pounds at a clip. And for a guy his size, Neff couldn't afford to lose _any_ amount. Yet, in noting Neff's small physique and weight, don't let any of it fool you. The guy has trained as a Brazilian jiujitsu ground fighter for a decade, owning and running several schools, and was recently awarded his black belt in the sport by none other than Royler Gracie, David Adiv, and Rosendo Diaz. Gracie and his family, all of whom hail from Brazil, are single-handedly responsible for bringing Brazilian jiujitsu into the States and making the sport what it is today.

The job of detective was a position you tested for. So Neff took the examination, passed, and was offered a desk and a badge.

In his four years as a detective, Neff had never testified in a jury trial. He'd been scheduled a few times, but the defendants pled out. Just as well. Like most detectives, Neff preferred being out in the field, solving cases, not necessarily having to explain them later in great detail in front of a room of strangers, some of whom are looking to tangle you up with your own words.

* * *

As Keith Neff walked the scene and looked for the opportunity to speak with Michael Roseboro, he considered the only case of an adult drowning he had ever seen. It was a man who had ingested way too much alcohol and had decided to swim across a lake—and failed to make it to the other side.

Neff noticed that Michael Roseboro was standing off in the back of the house inside the screened-in porch, surrounded by family, including his son Sam. The other three children, Neff and Larry Martin learned, were still sleeping. Neff later estimated that near "thirty people" were roaming around the scene—family, friends, neighbors, cops, medics, fire personnel. And even with everything going on, the children did not wake up.

Strange.

Neff spoke to a few of the medics, got their stories, then walked the perimeter of the pool, looking for anything different. The idea was to get a mental picture of the scene and then lock people down to whatever it was they wanted to say, all while getting to the facts of what happened. There was no cause for alarm just because the police were still present at the scene; it was protocol. Any death needed to be explained. Didn't matter how it happened.

"Mike Roseboro," someone close to the case later lamented, "stood off to the side away from where the body had been."

"He never came up and asked any questions," Neff said. "Or even, 'How's it look?' He just never asked anybody, 'How is Jan doing?' Where she was. Or what was going on. He had surrounded himself with this group of people who were, it seemed, protecting him."

The question was: From what? What did Michael Roseboro have to hide?

A family reputation, for one. The wife of a wealthy

undertaker drowns in her own pool. Sounded as creepy
as the guy's chosen profession. People were going to ask
questions. Point fingers. Michael Roseboro must have
felt the need to watch out for himself and his family.

It was near one o'clock in the morning. Officer Savage
called Larry Martin from the hospital. Savage had followed the ambulance and stayed with Jan. Savage told
Martin that doctors had found a noticeable "mark
behind the victim's ear." A pronounced wound of some
sort that went deep. One of the only reasons they noticed
the wound was because Jan had started bleeding inside
the ambulance on the way to the hospital as medics pumped
life back into her heart and it started beating, if only mechanically. Lying outside on the deck, Jan had not bled,
because her heart had stopped beating. But the head
bleeds copiously, like no other part of the body.

Martin spoke to Dr. Steven Zebert at the hospital. It
being such a small community, Zebert and Martin knew
each other. "What do you think, Doctor?" Martin asked.

"Man, this is a deep wound, Larry. It goes all the way
to the skull. I'm not even one hundred percent sure it's
not a bullet wound!"

Martin was shocked by the suggestion. "Huh?"

"But listen, I am going to send her downstairs for an
X-ray and we'll find out."

"Thank you, Doctor," Martin said, flipping his cell phone
closed.

This comment, at least for Larry Martin, made the situation a bit more fluid, if not downright mysterious.
Martin asked who was awake inside the house—and if
any of the kids were up.

He wanted to speak to them.

They were all sleeping.

The injury was later described as a "puncture wound . . .

to the left side of [Jan's] head . . . behind the left ear approximately one centimeter in diameter." About the size and shape, in other words, of a bullet wound. And wouldn't you know it, the wound was in the exact place a hit man or someone who knew how to kill would place a pistol and fire.

One shot.

Pop.

Done.

Detective Martin thought about it. *Bullet wound? Puncture to the back of the head?* If she had not been shot, had Jan fallen, hit her head, and maybe rolled into the pool and drowned? Perhaps Michael Roseboro was so distressed over the idea of not being there for his wife when she needed him that he was upset and wanted to crawl into a corner somewhere. That would explain his odd behavior. The guy was possibly blaming himself for what had happened.

Martin gave Keith Neff this new information. Yet it occurred to Neff after surveying the scene fairly meticulously that there was no blood *anywhere* outside. How could she have fallen, hit her head hard enough to produce such a severe wound, and not leave any blood behind?

"This rain," Neff said. It had come down hard, in intervals. It was one of those midsummer downpours that seem to come out of nowhere and dump bucket loads of rain and then abruptly stop, only to begin again minutes later. The rain could have washed away any blood, concealing where Jan had fallen.

"Of course, I don't want to overlook the obvious," Neff later explained, talking about what he was thinking as he walked the scene. "But I still need to stay focused and not get too zeroed in on *anything* in the beginning of an investigation."

Anything was possible.

* * *

According to Keith Neff's meticulous notes of that night, it was 1:07 A.M. when he approached Michael Roseboro for the first time. In his gentle manner, soft-spoken and congenial, Neff asked Roseboro, "I was hoping you could come down to the station and talk about what happened." Neff explained that the ECTPD was obligated to fill out reports and get statements from everyone it could. Since Roseboro was the person who had found his wife, his input might help clear up things. During this short conversation, Neff never told Roseboro that his wife had died at the hospital.

And Michael Roseboro never asked.

"Sure," Roseboro said, responding to a trip downtown.

The guy was preoccupied and flat, Neff observed. No emotion one way or the other. Family members nearby—Neff didn't know at this point whose side of the family they were from—gave Neff a feeling that he was not wanted. There was a sadness there for what had happened, implicit on the faces of everyone. But it was overshadowed in some ways by an eerie feeling of coldness, Neff later explained. It made the detective feel that in the Roseboro house, men in blue were the enemy. That Neff and his cohorts from the ECTPD were unwelcome guests and needed to leave at once.

8

Jan and Michael Roseboro's friends Rebecca Donahue and Gary Frees offered to drive Roseboro to the ECTPD so he could speak with Keith Neff and Larry Martin. It had to be done. Roseboro needed to clear up any confusion, add any details he could, so Detective Neff, now the lead investigator, could write his reports. After that was done, Roseboro could focus on perhaps the most important part of the ordeal thus far: preparing his three youngest children, who were still sound asleep back at the house, for what would be the worst news of their lives. Sam was the only Roseboro child to know what had happened. Sam was back at the scene, family surrounding him, some later claimed, walking around the pool deck area, smoking cigarettes, and, one might guess, searching for answers.

A teacher of special education, Rebecca Donahue lived about a mile away from the Roseboro house. She had known Jan for "a little over ten years," Rebecca later said, and considered herself to be Jan's best friend. Before Jan and Michael had moved into Jan's childhood home on West Main and Creek Road, they lived "two houses down from me, and across the street from my mother, and we were together often. My kids were at her house, and her kids were at my house, staying overnight and [on] holidays [and] birthdays." Rebecca Donahue had been over to the Roseboro house socially on Sunday and Monday of that week. It was gut-wrenching for Rebecca to think that Jan was no longer going to be there to talk to, or whiz by with the kids, stop in, maybe have a cup of coffee or a glass of wine. It was those subtle, everyday experiences we think are just simply part of our daily lives we miss the most after tragedy strikes. The way in which Rebecca was notified that something had happened to Jan was enough, in and of itself, to jolt her into the stark reality that Jan was gone forever. Rebecca had been sleeping. Susan Van Zant, Jan's sister, had tried calling, but Rebecca wasn't answering her phone. So Susan grabbed Mike Texter and drove over to Rebecca's house. Susan was frantic. Crying. Shaking. She had walked in, found Rebecca, and put it as bluntly as possible: "Jan's gone. . . . She had a heart attack and fell in the pool and drowned."

Yet no one, by that time of the night (near midnight), had said how Jan had died, or if Jan was even dead. Susan Van Zant, better known as Suzie, was telling people Jan was gone before the ER doctor had pronounced her.

During the quick ride, in which Gary Frees drove and Rebecca Donahue sat in the back, Michael Roseboro was quiet. Frees, Jan's sister Suzie's boyfriend at the time, had known Jan and Michael for just over a year.

Neff and Martin were ready and waiting for Roseboro, who walked into the lobby of the ECTPD through the glass doors around to the back of the town building. The ECTPD's foyer is about a five-by-ten-foot area of white-washed concrete cinder block walls. There are a few stiff and uncomfortable chairs for sitting on each side as you walk in. There's a bulletin board with posters reminding the public that crime doesn't pay and that drugs make you stupid and put you in prison. Directly facing people as they enter, there's a door leading into the small "squad room" office space, and another door, to the right, leading into the two-cell holding tank and booking station.

Small-town Andy Griffith stuff.

Sitting in the lobby, waiting for Detectives Neff and Martin, Roseboro was quiet. The room was well lit, and Gary Frees sat on one side of the lobby, Roseboro on the other, directly across from him, just a few feet between the two men.

Frees noticed that Roseboro "kept dabbing," as he later put it, at his face—and that something was "oozing," Frees added, from an area around Roseboro's chin and upper lip. Roseboro had recently grown a salt-and-pepper goatee. Still, "I took notice that he was wiping his upper lip," Frees said later. "Just . . . there was oozing coming out of his upper lip. He was wiping that with his finger. You could actually see it was oozing blood."

Watching Roseboro dab at his lip, that blood obvious in the fluorescent light of the ECTPD lobby, Frees wondered, *Did you cut yourself shaving?*

He decided, however, not to say anything.

Neff came out of the squad room and into the lobby. He asked Roseboro to follow him. All he wanted, Neff explained in not so many words, was a timeline from Roseboro of the day and night. He needed to know if Jan had been drinking. If, perhaps, she had been complaining of any pain the previous day, or later on that night. Was there anything out of the ordinary or odd that had struck Roseboro regarding his wife? Tests on Jan's blood would take time. Who knew if Jan wasn't some sort of a closeted alcoholic. Or maybe a drug addict.

Secrets . . . everybody's got 'em. When you die, they emerge gradually, like the grass over your grave.

All of this was fairly routine for the ECTPD. They needed to find out what had happened, and Michael

Roseboro might have that answer. No one was going to be shining a light in Roseboro's face and pointedly asking him tough questions. There was no crime, as far as the ECTPD could tell by this point.

The conversation would be fairly informal, unless something came up. In fact, Keith Neff was dressed in civilian clothes. He was not wearing any police equipment, didn't have his weapon, or even his badge.

"Thanks for coming in," Neff said as they got settled inside the small room. "I greatly appreciate this. I want to be clear here. You can leave at any time. If you need a break, at any time, just let me know, Mr. Roseboro. Okay?"

"Sure," Roseboro said.

Neff and Roseboro sat down, the cinder block walls, devoid of pictures, paintings, or any other distracting items, painted a nicotine yellow around them. Larry Martin sat, too, but he allowed Neff to do most of the talking. There was a walnut-brown Formica table with a few chairs. A three-by-five window (one-way mirror) on the north end of the room. And that was about it. The tone was going to be entirely conversational. Neff even felt bad, having to ask the guy questions so soon after what appeared to be a tragedy that would continue to grow in emotional magnitude before it got better for anyone close to Jan Roseboro.

At times, Martin got up and left the room, then returned.

Neff took out a laptop computer, opened it up on the table between them. He explained to Roseboro that he was going to type out a question and then wait for his answer and type that out before moving on.

Roseboro said he understood. "No problem."

After he gave Neff his full name and a few other personal details, Neff asked what time Roseboro got up the previous day, July 21, 2008, almost two mornings ago now.

That was an easy question for Jan's husband: "Five-thirty."

Roseboro's work schedule routine had started at the same time for years. Although he owned and operated the family business, Roseboro was a creature of habit.

"Was Jan with you when you woke up?"

"She did not feel well last night," Roseboro said. He seemed focused and detached, as if he were talking about somebody else's life. Roseboro spoke in a rather low monotone, soft and borderline effeminate. Neff could not judge the guy's emotional reaction one way or another. Maybe Roseboro's passive demeanor was the way he reacted to any social or personal situation? "She slept until about ten forty-five," Roseboro continued. "She took some NyQuil last night." He thought about what day that would be. Then: "*Monday* night."

"Did you sleep together Monday into Tuesday?"

"Yes."

"What was wrong with her?"

"We were down to Longstreth (a female sporting-goods store) Monday morning, and we stopped . . . and she came out and said she was not feeling well."

Neff rustled in his seat for a moment, tapping away on his laptop, trying to get more comfortable in the stiff chair. There was a delicate balance going on here between pushing Michael Roseboro too far at what was, Neff assumed, one of the worst nights of his life. Still, getting the facts so the ECTPD could hopefully close this case as an accidental drowning and move on was the goal. Nothing more.

"Um, did she see a doctor?" Neff asked.

"No. She thought it was a stomach virus. She did not feel good all of Monday. I went to the funeral home and came back around three-thirty P.M. and she was sleeping. She slept until four P.M. on Monday."

"What did you guys do on Monday?"

"We sat around and were playing cards. It was myself,

her and our three youngest kids. She had my oldest son [go out and] get Coke Slushies. He got them for her and the three kids."

Roseboro had no trouble answering questions. Here was a husband explaining an average day in the life of what appeared to be a normal suburban family.

"What did you do next?" Neff asked.

"Around nine P.M. on Monday night, she laid down and asked me to rub Vicks VapoRub on her back. I rubbed it on her back, and then she took some NyQuil." Roseboro ran a hand across the side of his face. It was getting late, somewhere near 2:00 A.M. He looked tired. Beaten down. "I went downstairs and watched TV until about ten-thirty P.M. and came upstairs and went to bed."

"Did she wake up during the night?"

"She woke up a couple of times to tell me I was snoring and to roll over to my stomach."

"What time did you guys get up on Tuesday?"

"I got up at five-thirty. She got up around ten forty-five. She told me she felt a lot better. I was home until about seven-thirty and then went down to the funeral home. I was there until about nine A.M. All the kids were home."

"What did you do when you got home?"

"I was swimming with the kids, from about nine-fifteen A.M. until she got up."

"When she woke up, what did you guys do?"

"She ate a bowl of cereal and then we played cards. It was me, Jan and [one of our kids]."

"What happened next?"

"Around noon, I went to get a shower, and she left and went to the bank and post office." Roseboro said that by the time Jan went out, she was feeling better.

Roseboro gave it to him, and said he had managed to get to the funeral home by about three o'clock that day. Then he corrected himself, explaining that his doctor's appointment was actually scheduled for one-thirty. It was near five o'clock when he finally returned home on Tuesday evening, July 22—the last night of Jan's life.

Neff asked for the doctor's name. Roseboro gave it to him.

"I jumped in the pool with all the kids and made burgers."

But Jan never went in the pool, Roseboro explained. She played cards with her two oldest daughters on the patio. It was near 85 degrees all day long, a perfect summer afternoon to hang out by the pool. They'd had such fun playing cards, Roseboro said. The game lasted all the way until about 8:45 or 9:00 P.M. They laughed and joked, and Jan felt so much better than she had during the two previous days.

It was about 9:15 P.M., Roseboro was certain, when he finally got out of the pool with two of his kids and went inside to go and get ready for bed.

"What did Jan do?"

Roseboro did not hesitate: "I was sitting on a step on the deep end of the pool. She was lying right behind me." He must have meant right before he went inside, although he never made it clear and Neff didn't ask.

"How long did you guys stay in the pool?"

"I left the pool around ten P.M. and went inside. My stomach did not feel too well. I asked her if I should put the torches out. She told me she was going to stay outside and watch the planes a little longer. She told me she would be in, 'in a little bit.'"

Neff was able to stay focused on what Roseboro told him; he could type and listen at the same time. If he missed something, he'd ask Roseboro to stop so he could catch up. The conversation never grew into anything other than two men sitting, casually talking to each other about an event they had probably wished had never brought them together.

Neff next asked Roseboro to explain what had

happened between the time he last saw Jan—10:00 P.M.—lying poolside, and the time he spied his wife floating in the pool, somewhere between the top of the waterline and the bottom.

Almost an hour had elapsed, according to Roseboro.

"In the summer," he said, "[our three youngest children] sleep on the floor in our bedroom. [Two of them] were sleeping, and [the other] was almost asleep. I told her good night. I turned off the TV and fell asleep."

"Did you wake up?"

"I woke up at ten fifty-eight P.M. I looked out and saw the torches were still lit. I went outside to put the torches out. I went to put the first torch out, and saw Jan."

Neff asked where she was.

Roseboro said Jan was on the "bottom of the deep end." So he "jumped in and pulled her out. I laid her on the deck and called 911. I started giving her CPR. Someone from 911 walked me through it. I kept going until the ambulance got there."

In succession—Neff considered as Roseboro spoke—this guy walked outside in his boxer shorts to blow out the torches, noticed that his wife was on the bottom of their pool, jumped in, swam down into the deep end, grabbed hold of her, pulled her out, laid her down on her back, *then* called 911. Roseboro was likely huffing and puffing after all of that. Out of breath and frantic.

Neff asked if Roseboro noticed "anything about Jan" that night that might have been different.

Roseboro ignored that question and instead said he felt for a pulse, but he did not feel one, adding that Jan never swam in the clothing he found her in.

"Did the kids ever wake up?"

"No."

It was after 2:00 A.M. Neff asked Roseboro if he needed to take a break and collect his thoughts, maybe just chill out for a bit, use the bathroom, grab a smoke, relax.

Roseboro said he would like that.

* * *

During the break, Larry Martin put in a call to Lancaster County assistant district attorney (ADA) Kelly Sekula. She had been informed of what was going on since Martin and Keith Neff had gone out to the scene and arrived back at the station house with a strange feeling there was more to an adult drowning in her own pool by accident. Martin had called ADA Sekula earlier and asked about boundaries and what the ECTPD should do in this situation. Sekula, in turn, woke up the district attorney (DA), Craig Stedman. They talked about the situation and agreed something didn't seem right. They had better work closely with the ECTPD to make sure everyone was on the same page. If it was an accident, they would find that out. If it was more, well, at least things would be done under the supervision of the prosecuting attorney's office from the get-go. It couldn't hurt.

Martin explained to Sekula exactly what had transpired thus far.

"I'll call you back," she said.

Sekula called Craig Stedman and conferred.

"All we can do is a consent to search," Stedman told his ADA. "Call me back and keep me in the loop as to what's going on." Stedman and Sekula talked for a brief moment more about what the ECTPD actually had—which amounted to nothing—and what they could do legally at this point.

When Sekula got back on the phone with Martin, she said, "We don't even have a crime here, Detective Martin. A consent to search is all we can do. But you need to get consent from Mr. Roseboro to go into his house."

Martin said, "Okay." He called Neff over. "Ask Roseboro if he'll consent us to taking a walk-through of his house."

9

Detective Larry Martin had walked in and out of the interview with Michael Roseboro, talking to various people on the phone, doing his job as detective sergeant. Keith Neff waited for Roseboro to return from his break, so they could continue discussing what had happened. One professional Martin needed to get ahold of was the county coroner. There was a good chance the coroner, when given all the facts of the case, would order an autopsy of Jan Roseboro's body, which might clear up things. Any type of "suspicious death" yields an autopsy. If Jan had had a heart attack, which was definitely on the minds of everyone, an autopsy would prove it and close the case.

In the state of Pennsylvania, the coroner is an elected position. A coroner needs no background in the field to get the job.

"The trash can," someone in law enforcement told me, "if elected, could be the coroner in this state. You get the idea?"

Coroners are not the same as pathologists. It's a suit-and-tie office job, a tradition in Lancaster County that goes back some two hundred years.

During the break, Larry Martin called the deputy coroner,

who happened to be a doctor. He was in Elizabethtown, about a forty-five-minute drive west of Denver. Martin explained what was going on.

"I'll drive down to the hospital, check it out," the deputy coroner promised, adding that it was going to be a while because he was tied up with another body. Unlike Denver, Reinholds, and those towns heading into Amish country from Lancaster City, downtown Lancaster was like any other major metropolis. Murderers and thugs and gangbangers were rather frequent creatures of the night.

As were dead bodies.

Martin said, "I'd like an autopsy." It actually felt good saying that out loud, Martin thought. They were finally getting somewhere.

It was going to be midmorning by the time he got out of there, the deputy coroner said.

That was fine, Martin told him. Then he called Dr. Steven Zebert, the attending physician back at the hospital Jan had been brought to, explaining to the ER doctor what was going to happen next, saying, "I want to be there when the autopsy's performed."

Zebert said okay. Then, seeing that he had Martin on the phone, the doctor mentioned that he had some news to share.

"What's going on?" Martin wondered aloud.

"It's not a bullet wound, Detective," Zebert reported. "The X-ray clearly spells that out."

So she slipped and fell, Martin thought as he hung up the phone. Being especially careful, Martin didn't want to rush to judgment.

"I didn't know it was a homicide," Martin said later. "I had to be cautious. If this was an accidental drowning and we completely nuked this guy, and his wife had just died, that wouldn't be right."

Because he knew Roseboro, and had met him professionally at times out in the field, Martin said, "When

Mike first told us his story, I probably gave it a bit more credibility knowing who he was. . . ."

All of that, however, was about to change.

At 2:19 A.M., Detective Keith Neff resumed his interview with Michael Roseboro. After Neff asked about any drugs or medications Jan might have been taking, Roseboro said his wife took ten to twenty milligrams of Adderall every day. An amphetamine, Adderall is said to stimulate the central nervous system, influencing different chemicals in the brain, specifically those nerves that lead to hyperactivity and impulse control. It is prescribed to treat narcolepsy, a sleeping disorder, and attention deficit hyperactivity disorder, the ever-more-popular ADHD. According to her husband, Jan suffered from attention deficit disorder (ADD) and needed the medication to maintain a stable life, free of symptoms. This could turn out to be imperative to the investigation— that missing puzzle piece. Had Jan taken too much medication, or not enough? Maybe her meds had caused Jan some trouble with equilibrium and she accidentally slipped and hit her head? Was it possible Jan had gone into a state of shock or had a seizure while walking into the house from her seat at the pool?

All good questions.

But Neff's next query centered around a possibility it seemed everyone else, besides Michael Roseboro, had answered: "Were either of you drinking?"

"Jan did not drink anything," Roseboro confirmed. "I had a few beers."

There was one other pending question that needed to be asked, regardless of what, on the surface, appeared to be an ideal marriage between two people who seemed to have it all: love, loads of money, four healthy kids, a successful family business, and a home fit for a segment of MTV's *Cribs*.

"What is your relationship with Jan?" Neff asked, looking for some insight into the Roseboro marriage.

"Good," Roseboro answered quickly. "I had a plan to renew our vows on the beach, the Outer Banks (in North Carolina). We were going to go on the tenth to the seventeenth of August." There seemed to be a shake of the head by Roseboro there, as if the thought of the trip now not happening made him suddenly question things.

"Who was the person who was going to renew your vows?"

"Leslie Buck-Ferguson," Roseboro said, as if he had just spoken to the woman before sitting down. "She does beach weddings in the Outer Banks. I found her on the Internet."

Roseboro explained how he and Jan had not argued at all on Tuesday, this after Neff pried deeper into how they had gotten along as husband and wife. Ditto for when Neff asked if Roseboro ever had a "physical confrontation with Jan."

In May, Roseboro said, just two months ago, it had been nineteen years of marriage. Sure, they'd had their ups and downs, and fights, throughout the years, like any married couple. But they were generally happy people, in love—at least from the impression Neff got from Roseboro as the mortician talked about renewing his marital vows, playing cards, and swimming with his kids.

After answering another question about Jan having any major medical issues to contend with, besides ADD, Neff asked Roseboro if his wife could swim.

"She is not real proficient," Roseboro said, "but she can get around the pool."

Roseboro cleared up how deep the pool is after Neff asked: "Three to six feet."

It was getting close to 2:30 A.M. Neff asked Roseboro, "Would you consent to a walk-through by us of your home?"

"Of course. Yes."

Neff left the room, grabbed the "consent to search" form, returned, then asked Roseboro to sign it, explaining that he and Detective Martin would be heading back out to West Main Street immediately. Was that going to be a problem for anyone?

"No. . . . Sure," Roseboro said again.

Neff read back the Q&A he had typed on his laptop from their conversation. Then he asked Roseboro if he agreed with it.

"Yes. Sounds accurate."

"Can you sign the bottom of each page?"

It was four pages long.

When he was finished, Roseboro stood and walked into the foyer to meet up with Rebecca Donahue and Gary Frees, who drove him back home then.

Watching Gary Frees drive away from the ECTPD with Rebecca Donahue and Roseboro in the car, Larry Martin and Keith Neff considered the fact that not once during the entire interview did Michael Roseboro ever ask about the status of his wife. How was she doing? Did the ECTPD know if she was alive? How might she have died? Was she alive when she got to the hospital? It was 2:34 A.M., almost three hours after Jan had been taken away from her home in an ambulance, and her husband of nearly two decades had never inquired about her, nor had he gone to the hospital. In fact, as Martin and Neff learned, watching those swirling clouds above prepare for another round of powerful thunderstorms, not once did Michael Roseboro, or any one of his family members or friends, call the hospital to see if Jan was going to pull through. No one had asked when—or if—Jan had been pronounced dead. It was, quite oddly, as if they all knew not only that Jan had died, but how.

"And that's why we . . . asked if we could do a walk-through," Neff said. "To find out what happened to this forty-five-year-old mother of four kids."

10

What did Michael Roseboro do during that period of time when paramedics took his wife away from their home in an ambulance and a posse of family members and friends showed up at the house? For starters, how did everyone find out so quickly what had happened to Jan Roseboro? When it was looked at later, it was as if Roseboro had sent out a press release, or a text message, to a predetermined list of people.

The first call Roseboro made was at 11:23 P.M., thirty-four minutes before the doctor at the hospital had pronounced Jan Roseboro dead. The doctor later said that a "pronouncement" is not necessarily the actual time of death; it is, for hospital personnel, the exact time efforts to bring a person back to life are suspended.

Roseboro called his father, Ralph Roseboro, at his dad's house. Ralph lived across the street from the Roseboro Funeral Home in downtown Denver, with Michael's mother, Ann, who happened to be in Vermont at the time on a bus trip with a tour group.

Two minutes after calling his dad, Jan's husband called the Roseboro Funeral Home for some reason that no one could later discern. The ECTPD could never get out of Ralph Roseboro what his son had said to him, if anything. Ralph didn't say one way or another if he was not at home but across the street at the funeral home, which would be a good reason why Roseboro called there after calling his parents' home.

Five minutes after calling Ralph, at 11:28 P.M., as the Roseboros' yard filled with law enforcement, fire personnel, friends, and family, Roseboro called Susan Van Zant, his sister-in-law, at her home.

Suzie picked up after just a few rings.

"She's gone . . . ," Roseboro told his sister-in-law without further explanation. Then, more quietly, "She's gone."

"What do you mean?" Suzie asked. "Who's gone?" Was the guy half in the bag? Did he know what the heck he was talking about?

"Jan," Roseboro said. "I couldn't save her."

Suzie still didn't understand. "I'll be right up," she said. Suzie lived minutes away, in downtown Denver, directly across the street from the Roseboro Funeral Home.

"Okay" was all Roseboro said before hanging up.

Suzie got off the phone, thought about it a moment, and considered the idea that Jan might have had a heart attack and had fallen into the pool. At some point after cradling the phone, those words hit her: *"She's gone."* Jan was dead. It had to be an accident. What else could have happened?

Jan's sister called one friend, who didn't answer. Then she phoned another, explained what was going on, as best she could, and asked her for a ride up to the house.

"Sure."

"I'll wait outside," Suzie explained, more frantic and worried now.

Standing in front of her parents' home where she was staying, waiting for her friend, Suzie heard a siren. She looked up. An ambulance went screaming by at a high rate of speed.

Speaking through an avalanche of emotion and tears,

Suzie later said, "I saw the ambulance go by. It had my sister's body in it."

But Suzie didn't know that as she waited for a ride to her sister and brother-in-law's house. Jan, whom Suzie later described as "a rock to me," someone who was "there for anyone, anytime," was arguably fighting for her life inside that ambulance.

Inside the car on the way to the house, Suzie's friend, noticing how quickly Suzie was falling apart ("losing it"), said, "Just get it together for those kids."

And that was what Suzie began to focus on: "My concern was for the children," she later said. "And that's what I did."

After talking to Suzie, apparently convinced that his wife was dead by the way she looked when the ambulance took her away moments before, Michael Roseboro called Brian Binkley, Jan's brother.

Brian didn't answer. So Roseboro left his brother-in-law a message.

Then, at 11:50 P.M., Roseboro called the family's Lutheran pastor, Larry Hummer.

The final call—six in all—that Roseboro made within that time frame before Jan was pronounced dead was to his sister's house, which led to a series of calls to other Roseboro family members, sending them all flocking to the West Main Street home.

11

No one in law enforcement had reported seeing anything out of place at the Roseboro residence, both in and around the concrete pool decking area, besides those two stones, Jan's cell phone and reading glasses on the bottom of the pool. Nothing had been disturbed. There was no blood. No indication whatsoever that a struggle had ensued between two people, or that a woman had fallen, hit her head, and drowned. There was a bucket full of what appeared to be cleaning fluids, a red rag floating on top.

And that was it.

By now, the ECTPD had found out that the wound Jan had sustained on the back of her head was no surface bump or bruise. Jan Roseboro had a deep gash, the size of a nickel, shaped roughly like the letter *L*, on her scalp in back of her left ear, which burrowed all the way down to her skull. This was not a wound that had come to Jan easily, without pain or violence. Both the doctor and Detective Larry Martin were convinced there had to be evidence somewhere in or around the house explaining how Jan had received such a blow. Be it an overturned plant holder, remnants of hair and tissue on the corner of a kitchen countertop, or some other explanation. But a person does not receive a blow like the one Jan had sustained without leaving a clue behind as to how it got there.

Police had not gone into the Roseboro home. They had no reason to. Which was why Detective Keith Neff had asked Michael Roseboro—who graciously agreed—to sign the "consent to search" form for the interior of the home.

Heading back over to the house, Neff and Martin got to talking. Neff was more than a little concerned by now. Roseboro had not once asked about his wife, what happened, or what the police thought *might* have happened. He had never shed a tear that Neff or Martin had seen. Stranger still, the ER doctor at the hospital had reported that in over thirty years of experience in dealing with death in the ER, he had never had a family member—wife, husband, sister, brother, mother, father—fail to show up at the hospital or call during a situation similar to Jan's. Roseboro not only had never gone to the hospital to inquire about his wife's well-being, but had never called, either. No one in the family had, for that matter. And yet they were all under the impression that Jan had died.

"That is not the appropriate reaction that I am used to seeing when talking to someone who has just lost a loved one," Neff remarked. "Mike Roseboro was pretty much quiet. He was not asking me questions: 'What do you know? What's going on?' That sort of thing."

Martin was a bit more guarded about his judgments concerning Roseboro. With more investigatory experience, Martin was taking the case in, a breath at a time, following the evidence. Neff was too, it should be noted, but Neff had a sneaky suspicion (maybe a gut instinct) that all was not what it seemed, and that the answer could very well be found inside the Roseboro house.

When they arrived that second time, early morning, July 23, 2008, the heaviest rain of the night began. Cats and dogs. Buckets upon buckets of thick, slanted rain, with thunder and lightning, to boot. If there was any sign of blood outside the house, on the lawn, or around the pool, consider it washed away by God's hand at this point.

Gone.

Inside the Roseboro residence by 2:52 A.M., Neff explained, there was, "and I am going to estimate here, between fifteen to twenty family and friends walking around the house."

Neff and Martin knew going into the situation that Roseboro could yank the "consent to search" form out of their hands anytime he felt like it, then demand they hightail it out of his house at once. So they had to be careful with their reactions and what they said, making the visit as quick and thorough as they could under the circumstances.

"That house was cold," Neff said later, referring to the reaction from Roseboro's family and friends as he and Martin began their walk-through. Nobody wanted them there, and they were not concealing those feelings for the officers as Martin and Neff entered.

"I just kept my head down," Neff added, "and did what we had to do."

The house itself was "confusing to navigate," Neff explained. Which was one of the reasons why they asked Roseboro to show them around. The other problem was that everyone in the house was startled by their presence this second time: *Why in the heavens are the cops back here again?* Jan had drowned accidentally. Everyone at the house had signed off on that as a cause of death. Heart attack. Fall. Drowning. Jan's death was a tragedy enough all by itself. Did the police have to make matters worse by continuing to pester this grieving family?

"We were not welcome with open arms," Martin said. "I'll leave it at that."

There was a lot of strange feelings in the house, too, Martin felt. The pastor from the Roseboro's church, Larry Hummer, who also happened to be the ECTPD's chaplain, was inside, talking to Roseboro friends and family, helping out where he could. Many of these people inside the house were professionals: doctors, lawyers, businesspeople.

Martin had called ADA Kelly Sekula back and asked if the ECTPD had any chance of obtaining a search warrant.

"You just don't have enough," Sekula said. Most in law enforcement will admit that Pennsylvania is one of those states where getting a search warrant is tough business. It's not as easy as people might think. Here, in this situation, the ECTPD had absolutely nothing: speculation and theory, a cop's gut instinct. But no evidence whatsoever—the "probable cause" a judge wants to see—showing them Roseboro had anything to do with his wife's untimely death.

That would all change the instant Neff or Martin spotted something in the house that could kindle a search warrant: a bloody towel on the floor, hair or blood in the washer or dryer, a bloody weapon of some sort, maybe some furniture out of place, a broken vase, anything of concern. But they were walking on eggshells, being hawked and watched as if they were intruders.

Larry Martin pulled Michael Roseboro aside before they started. "Mike, listen, is there anything strange or out of place—i.e., somebody who could have broken into the house, robbery, burglary, or evidence of an intruder—that you see?"

There was always the possibility that while Roseboro was asleep, which he had claimed to be during that crucial hour Jan had died, a home invasion could have been uncovered by Jan, who died trying to bust it up.

Roseboro did not hesitate with his answer: "Nope. Everything looks normal."

Martin made note of what Roseboro said.

Both detectives "would have loved to lay on the floor and shine flashlights under beds and in back of furniture,"

Martin later lamented. But considering the intense disgust
they were feeling from others about them being there, in
the first place, and the fact that Roseboro could ask them
to leave at any moment, a more thorough search was not
going to be possible.

There were several people, including Roseboro, following so close behind as they walked through, Neff and
Martin could literally feel their breath on their backs.

Martin opened the door to the master bedroom,
where the kids were still sleeping. He walked in.

One of the children, sleeping in the large bed, rose up.

Someone came up from behind. "Get out of there!
No! Don't wake the kids!"

Keith Neff and Larry Martin backed off.

"Look," Martin said later, "if I pushed this issue, we
don't get any walk-through. They throw us out."

It was remarkable to the detectives that the kids were
still asleep and had not woken up once throughout the
entire ordeal.

In the laundry room, there were a pair of each: two
clothes dryers and two washers. Martin took a careful
look inside both.

He found nothing.

Without moving anything, they quickly looked in trash
cans for blood or any obvious signs of violence.

Zilch.

"This," Martin said, "was certainly not the search I
would have liked to conduct."

They wanted to go through the outside garbage cans
and the turkey house out in back, but knew there was no
way Roseboro was going to allow it. Heck, they were already on borrowed time; pushing the matter would only
get them tossed.

What they needed was a search warrant.

"*Legitimately,*" Martin said, emphasizing the word, "it
was a walk-through in every manner of speaking."

Nearing the end, Martin asked if they could take a

look inside the pool house connected to the patio area. A nice room, with a fireplace and cozy couches, plush carpeting and fieldstone for the mantel, it was an area of the house where there had no doubt been lots of family fun. Memories, even though the addition was just months old, seemed to seep from the walls like laughter as they entered. It was hard not to picture Jan and her kids inside this room talking about life, joking around, reminiscing about a cookout or a family function, a swim meet, schoolwork, a lacrosse game, playing cards, talking about the future.

Sad, too, that none of this would ever take place again. Three young kids—still sleeping, unaware—had gone to bed with a mother and would wake up without one.

A tragedy, indeed.

Roseboro followed Neff and Martin into the room. It was just the three of them now. The two detectives had finally gotten Roseboro alone.

Martin asked Roseboro to have a seat. They wanted to speak with him, he said, if he didn't mind. Just for a moment. Martin said they had some new information they wanted to share. It was important they gave it to him personally.

"Mike, hey, listen," Martin said in his gentle manner, "that injury on Jan's head . . . Well, that thing is deep and wide. Do you realize how much pressure and force it must have taken . . . to go all the way to the skull? Do you have *any* idea what happened?" Martin looked at Roseboro with a seriousness neither he nor Neff had yet to project on the mortician. They wanted to let him know, delicately, that things had taken a turn into a more sobering, more serious direction. They were not simply going to write the case off as an accidental drowning because Roseboro had said so. Not with an injury as pronounced and deep as the one on the back of Jan's head. They needed to find the answer to how the injury got there.

"Oh, okay," Roseboro said. It was an odd answer. And that was it.

Neff and Martin looked at each other.

The comment caught Neff "off guard"— *"Oh, okay."* So he piped in, "Do you have any questions for *us* about that, or anything else?"

"No. I didn't see the injury," Roseboro said nonchalantly.

"You have *no* questions, Mr. Roseboro?" Martin asked. He and Neff looked at each other again. *What's going on here?* They couldn't believe it. Both had pictured themselves in the same situation, their wives dead, the same injury on the back of the head. They'd be banging down doors to try to find out what happened. Climbing the walls. Crazy for answers.

"Nope," Roseboro said. He was calm. Undistracted. Unworried.

This answer struck both men as abnormal—that is, considering the circumstances of the conversation. They had just told Jan Roseboro's husband that she had suffered a severe blow and gash to the back of her head. One that was likely the impetus leading to her death—and the guy did not even wonder how it might have gotten there. He didn't even ask if they had a theory. It was as if what he didn't know wouldn't hurt him.

"That was the point during the conversation," Neff recalled, "where, for me, the trigger hit the hammer."

The other aspect of this scenario that Neff and Martin were perhaps overlooking to a large extent was that Roseboro had been a funeral director and worked in a funeral home. The guy had been around dead bodies all his life, had drained blood from corpses and replaced it with embalming fluid. He had taken mangled children and repaired them enough for an open casket. He had caked makeup on the dead and combed their natty hair, clipped their nails and sewn their mouths shut. The man was likely desensitized to death. To him, perhaps, death was a *thing*. A part of the job. He was turning to that well of emotion for this situation. Using it to get through it all. Was this Roseboro's poker face? Had it helped him cope and deal with Jan's demise—that same somber look he had assumed like a mask for the hundreds of families throughout the years who had come in and out of the doors to the funeral home?

Larry Martin and Keith Neff were concerned on many levels as they drove away from the Roseboro residence. So Martin called ADA Kelly Sekula as Neff drove. It was now somewhere in the neighborhood of 3:30 A.M.

"Kelly, is there *any* way that we can hold this residence until we can get a search warrant?" Martin was certain the answer was inside the house. But every minute that passed was another chance that whatever evidence was in the house would be found and discarded or cleaned up.

It was a situation akin to an infant death, ADA Sekula explained, using the analogy to make an important legal point. Sadly, the Lancaster County District Attorney's (LCDA's) Office sees more infant deaths these days than ever, and yet they are some of the most difficult crimes to investigate and prosecute. An infant dies. The parents claim crib death. Cops have a feeling it's more than that. But there are no outward signs of a crime. The investigating officer, nine out of ten times, is forced to release what he or she strongly believes is a crime scene with evidence—and there's nothing the police can do about it.

ADA Sekula hung up with Martin, called DA Craig Stedman, asked him about a search warrant.

Sometime later, she called Martin back: "No, Larry. Cannot do it."

Martin hung up his cell and stared out the window.

Tomorrow was another day. Perhaps something would turn up? Maybe somebody saw something? Possibly the autopsy would divulge a clue or two, maybe enough to secure a warrant?

Either way, Martin considered, he wasn't giving up on Jan Roseboro.

12

Jan Roseboro's father, Samuel Binkley, was a well-known Denver resident and banker throughout Lancaster County. Binkley owned Denver National Bank, later bought out by Fulton Bank, where Jan had been branch manager before becoming a full-time stay-at-home mom in 1995. It was Sam Binkley's house on West Main Street that Jan and Michael Roseboro put a $600,000 addition into recently, and had relocated from their home on the other side of town after Christmas, 2007.

"Mr. Binkley was a very nice guy," said a former neighbor. "Jan and Mike spent about a year remodeling that house."

For a time, they were living in both houses, going back and forth between the two. Jan had grown up in the West Main Street house with her sister and brother. Jan's father, a gentle man, was that *It's a Wonderful Life*–type banker you went to in a small town, hat in hands, eyes on the floor, when times were tough and everyone else turned you down. Binkley was a smart businessman, knowing that if you treated people the way you wanted to be treated, they would be loyal customers forever. A straightforward, effortless business model small-town people had no trouble accepting.

"Mr. Binkley would just sit outside with his dog in the evenings," that neighbor added, "and just keep to himself. He was a simple man. I'd say hello and he would nod."

Cassandra "Cassie" Evanick Pope grew up around Jan and Michael Roseboro; she and her family knew them long before they moved next door to where Cassandra and her husband, Richard, now lived on West Main Street. Before she was married, Cassandra lived southeast of the Roseboros' West Main Street home with her parents on the outskirts of Reinholds, about two miles away. Jan and Michael Roseboro lived in the same neighborhood. Cassandra was familiar with the Roseboro family: picnics, block parties, get-togethers. Of course, anytime a family member, friend, or someone in the neighborhood passed, there was Michael Roseboro taking care of everything. There was not another funeral home any one of the Roseboros' neighbors would dream of using. Roseboro, said one of his customers, "was the kindest, nicest man to our family when my father died."

At neighborhood parties, Roseboro insisted on being the bartender. He made strong drinks, some said, especially for the women. He liked to frolic around, too, others added, raising eyebrows to the ladies, maybe commenting on a tight pair of jeans or short skirt.

"I was seventeen," one former neighbor told me, "when he hit on me the first time at one of the block parties. That was Mike . . . always eyeing the young girls. Very creepy."

"Jan was the typical soccer mom," Richard Pope said of his former neighbor. At the time Jan died, Richard and Cassandra lived next door, the first house after the Roseboros' heading down West Main, after taking a left off Creek Road. "She was always running around . . . and taking the kids here and there. Very pleasant woman." Living next door to Michael and Jan Roseboro, Richard watched the new addition go up. He also saw Jan once a month, because Jan and her siblings owned the two-story house Richard lived in with Cassandra and their newborn. So Richard Pope would walk over and hand Jan the rent check every month. They'd chat. Jan was always sociable and talkative. "Whenever I had any problems in the house, I just called Jan and she'd take care of it. I never dealt with Mike."

A good-looking woman, Jan had kept herself physically fit and reasonably trim. She was in good shape. "She wasn't bone-skinny, like a model," Marcia Evanick, Cassandra's mother, later said. "She ate, but took care of herself. Jan was constantly with her kids. Anything having to do with her kids, Jan was there! Her younger ones were on the swim team. . . . That's why she was gone every morning—to watch them practice. . . ."

Whereas, some later said, the Roseboro clan weren't afraid to show what they were worth, and buy the toys and finer things in life they wanted, the Binkley family never flaunted what they had.

"They were humble people, I'd say so, yes," Marcia Evanick added. "Jan had the fancy jewelry and everything . . . but you always saw her in shorts and jeans."

Flip-flops, with her hair pulled back in a ponytail.

Marcia called Jan "*the* mother. She'd jump rope with the kids, be out there swimming and playing."

"For a mother of four," Michael Evanick, Marcia's husband, said, with a respectful laugh, "Jan had it together. She was hot! All those firemen across the street from the house, they would all look over at Jan if she was out at the pool and they were heading out for a fire or just driving by."

This was why, on the night of Jan Roseboro's death, that same team of firefighters, heading off to an alarm in town shortly before the call came in about Jan being found, unresponsive, in the water, didn't notice Jan outside at the pool. Many of them later said they would have definitely noticed if Jan was outside, not only because they had actually looked for her whenever they drove by, but all the lights surrounding the pool—at least near 10:30 P.M. when the fire alarm was called down the street—were off. The back of the Roseboro house, which was an extremely rare event, if not odd, was pitch dark. Even the dusk-to-dawn light, a light that required no human contact to turn on or off, was out. The only way to shut that light off was to flip the breaker in the fuse box, or pull the plug from the socket (if you knew where it was).

"For this one night, during this particular time frame," someone close to the case later said, "no lights were on in the backyard of the Roseboro house."

Over a half-dozen others claimed to have seen the same thing.

Yet, when paramedics and law enforcement arrived, all the lights, including the tiki torch lamps, which required fire to be lit, were on.

13

Cassandra Pope liked to get her six-month-old, Dakota, into bed by nine o'clock on most nights. That way, Cassandra could catch the nightly news and then watch a rerun of one of her favorite shows, *Friends*.

Habit. Every new mother relied on those ordinary—however routine and instinctual—things she did every night, whether she realized it or not.

On the night Jan Roseboro was found lifeless and not breathing, Cassandra had run up to the local Getty Mart store—two minutes from her home on West Main—and returned at nine-fifteen. She was just about to step into her nightly routine and put Dakota to bed upstairs, when she realized that her husband, Richard, had already done so. Checking in on Dakota, Cassandra gave her baby a kiss. Then she went in and did the same to Richard, who was in bed, but he had rolled over and groggily said something before falling back out.

Cassandra now had a chance to relax with some television.

People often recall certain circumstances of a particular moment based on what they were watching on television. Cassandra later said, "That's how I knew what time it was. I watched the news and was waiting for *Friends* to come on."

The first thing Cassandra heard on the night Jan died was a siren. It was close to 10:30 P.M. A fire alarm had been called in down the road. And the fire department being so close by, Cassandra heard the blaring of the horns and high-pitched sirens. Looking out the window, she watched as the trucks whizzed by on West Main Street.

Just after the sirens passed and the nightly news was scrolling ending credits, Cassandra settled back down in her seat in the living room to that familiar "I'll Be There for You" pop song by the Rembrandts, letting her know that *Friends* was starting.

And that's when she heard what would become known as "the scream." A terrifyingly loud—like in a horror movie—shriek.

What the . . . , Cassandra thought.

Then got up and walked toward the window.

Cassandra and Richard had an old air conditioner in the living-room window, which was loud when it kicked on and off. Cassandra thought maybe a belt in the machine had squealed. Perhaps when the thing turned on, it shifted inside the window, scraping against the glass or something. Who knew?

"I didn't think anything of it," Cassandra later said, "at that time."

As she looked at the air conditioner, realizing there was no way it could have made such a shrill sound, she now knew it was definitely a scream. No doubt about it. And it had to have come from the Roseboros' backyard, Cassandra was certain. She knew this because the Roseboro family had just opened their pool and the kids "were out there all the time, yelling and screaming."

At all hours of the night.

After a moment, Cassandra told herself it was just the Roseboro kids outside having fun. The kids had been known to be out in the pool playing, until ten or even eleven o'clock. All the kids. They never went to bed at a reasonable hour. Even the young ones. They were always running around the yard, chasing one another, playing.

Thinking about it a bit more after she sat down, this particular scream was different, Cassandra considered, and it was beginning to frighten her and cause some anxiety. So much so, Cassandra got up and went to check on Dakota. Just to make sure.

"I'm a paranoid mom, you know," Cassandra explained. "And I don't know why I went to check on her, because I heard the scream *outside*. Motherly instinct, I guess."

The other notion Cassandra had considered as she came back from checking on Dakota, who was fine, was how the youngest Roseboro boy "when he screams, chasing his sister around, kind of sounds like a girl."

That must have been it, she told herself.

So Cassandra looked out the window. But she didn't see anything. It was dark outside. No one was swimming in the pool. Odd that it was so damn dark. And so early.

Cassandra went back to her television show. It must have been the kids, she believed, chasing each other around the yard.

By 11:30 P.M. on July 22, 2008, Cassandra had forgotten about the "female scream," as she later described it. Before heading off to bed, she looked outside one last time. Now there were all sorts of people combing around the Roseboros' backyard. There was an ambulance and several fire trucks parked in and near the driveway, lights flashing and pulsating in the dark night, blue and red colors bouncing off the trees and the sides of houses. She couldn't really see the pool from her viewpoint, but Cassandra could tell it was all lit up out there now.

What in the world?

That scream meant something—Cassandra was sure of it.

"And then I . . . thought something happened to one of the kids."

So Cassandra got dressed and went outside to see if she could find out what was going on. As she later put it, she started "snooping around." What scared her was the Roseboro dogs, Jan's prize possessions. They were always outside roaming around the yard. They often barked at Cassandra whenever she went out on the steps of her front door to have her late-night cigarette. Come to think of it, when Cassandra had gone out for a smoke earlier, the dogs had not approached her or barked. Cassandra couldn't recall a night or day when Jan was outside *without* her dogs.

Jan's neighbor didn't want to run into one or both of the dogs as she walked around the Roseboro property at 11:30 P.M., trying to find out what was going on, so she went about her snooping in a cautious manner.

"I thought it was strange that not one cop came up and asked me what I was doing."

By then, she noticed there were cops everywhere.

Cassandra wandered over to the side of the Roseboros' house and watched for a few moments. She saw Sam, Jan's oldest son, arrive home with a friend, and she watched as people stood around, with dumbfounded looks on their faces.

When she went back into her home, Cassandra woke Richard up. "Something's going on over at the Roseboros'," Cassandra told her husband.

Richard didn't want to get up. The guy worked long, hard days. He needed to rise early. Richard said something Cassandra couldn't understand, rolled over, and went back to sleep.

Cassandra wasn't going back out there. Not now, at this hour. So she lay down next to her husband and fell asleep.

14

Early the next morning, Wednesday, July 23, 2008, Richard Pope got up before his wife. Richard was outside getting something in his garage, when Suzie Van Zant walked over. Suzie had a somber, dark look about her. It was fairly obvious to Richard that Suzie had been up all night. She looked tired and spent. Pale as pizza dough.

"Hey," Richard said. He noticed all the people still hanging around the house, inside and out, but he didn't think much of it. There were cars parked along the road and in the Roseboros' driveway in back. Looking around, Richard vaguely recalled the night before, when Cassandra had woken him and told him something was going on next door.

"Did you hear what happened?" Suzie asked.

If you stood in the front of the Popes' small brick garage with the white door, you can see clear across the Roseboro yard to the pool. The turkey house would be to your right. The Roseboro house to your left. The pool in the center.

"No," Richard said, wondering why Suzie was asking him this question so early in the morning.

"Jan died last night," Suzie said.

"What?" Richard walked closer and hugged her. He could now tell Suzie was nearly shaking. "What happened?"

"They think she fell and hit her head," Suzie said. Then she explained how "they" had found Jan in the pool. ("But I don't remember Suzie telling me that Jan had drowned," Richard later recalled.)

After they talked for a bit (Richard telling Suzie that if there was anything he could do, just say the words), Richard went inside and told Cassandra. It would certainly answer some questions Cassandra might have had about the previous night.

Cassandra couldn't believe it. Stunned, she walked over to the window, looked toward the Roseboro house, and asked Richard, "Why are so many people over there? What are they doing? Jan was just murdered."

Who said anything about a murder?

"What?" Richard asked. Maybe even a roll of the eyes. The statement was shocking. Jan had fallen into the pool, Richard said again. That's what Suzie had told him.

"Well, Richard," Cassandra answered, explaining herself, "they just built that pool—and now they find *Jan* in it? Come on!"

Two plus two, by Cassandra's count, equaled four. It was clear.

As the morning continued, it was troubling, Cassandra Pope later explained, to watch as "family members," she wasn't sure who the people were she was looking at, and "kids," as she described them, "picked up pool paddles and walked around in the pool area, using the skimmer . . . putting things in the pool, just playing around near where Jan had died."

Cassandra soon found out that Jan was in the pool when Michael Roseboro found her. It seemed almost morbid and in terribly bad taste to see so many people out there parading around the pool deck. Throughout the morning, it had remained partly cloudy. Any rain was light, returning on and off. If Jan had died inside the pool, Cassandra thought, why were the children and some adults out there near the scene? Didn't they think it was in bad taste, at the least, to stand around and look at the water from where Jan's body had been pulled? What was more, Roseboro was out there, Cassandra noticed at one point, sitting, smoking, just staring blankly into the blue water as if it held answers.

An additionally unnerving—or perhaps interesting?—period of the morning for Cassandra came when she saw "people" taking the Roseboros' trash out and, not only tossing it into the garbage cans in the dawn-to-dusk garage, "but going through it. They were definitely cleaning the house." There was one time when someone "washed out the garbage cans," using a water hose to flush the cans out for some reason.

The timing for this was odd, or suspect, to say the least.

"These were older people," another source told me. "Here it was, right? Someone had been murdered, and they're cleaning out the garbage cans!" Then there was another "family member," that same source added, "actually going through the trash. They were taking the trash cans out and going through the garbage. . . ."

Piece by piece.

One had to wonder: Why would someone—presumably a Roseboro family member or friend—be going through the Roseboros' trash? What were they looking for?

15

Larry Martin had a feeling that Jan Roseboro's autopsy was going to shed some light on what the ECTPD was looking at: homicide or accidental death. Martin got in his cruiser and headed out to the Lancaster County Morgue, located in the basement of the Conestoga View nursing home, an eight-story brick building on twenty-six acres, with close to five hundred beds. The View, as it is called, was owned by Lancaster County until 2004, when it was sold to a private company. At one time, locals referred to this establishment just six blocks from downtown Lancaster as the "County Home." Go back a few more generations than that and it went by the insalubrious name of the "County Poorhouse."

Aptly located in the basement of the View, the Lancaster County Morgue is an L-shaped room about twenty feet wide, fifteen feet long, a small office attached to one side. The morgue was opened in June 1968 and still very much holds on to its original framework, with the exception of an added positive air-pressure system. The room contains one examination table, where Jan Roseboro's body was lying in wait for Martin and the pathologist, surrounded by stainless-steel casework. There's a walk-in refrigerator for, you guessed it, bodies and body parts. The walls are ivory-colored tile. For cops like Larry Martin, the one thing that bothers them about being in the morgue is not the sight of dead people, or organs lying around in stainless-steel dishes. It is the smell. The absolute unmistakable odor of decomposing flesh. The Lancaster Morgue has portable shelving on the walls that contains masks and gowns and other supplies to keep things clean and the smell to a minimum. Yet, the one way the county forensic pathologist, Dr. Wayne Ross, has managed to contain and control the rank odor of death, keeping the horrible stench to an acceptable level, is to burn candles.

Martin met with Dr. Ross and his assistant after walking in that morning, July 23, 2008, somewhere near nine o'clock. Before they got started with the actual dissection of Jan's body, Martin briefed Ross, who had been with the Lancaster County Coroner's Office since 1994. He told the doctor what had happened, filling him in, thus far, on the investigation—if it could even be called such—pointing out the wound on the back of Jan's head, which the hospital ER doctor had discovered. Martin explained how important he believed it was to the investigation to find out how the wound got there.

Now that the pathologist had a chance to cut open the hoodie Jan was wearing at the time of her death, spread it apart, and take a look at the inside, quite a bit of bloodstaining was revealed.

Martin looked; he had not expected to see so much blood.

"Wow."

Where had it all come from?

"Extensive bloodstains," Dr. Ross later called them. He checked the hoodie front to back, "looking for various bloodstain patterns." A lot of times, "bloodstains tell their own story," the doctor said, adding, "I could see a lot of what we refer to as transfer bloodstains over the front of the sweatshirt. In particular, I could see there was a cut noted through the front of the sweatshirt. It went right through a bloodstain. So we know that bloodstain was deposited before any of the emergency medical personnel had done a cut to remove that hoodie."

There were also bloodstains, the pathologist observed, on the hood of the sweatshirt. There was a fairly prominent stain in the area of the hood where Jan had received that nasty gash to the back of her head.

"Suffice it to say," the doctor concluded after checking the sweatshirt, "there were bloodstains all over the hoodie."

One scenario that law enforcement had to rule out, as bizarre as it might have sounded, was a lightning strike. Had Jan been sitting poolside, enjoying the night sky as that thunderstorm rolled in, and been the victim of a direct lightning bolt strike? Although highly improbable, and perhaps against all odds, it was definitely possible. Perhaps that gash in her head was the lightning strike entryway or exit?

"In the beginning, I keep an open mind," Dr. Ross later explained, "as to what I was looking at. There was no evidence of a lightning strike. I ruled that out. I excluded that."

There were no burn marks, for one, on Jan's body. And the injuries, which now looked to be substantial and plentiful, were consistent with blunt-force trauma.

Nothing else.

Jan had been beaten.

Savagely, in fact.

Ross found bloodstains, for example, on Jan's bra and underwear.

"Transfer bloodstains," Ross explained. "This means the blood had been transferred from an object or from clothing or something *on* that clothing. So bloodshed had already occurred, had already taken place, and then the blood was *transferred*."

A new picture was slowly emerging.

But how? Where had all this blood come from—that one wound to the back of Jan's head?

One of the first things Ross did was study the body and write down all of the injuries he felt Jan had endured during whatever incident had occurred. Once she was naked and lying on the gurney with high-powered lamps shining down, Ross could see how many injuries Jan had actually sustained. This was pure science. Ross made it clear in court later that an "abrasion is a scrape," while a "contusion is a bruise, and a bruise is basically bleeding underneath the skin."

Most interesting to Larry Martin was how Ross explained that contusions do not typically take place *after* death.

"Under some circumstances," the doctor said, "somebody might raise that issue, but that's why you've got to look at the amount of the contusion. You've got to look at it microscopically and that tells if you're dealing with something that occurred before or after death."

In Jan's case, the list of contusions and abrasions alone turned out to be enormous. In between her breast, for instance, there were "two bruises and abrasions. . . . There were actually some stippled hemorrhages on [there]." (A fancy word for spotting.)

On the lower region of Jan's abdomen, there were two additional sets of abrasions or scrapes. Her upper left arm had three circular bruises; on the back of her left arm, near the elbow region, there was another "roughly" circular bruise; another bruise near her wrist. This was all consistent with someone grabbing Jan firmly and holding on to her. Wrestling her around, perhaps. Moreover, inside her right arm had a bruise. Her lower legs, both of them, had several bruises on the front and back. There was an abrasion or scrape again on the top of her right foot. And quite fascinating for Martin, when looking at the scenario as a homicide—the drowning as a possible cover-up—was that there were no bruises, other than two small spots on her lips, to Jan's face, and nothing on her forehead.

"It's pretty much clean," Ross said, referring to Jan's face.

Many of these bruises and contusions, the doctor knew from studying them, had been made on Jan's body *before* her death.

At that point during the autopsy, after observing all the wounds Jan had sustained, the doctor said, "I have what I refer to as significant stuff. . . . I'm concerned about what is going on here."

Still, Ross had not concluded on a cause of death, but the more he looked at Jan's body, the more it seemed she had been the victim of murder.

Before concluding his assessment of Jan's body, Ross took scrapings from underneath all of Jan's fingernails and placed them into evidence bags for shipping off to the forensic lab. There seemed to be "something" underneath the fingernails on Jan's left hand. Ross noted that Jan had short fingernails, generally speaking, as compared to most women with long fingernails. On her left hand, however, Ross was able to obtain scrapings from only four fingers. Years ago, Jan had purchased a juicing machine. While juicing some vegetables and fruits one afternoon, she accidentally stuck her hand down into the juicer and it ground her left middle finger (the "F-U" finger) past the cuticle part of the fingernail down to the first joint. Jan had no left middle fingertip to extract any trace evidence or clippings from. Just a stub. Or "amputation," as the doctor noted.

Still, that one small variable, that Jan had only four fingers on her left hand, would become one of the more important pieces of evidence the ECTPD would uncover throughout its investigation.

After he finished documenting all of the bruises and

abrasions on Jan's corpse, bagging those clippings and scrapings from Jan's nails, Ross took his scalpel in hand and began to fillet Jan open. That was when things truly became interesting, as Martin and the doctor began to wonder how, in fact, Jan had died.

16

After Dr. Wayne Ross shaved Jan Roseboro's head, he and Larry Martin could see that the wound to the back of Jan's scalp was even more pronounced than they had originally thought, simply because now it wasn't buried underneath her thick mane of blond hair anymore.

The next thing Dr. Ross did, as Martin stood nearby and watched, was make an incision with his razor-sharp scalpel above Jan's forehead and back down over each ear. He then peeled the scalp back—as if it were a rubber wig—and let it hang from the back of Jan's head. This exposed Jan's skull and the tissue underneath her scalp.

Larry Martin stood next to Ross in the autopsy suite staring down at Jan's skull. With Jan's scalp stripped off her head, Martin couldn't believe what he was looking at.

Before Ross even said anything, Martin thought, *She was beaten over the head and killed.*

The bruising was distinctive and noticeable, now that Jan's skull was bare.

Wow, Martin thought.

"There was other bruising on the top of the head," Martin recalled. "This was *very* clear to us."

It wasn't just a few localized bruises in a certain quadrant of Jan's head, as if she had maybe fallen and bumped herself on a plant container, the side of the pool, or a table. There were sections of a white, milky substance—indicating violent contusions present (made) before death—overwhelming the blood vessels and muscle tissue.

As they stared at this, there was no doubt in either of their minds.

Jan had been beaten over the head.

Ross focused on the bruising. "Look, Larry, I want to check some other things out first, but this is looking more and more like it is going to be a homicide."

Murder one.

Martin shook his head, agreeing. Then he asked the doctor to stop the autopsy. Martin wanted to call in Scott Eelman, a detective from the East Lampeter Township Police Department (ELTPD), who also happened to be the coordinator for the Lancaster County Forensic Unit (LCFU). Law enforcement liked to work together in Lancaster County, supporting one another. Where one department might lack a certain resource, it could call on another department specializing in a particular field to come in and help out.

Larry Martin had a digital camera with him, but Martin was the first to admit he was no Annie Leibovitz. On top of that, Ross wanted someone from forensics to take photos for his reports. Eelman was good at what he did.

"Get over here with your camera," Ross told Eelman.

Along with Eelman, Kelly Sekula and one of the investigators working for the LCDA's Office showed up. Not only was Eelman good with a camera, but when (and if) it came time to seal off any crime scenes that might be connected to Jan's death, Eelman was going to be one of the crime scene investigators coordinating that effort. Bringing him into the fold now was a smart thing to do.

With everyone standing around twenty minutes later,

Ross continued with his autopsy. As he worked from Jan's head down, opening up Jan's neck, he found something else: bruising on both sides—directly along the linear line of both carotid arteries on each side of Jan's neck.

The evidence was clear: Jan Roseboro had been choked at some point.

Ross moved in, asking Martin to take a closer look.

"Strangulation," Martin said. "I remember Dr. Ross showing me that. By then, I was sold that Jan had been murdered."

The horror of Jan Roseboro's final few minutes of life, however, didn't end there. Down inside Jan's chest, after Ross cut her lungs open, a frothlike, watery substance poured out.

Foam?

"I had been to enough autopsies of drowning victims to know," Martin later commented, "that Jan had drowned to death."

The most incredible part of all of this was that the water in Jan's lungs proved she was alive inside her in-ground pool. Jan had drowned. This after being beaten and strangled.

Incredible, Martin thought. *This is remarkable evidence.*

It was near noon when Ross finished. Martin called Keith Neff.

"He ruled it a homicide," Martin told his lead detective. "Multiple head injuries, strangulation, and drowning."

"My goodness," Neff said.

"You start thinking," Martin recalled, "and you don't want to be close-minded about it, but you start to ask yourself, 'Who was the last person to see Jan alive?' and 'Who was the person who found Jan in the pool?'"

Michael Roseboro.

"From that person, you begin to work outward," Martin added.

Larry Martin collected all of the evidence from Ross—the fingernail clippings, vaginal and rectal swabs, that plastic tube the EMTs put in Jan's throat, nasal swabs, clothing, any tape lifts the pathologist took from all over the body, blood—and brought it back to the ECTPD station house, where it would then be sent out to various labs for testing.

17

When Larry Martin returned from the autopsy, he and Keith Neff sat down inside the ECTPD conference room. It was close to one o'clock, the afternoon of July 23, 2008. While Martin was at the autopsy, ECTPD office manager Heather Smith set it up so they could hear Michael Roseboro's 911 call from the previous night. Neff and Martin would eventually get an actual recording of it from the communications center, but they had wanted to hear the 911 call as soon as they could.

There was a speakerphone in the middle of a conference room table with the 911 call on the other end of the line.

Certain things Roseboro had said were, at best, suspicious; at worst, these were the words of a guilty man. The 911 call could clear up some of that confusion, or, as the case would soon be, cause more problems for Roseboro. His wife's death had been ruled a homicide. The ECTPD had a lot of work to do. Part of it started with this call.

The dispatcher on the other end of the line asked if they were ready. Neff, Martin, and the other officers in the room indicated they were.

"Go ahead," someone said, "run that tape."*

The call had come in at 11:03 P.M. the previous night to the communications center. It was made from the Roseboros' landline number. The male operator said, "Lancaster County 911?"

"I believe my wife just drowned," Roseboro said matter-of-factly. There was no emotion in his voice.

So abnormally soft was Roseboro's voice, the 911 operator said, "I'm sorry?" as if he could not hear Roseboro.

What's important is, according to Roseboro, this was just seconds after he had gone outside and found his wife in the deep end of the pool and pulled her out of the water. Yet, he was subdued and nonchalant, saying, "I believe my wife just drowned."

The first question had to be: *how could he know she had drowned?*

"What's your address?" 911 asked.

As Neff and Martin listened, they sat up closer to the speakerphone, looking at each other. It was an odd call. Roseboro sounded too calm and collected for a man describing the possibility that his wife was dead, or, at the least, in big trouble.

Roseboro told the operator the address and the township he lived in.

Then, "Okay, and what happened?" 911 queried.

Without hesitating, again without any emotion or fanfare, Roseboro said, "I had gone to bed about an hour and a half ago and she was outside, and I came out and saw the lights on by the pool, but—oh, God—her shorts and shoes are still on. I came out and found her in the deep end of the pool."

"Okay, is she breathing?"

"No, she's not."

"Is she still in the water?"

---

*You can go online and hear this 911 call. Conduct a simple search on any reputable search engine.

"No, I pulled her out."

"Okay, do you want to try to start CPR on her?"

"I will, I will. Yeah."

"Okay, do you need help to do that? I can give you instructions on what to do."

"I was a lifeguard. I know."

Martin and Neff looked at each other again while listening: *What an odd thing to say at what you would assume to be a frantic time.*

"I was a lifeguard."

Why wasn't this guy in stage-four panic?

"Okay, do you want me to help walk you through it?" 911 asked.

"I . . . Just compressions under the breast?" Roseboro said.

"Right. I can walk you through it, if you want help?"

"I wanna get her out of the pool."

What? Neff thought. *He said earlier that he had gotten her out of the pool. How could you confuse such a thing?*

"What's that?" 911 wanted to know, a bit of confusion in his voice.

"I wanna get her out of the pool," Roseboro repeated.

"She's *still* in the pool?"

There was a beat of silence. Thinking, perhaps. Then, "Yeah," Roseboro said clearly.

"I thought you said she was *out* of the pool?"

"I . . . Oh, my God"—and again, he sounded as though he were being forced into this reaction—"I'm sorry, she's out of the pool. Uh, yeah, help me through it, please."

The 911 operator wanted to reaffirm that Jan was out of the pool.

Roseboro said yes, she was.

Then 911 asked Roseboro, where was he at that moment?

"I'm right beside her. . . ."

That was assumed. He meant, where in the backyard?

"I'm on the deck."

"You're on the deck? Okay. What I want you to do . . . Is there anybody else there?"

"My children are asleep."

"How old are your children?"

"Twelve, nine, and six."

"Okay, what we need to do is get her on her back."

"Yes, sir."

"You have her flipped over on her back?"

"She's on her back, yeah."

"Okay, I want you to check and see if she has a pulse. Do you know how to do that?"

"I do."

"Okay."

A second later, "There's no pulse."

Martin and Neff wondered how the guy could have checked for a pulse in such a short period of time—this, with the phone apparently cradled in his shoulder. It took seconds, if not more, to find an artery. Even longer to determine if there was a heartbeat. Neff leaned back in his chair as the tape continued to play.

Come on. . . .

"There is none?" 911 asked.

"No, there's not."

"Okay, what I want you to do . . ." The operator then explained how he wanted Roseboro to get his wife on her back, and look in her mouth to see if there was anything blocking the airway. "Vomit or anything like that?"

"No."

"No?" 911 asked, surprised.

"No."

911 then told Roseboro where to place his hands in order to tilt her head back, so he could put his ear next to her mouth to see if he heard breathing.

After another brief exchange, it was determined that Roseboro could not feel or hear any breathing coming from Jan's mouth. She was definitely unconscious, if not dead.

911 explained how to start CPR. "Keep her head titled back. Pinch her nose. Cover her mouth with yours and give her two deep, regular breaths, about one second each."

"Okay."

After doing it a few times, Roseboro said he could feel air going "in and out" of Jan's lungs.

"Okay, stay on the line with me . . . ," 911 said. ". . . We're starting . . . The ambulance is on the way."

"Okay."

"What I want you to do is, we are going to start compressions. Okay, listen carefully, and I'll tell you how to do it." From there, the dispatcher explained how he wanted Roseboro to conduct the CPR compressions to Jan's chest. You could hear sirens now from afar in the background of the call, and the 911 guy noted the noises, asking, "Okay, is that the siren from the fire department there [nearby]?"

"Yeah. Hold on," Roseboro said. "I have to throw up. Please hold on."

"Okay."

"I'm sorry."

After being asked, Roseboro said nobody was there with him.

"Okay, what we're going to do is start the compressions, okay? Go ahead and put your hand on her chest like I told you. I want you to pump her chest hard and fast, about thirty times, about twice a second."

That would take, at the least, fifteen seconds, plus the time to position yourself to proceed. More than that, Neff and Martin considered as they sat and listened, trying to picture in their minds every movement Roseboro made, it would take two hands. Yet, there was never any indication that Roseboro put the phone down, or was wrestling with it, trying to cradle it in his ear and shoulder.

"Okay," Roseboro said after 911 told him to make sure he let the chest come up between pumps.

"Let me know when you've done it thirty times."

"Okay."

"All right, go ahead and do that."

A few seconds later. "Okay."

"You did it about thirty times?" 911 asked, shocked.

"Yes, sir."

911 asked Roseboro to check Jan's mouth to see if the compression and the breathing brought anything up from her lungs.

"No, there's not," he said.

"Okay. . . ."

"Oh, my God."

"Okay, what we're going to do is continue, okay?"

"All right."

911 told Roseboro to continue keeping his hand under Jan's neck, pinch her nose closed, tilt her head back, giving her two more regular breaths, and then pump her chest thirty *additional* times.

It took Roseboro a second or two to say, "Okay. . . ."

"Okay?" 911 asked with some confusion. *Okay, you understand me? Or, okay, you've done it?* There just didn't seem to be enough time in between the okays to perform such a procedure.

"Okay . . . okay," Roseboro said.

"Okay, go ahead and give her the thirty chest pumps, okay?"

"I did. I did."

"You did do that?"

"Yes."

911 asked if there was any sign of life.

"No."

911 then instructed Roseboro to continue with CPR. "I want you to keep doing that [until the ambulance arrives]."

"The ambulance is here, sir."

". . . Okay, sir, go get them."

"Okay, thank you," Roseboro said.

Neff was floored by that last comment. . . . *"Thank you"? Your wife is struggling for life, possibly even dead, the ambulance is just pulling up, and you are thanking the 911 dispatcher instead of dashing off to flag down the medics?*

"Strange," Martin said as the call ended. "We need a copy of that so we can break it down line by line."

"You got it," Neff said.

18

Jan Walters had been a Lancaster County detective for eighteen years. Altogether, Jan had nearly forty-plus years of law enforcement experience by the time Michael and Jan Roseboro's names crossed his busy desk at the LCDA's Office on North Duke Street, downtown Lancaster. The LCDA did not want to step into the situation like cowboys and take control from the ECTPD, now that the pathologist had made the pronouncement cause of Jan's death as blunt-force trauma, strangulation, and drowning, the manner of death homicide. DA Craig Stedman and ADA Kelly Sekula were adamant where it pertained to helping the ECTPD in a supporting role. But Stedman—according to almost everyone in law enforcement I spoke to later—was going to now begin driving the bus. The investigation was the ECTPD's; Keith Neff was the lead. That was not going to change. But in the reality of the situation, Neff had never investigated a homicide. A seasoned investigator like Jan Walters, with decades of murder investigation experience behind him, could help Neff along the way and, Neff knew, probably show him a thing or two about solving a case.

"I welcomed Jan's help," Neff said later.

"I have known Jan Walters for years," Larry Martin recalled, "and have the utmost respect for him. I knew he would do a great job for us."

Perhaps by rank alone, Martin had become the case manager of the investigation, which would keep him at the station logging and posting what each investigator did during the course of his or her day. There were now between ten to fifteen investigators activated for the Roseboro investigation. The media was sniffing around, looking for a crumb to run with. This was huge news in Denver/Lancaster, where the Roseboro name carried some serious social weight. With all of the media coverage that would ensue as soon as word got out that Jan had been murdered, and the presence of so many investigators coming to help, Larry Martin needed to keep everything tight. As the night and day shifts investigated different aspects of the case, both would need to know what the other was doing; and now with so many additional investigators part of the case, Martin had to delegate jobs and keep everyone on the same page while, at the same time, utilizing each investigator's talents and experience.

The other advantage to having a case manager was so Martin could check off assignments as they were completed.

"You didn't want to find out two weeks after the fact that this person was never interviewed, or that was never looked into."

Coordination. Information was going to flood in. Someone needed to pore through it all and manage it. In addition, with extended families on both sides—the Roseboros and the Binkleys—scores of interviews were going to be conducted.

"And so," Martin said, "we all got together and decided what to do next."

The other important piece in managing the case was Heather Smith, the ECTPD office manager. Neff pulled

Martin aside and told him, "We need her to help with organizing—she is great with computers and putting things together."

Neff didn't need to be sold on the idea. Heather, with twenty years on the job, was good at what she did.

"Heather was always willing to help," Martin said. To Neff, "Absolutely."

Indeed, Smith's input would prove crucial to the case, as Heather began to painstakingly keep track of what everyone was doing and how the information coming in was stored and categorized. When it came time to track people down via phone numbers, Smith would be the one to make those calls, look up the numbers, find addresses, and then put all of the info into some sort of graph or chart that the detectives could easily understand, plus coordinate for a possible (and potential) prosecution down the road.

Routine morning meetings between detectives, which Martin and Neff began right away, would soon prove to be essential in solving this case.

Whenever a murder is committed in Lancaster County, the county's Major Crimes Unit (MCU) is officially activated. There's no Bat Cave button to be pushed, or alarm sounded. The MCU is not a separate team of investigators, as the name might suggest. The MCU operates like an ad hoc force that forms on an as-needed basis. What this meant to the ECTPD and the Roseboro investigation was that the ECTPD would have the help it needed from any law enforcement agency in the county.

For Detectives Keith Neff and Jan Walters, who had shown up at the ECTPD that afternoon, July 23, the first job in front of them was to contact Michael Roseboro and see when he would be available for another little sit-down.

ADA Kelly Sekula got busy on the DA's end, writing a search warrant for the Roseboro residence. The Roseboros' pool was a crime scene, along with the entire house.

As Sekula wrote inside the ECTPD in Denver, Neff and Walters got together and talked about how they were going to approach Roseboro. What was the best way to talk to the guy, now that Jan's death had been ruled a homicide? This would be a far different conversation from the one Larry Martin and Keith Neff had with Michael Roseboro the previous night.

Surprise was the best way to go about talking to Roseboro at this point. Go over there and knock on the door; see what he says when he's given the information that his wife's death was no accident. Reaction during a situation like this is *everything* to a cop. Ever since Jan's death, Roseboro didn't seem to have any emotional response whatsoever. Nearly everyone close to him during this time period later agreed that his demeanor was flat. Nonverbal.

Not even detached. But just, well, level.

Was Roseboro mourning the death of his wife?

In addition, Neff said later, the other purpose of the interview was to get an account from Roseboro of how he had removed his wife from the pool.

It was 2:11 P.M. when Jan Walters and Keith Neff knocked on the Roseboros' front door. Michael Roseboro's black SUV was parked in the driveway alongside a few other vehicles. It was clear that he was home, and not alone.

"Can we talk to you again?" Neff asked after Roseboro opened the door.

"Sure . . . yeah, that would be okay," he said.

Roseboro invited the investigators into the newer section of the house. The kitchen and living room were connected to each other. It was just the three of them. Everyone else was in another part of the house.

"We need to get some detail about what happened," Neff said.

"Sure, sure."

"Okay, we're trying to figure out what happened to Jan. Can you just go through your night once more for us, Mr. Roseboro?" Walters asked after Neff introduced him as a detective from the DA's office in Lancaster.

Roseboro did not hesitate. "I went to bed at about ten. Woke up at ten fifty-eight. Saw one of the torchlights were on and went outside. When I got to the first torchlight, I saw my wife in the pool."

Neff was thinking of the 911 call that he and Larry Martin had listened to earlier that day and the statement Roseboro had given him—and Patrolman Firestone—the previous night. This statement—*went to bed at ten, found her in the pool near eleven*—was becoming the Roseboro mantra.

Like he's reading from a script, Neff thought.

Walters watched Roseboro as he spoke, studying his movements and facial expressions.

"How did you get her out of the pool?" Neff asked.

It was odd to Neff, now that he'd had more time to think about the situation, that Jan Roseboro was found on her back in the deep end of the pool, then placed on the deck, one leg hanging over the edge, barely in the water. How had Roseboro hoisted her out of the pool?

"When I got to that first tiki torchlight," Roseboro explained, "I noticed Jan was in the deep end of the pool. Her face was facing away from the residence. So I jumped into the pool, swam to her, and started pulling her out by her sweatshirt . . . toward the two sets of steps in the deep end of the pool. . . . When I got to the steps and the ledge, I started pulling her up." Roseboro demonstrated his actions as he explained what happened. "I reached around her, crossed her arms, reached around her, and was using her forearms, the wrist area, kind of her shoulders, to pull her up onto the deck."

Some struggle that must have been, Neff considered. Literally, Jan was dead and wet weight. Any husband would have had anxiety and fear and shock undoubtedly flowing through his bloodstream like adrenaline. Being a heavy smoker and drinker, Roseboro must have had a difficult time getting his wife out of the pool.

"Go on," Neff encouraged.

"When I got her . . . to the deck, I had pulled her out by the sweatshirt. I checked for a pulse and started pushing her on the chest. _Then_ called 911."

Keep him talking. . . . "Okay. Then what happened?"

"The 911 operator instructed me to check for an airway obstruction and then told me how to do CPR . . . which, I believe, it was, um, two breaths for thirty compressions."

As he told this part of his story, Roseboro acted it out. "He told me," Neff later said, "that she was . . . He was demonstrating it and was leaning forward with his arms out and said that she was submerged in the water in the deep end of the pool" as Roseboro pulled her out. "I wanted to make sure his handling of her body could not account for the injuries."

It all seemed so awkward. Who would pull someone out of the water like that—better yet, his own wife?

As the ECTPD, now with the help of the MCU, began to branch out and conduct a widespread investigation into the death of Jan Roseboro, one of the first things on the list was to create a victimology report, which took a look into Jan's life to see what type of person she was and if anyone had a good reason to kill her. Who knew, really, if perhaps Jan had been living some sort of secret life? Or maybe was having an affair, broke it off, and her lover returned and drowned her as payback? What about a home invasion gone wrong? There were scores of possibilities to consider. At this time, nothing could be ruled out.

"We were looking at about two hundred fifty people

to interview in the early stages of the investigation," Neff said.

And yet, it all started with Michael Roseboro, Jan's husband. The guy who had found her dead. The last person who had seen her alive.

As Neff and Walters talked to Roseboro, near 2:30 P.M., Neff was still not convinced that Roseboro was being honest with them. Neff was now working under the assumption that Roseboro had killed his wife and tried to cover it up. The fact remained that if he had pulled Jan out of the pool by her arms, as he had explained in detail, why were there no scratches on Jan's back or belly? The pool coping (edge mold) is rather rough, scratchy, like sandpaper. Why weren't there scratches anywhere else on her body, indicating that she had been dragged?

Something wasn't right.

Staring at Michael Roseboro, listening to him finish his explanation, Keith Neff noticed something else that began to bother him.

Scratches. Three of them. On Roseboro's face. They were more pronounced now that they'd had time to scab over.

When he noticed the scratches, Neff thought, *Whoa.*

There were two scratches on the left side of Roseboro's mouth, one on the right. Although Neff and Walters didn't know it yet, the number and placement of the scratches were significant. Jan Roseboro had that hand with one fingertip missing. Just a stub, actually. So if—a big *if,* mind you—she had scratched her husband with that hand, it would leave only three scratches, as opposed to four from a normal hand.

"I have a lot to do," Roseboro said. "I need to write Jan's obituary . . . and meet with the church people to set things up."

"We understand," Neff said. "Is there a time we can talk to you again? We need to go over a few more things."

"Ah, maybe five-thirty today would work."

"At the station, okay?" Neff told Roseboro.

"Yeah, okay. I'll be there."

As they walked away from the house, it occurred to Keith Neff and Jan Walters that Michael Roseboro had not asked one question regarding what had happened to his wife. Or, now that her death had been ruled a homicide, if they had a suspect.

19

Keith Neff and Jan Walters waited at the ECTPD for Michael Roseboro to show up. He said he'd be there at 5:30 P.M.

Wouldn't you know it—as the big hand hit the six, the little hand the five, there was the man of the hour: Michael Roseboro stepped out of his friend Gary Frees's vehicle and walked into the station house.

Roseboro came through the door with the same demeanor he'd had throughout the previous night. Some called it stoic. But "stoic" implied that Roseboro was struggling emotionally with his wife's death and holding it together. That was not the attitude Keith Neff and Jan Walters observed.

To them, Roseboro seemed like a guy who didn't give a hoot.

"Thanks for coming in, Mike," Neff said, greeting him with a handshake. "Can you come on back into the interview room for us?" Neff and Walters stood with Roseboro and Gary Frees in the lobby.

"Yeah, okay."

Walters, Neff, and Roseboro sat down in the interview room. Frees waited in the lobby. As soon as they got situated, Walters came right out with it, perhaps at the risk of laying some of their cards on the table. "Mike," the experienced detective said, "I want to thank you for coming in. Look, your wife's death was *not* an accident. She was beaten and drowned."

Not a flinch. Not a movement. Not a word.

Zombielike.

"Nothing," Neff said later. "The guy did not say or do *anything* when we gave him that news. He just sat there."

"There was no reaction," Walters later added. "He said nothing. No gestures. Nothing."

Not even close to an appropriate reaction, Neff considered as he stared at Roseboro as Walters delivered the news. *What is going on with this guy?*

"Mike, listen," Walters continued, "since you're in a police station, it would be proper if we advised you of your Miranda rights."

Roseboro had his head down. He made little to no eye contact with either Neff or Walters as they spoke.

Neff took out a sheet of paper and read Roseboro his rights. They were not accusing him of the murder, officially. But they wanted Roseboro to understand that he didn't have to speak to them without representation if he didn't want. Essentially, Walters and Neff were saying that the questions they were going to be asking could get a bit more intimate and accusatory, so it would be best if he watched what he said or called his lawyer. The choice was his to continue.

"Mike," Walters asked, "can you read me a portion of it out loud?" Standard procedure. It was to show the detectives that Roseboro understood and comprehended English.

Roseboro read. When he finished, Neff handed him a pen. Roseboro needed to sign the form indicating that he was willing to answer questions without a lawyer present.

He signed the Miranda form. As he did this, Neff

and Walters looked at each other with a bit of *Okay, yes, this is good.*

Walters said they needed an explanation from Roseboro about what happened out at the pool. All those injuries the pathologist had reported on Jan's body. Especially that gash in the back of Jan's head. The fact that her lungs contained a soapy liquid meant she was alive when she went into the water. They never gave Roseboro all these details. But instead, Walters said, "Mike, it was just you and your wife at the house, except for the kids, who were sleeping." The detective paused. "Mike, we need an explanation from you. You're free to leave at any time. You are not under arrest. But we need to know *what* happened out there."

"No," Roseboro said. Then, after a brief gap of silence, as though a lightbulb went off and he suddenly understood what was going on, Roseboro pointed at himself and said, "Hey, are you saying *I* am a suspect?"

Walters didn't hesitate. "Yes, Mike. Of course. You must have known it would come to this. It was just you and Jan out there."

Roseboro looked at the two of them. He didn't like the tone or where this was obviously heading.

"Can you think of any other explanation?" Walters asked.

"No," Roseboro said. Then he broke into that familiar monologue: "I got up around ten fifty-eight. . . . I saw the torchlights were on and I went out and found her."

Robotic. Rehearsed. Scripted.

"Well, Mike, put yourself in our place," Walters said while Neff studied Roseboro's reactions.

"I understand."

"Mike, do you have *any* other explanation?" Neff piped in and asked.

"I don't have one."

Roseboro wasn't looking down at the floor any longer.

Walters later said that he was "basically looking past us, down a little bit, but *past* us." Walters was sitting in front of Roseboro, Neff to Roseboro's right.

"Can you tell us about those scratches, Mike?" Walters asked.

"Oh, this," he answered, touching his face. "I got those from my daughter. We were playing basketball at the house, inside the pool."

"Can we photograph those scratches on your face, Mike?"

"Sure . . . sure."

Walters got up and walked out of the room, presumably to get a camera.

When Walters was out of sight, Neff asked Roseboro, "What type of basketball did you play?"

"The net, in the water." Neff understood it to be one of those floating basketball hoops.

"Mike, we really need an explanation from you about what happened to Jan. You don't have *anything* you can tell us?"

"No."

Neff decided to go for it. Give the guy a way out of this mess, if Roseboro wanted one. In a genial manner, one that said he was there to help Roseboro through this, if he wanted, Neff said, "Mike, we know this was something that either happened in the heat of passion or was planned out. But I don't want to believe it was planned out."

Neff was trying to tell Roseboro, without coming out and saying it, that there might be a way to escape real prison time—if only he came clean. Maybe it was manslaughter? Perhaps he and Jan got into an argument and Roseboro snapped?

"I didn't do this," Roseboro said in a near whisper. No defiance in his voice, or anger at the fact that two detectives were accusing him of brutally murdering his wife, a woman Roseboro had claimed he was going to renew his marriage vows with in a matter of weeks.

"I am past that, Mike." Neff heard Walters coming back into the room. "Do you have *any* questions for us, Mike?" Here they were telling the guy his wife had been murdered, pointing a finger in his face, and he had not asked them one question. They expected Roseboro to have *nothing but questions.*

Roseboro thought about it. Then he said, "No."

Another detective took photographs of Roseboro's goatee area, where the three scratches were located.

"Thanks for coming in, Mike," Walters said. "We appreciate it."

Roseboro left.

Neff and Walters needed to get a search warrant in hand and head over to the Roseboro residence and comb through that house, inch by inch—without anyone breathing down their backs. They needed to find evidence to arrest Roseboro on first-degree murder charges. As the officers stood and watched Roseboro leave, the ECTPD had no evidence and no motive. Just a few scratches and a hunch. The Roseboro family had money. Jan and Mike's marriage appeared to be solid. Why would this guy kill his wife?

Soon after Roseboro left the parking lot, Neff grabbed one of the patrol officers and drove out to the Roseboro house, saying later, "We needed to take that house." Seal it off until the warrant came through.

By now, they were told by Kelly Sekula that a search warrant was imminent. It was only a matter of time and a judge's signature.

When Neff arrived with several officers, there were approximately thirty people at Michael Roseboro's house, inside and out. The officers took down names as they explained that a search warrant was going to be served and everyone needed to leave.

As Neff stood outside the house, he had no idea that the case was about to yield its first major twist (or break, depending on how you looked at it). It would soon be revealed that one of the most popular motivating factors for murder had been right underneath the ECTPD's nose all along. It would have nothing to do with the Roseboro house or what the ECTPD was about to uncover inside, but everything to do with the type of human being, husband, and father Michael Roseboro was—something that would turn the small town of Denver, Pennsylvania, on its heels.

20

The first of two search warrants was signed by Judge Nancy G. Hamill, of the court of common pleas, on July 24, 2008, at 1:40 P.M. The ECTPD had two days to go through the Roseboro house. The warrant stipulated some of the items the ECTPD was looking for: trace evidence, including hair fibers, blood, bodily fluids, and fingerprints, along with any items with bloodstains or apparent bloodstains. It allowed the ECTPD to process the entire residence: pool area, patio, and any other common area, for blood spatter analysis. The fact that it had rained so heavily the night before and continued, on and off, throughout that day, worked against the CSI team. Yet luminol could reveal blood hidden in plain sight. Little mist here, a bit over there, and *boom!*—there it is, like invisible ink—that Day-Glo light indicating the presence of plasma.

East Lampeter Township Police Department detective Scott Eelman, the coordinator for the Lancaster County Forensic Unit, was called back into the case as part of the MCU. Eelman had processed "hundreds" of crime scenes. It was Eelman who had checked the radar the night before. Learning that more storms were moving into the region, he chose to forgo the search on the night Keith Neff took the house and instead decided to begin the following morning.

"We elected to wait until the twenty-fourth," Eelman said. "It had already rained . . . and one more time wasn't going to do anything to harm the situation."

After photographing the inside of the house and the outside yard, which familiarized members of the LCFU helping Eelman with the layout, they started in the backyard. Inside the pool deck area, it was clear that people had been hanging out at the pool recently.

"It appeared that there were several drink containers," Eelman reported, "glasses, bottles, that sort of thing, lying around the pool area up on the table and surrounding areas, and it appeared that there were . . . that there had been people there after the initial incident."

One neighbor said she was appalled to see kids and adults swimming in the pool in the days after Jan had been found dead in that same water.

"I could not believe my eyes," the neighbor said.

"Disgusting," said another neighbor. "It was incredible."

Nonetheless, Eelman had to deal with it. There was the chance that if they found anything outside near the pool, it would be worthless, anyway. There were so many variables at work here—albeit rain and people—searching for evidence of value outside near the pool was more or less a formality at this point.

After spending hours going through the house and the outdoor areas, Eelman and his team found "nothing of great significance," he later described, that "really stood out. Nothing really jumped out as evidence."

Along with computers and cell phones and everyday electronic gadgets that all search warrants covered these days, the team did not take much forensic evidence out of the Roseboro home. They listed: *two hairs from the edge of the pool coping near the gate* and *two white tissues/toilet*

paper and two Band-Aids all with blood staining, along with
*one pair of red & white swim shorts/suit—XL size, Counter
Culture brand.*

The swimsuit was an interesting discovery. It turned
out to be the one Michael Roseboro wore on the night
EMTs and ECTPD showed up after his 911 call. On the
front of the garment, it appeared to have stains of some
sort. The LCFU found the bathing suit inside the Roseboros' downstairs bathroom. Yet, when the state police
lab later tested it, the stains turned out to be nothing of
any consequence to the investigation.

Even after they sprayed the entire pool deck area
with the chemical leuco crystal, which turns traces of
blood purple, and another chemical compound called
Starlight Bloodhound, which works more like straight
luminol and makes blood essentially give off a glow,
there was not one trace of blood anywhere. Not even a
speck. This after several members of the CSI Unit got on
their hands and knees with flashlights and searched inch
by inch along the concrete, looking for any, however
remote, trace that blood was present on the concrete
near the area where Jan's body had been worked on.

If Jan had bled outside, someone knew what he was
doing when cleaning it up.

There were several large planters around the pool. But
not a trace of blood or hair was located on any of them.
The accidental slipping idea—Jan could have fallen on
one of those planters, cracked her head open, and then,
dazed and dizzy, fell into the pool and drowned—was
superseded by the fact that there was not one single piece
of trace evidence to suggest such a scenario.

Given that news, Keith Neff thought it was possible
that Jan could have been killed inside the house and
brought outside.

But there was no trace of blood inside the house—
carpets, floors, furniture, walls, ceiling, doors, anywhere—

or outside on the lawn, pool deck, or anywhere else. None of this made sense. Jan had definitely bled profusely; yet there was no indication that she had bled anywhere in or around the house.

Then again, Neff considered, *Jan could have been killed outside, near the pool?* . . .

There was one substance just about every household had on hand that could clean any trace of blood and throw off the luminol tests the LCFU had conducted with meticulous precision.

Hydrogen peroxide.

It was the only solution available to the average home owner that could distill blood enough to make it disappear.

Yet, the LCFU did not find one empty bottle of hydrogen peroxide or a trace of it anywhere inside or outside the home.

By the end of the day, Neff was scratching his head.

No motive. No forensic evidence. Very little circumstantial evidence.

"We had nothing," Neff observed, "besides a feeling."

Michael Roseboro *appeared* to be guilty. But a feeling or instinct was not going to get an arrest warrant signed.

Opportunity was another thing. Roseboro said he was sleeping when Jan was murdered. That meant he had an opportunity to kill her. So Neff and his team knew they had to see if anyone had seen or heard what had happened in the Roseboros' backyard between 10:00 and 11:02 P.M.

Neighbors. It was time to canvass the neighborhood and see what people had to say about the night of July 22, 2008.

There was a house directly across the street from the Roseboro pool, on Creek Road. A raised ranch-type house with two floors, it was set back about an acre from West Main Street and faced the Roseboro pool, looking south. If a person stood on the upper floor, the second story, and peered through a window, he had a straight shot directly into the Roseboro pool area.

This was as good a place as any to start.

For the past fifteen years, September Malamon lived in the house with her husband and three Siberian huskies. September had a schedule, or routine, with the dogs. The last call to go outside and do their thing was at 9:00 P.M., September told the ECTPD. She took them herself every night. This worked out well, because September worked third shift at a local Denver Pepperidge Farm plant. She took the dogs out, got her lunch ready, and generally left the house by 10:15 P.M. Her car was parked in the garage. When she left, she'd have to drive out of her driveway and, facing the side of the Roseboros' house the pool was on, look directly at the Roseboros' as she pulled onto Creek Road and headed into downtown Denver.

That night, September said later, the Roseboro residence was "pitch black." There were no cars in the driveway, nor were there any lights on outside.

She was sure of it.

This scene was oddly unfamiliar to September, because the Roseboros *always* had the backyard lit up like a high-school football field—which was one of the main reasons why she noticed the darkness.

As September was changing that night, getting ready to go to work, she recalled standing in an upstairs room, looking out at the Roseboros' backyard. This would have been, September remembered, around ten, a little after. Roseboro had said he left Jan outside at that time and all the lights were on.

Supposedly, Jan was enjoying the night sky, but with the lights on?

September said she looked across the street and had not seen anybody, admitting, "There are parts [of the yard] blocked from my view. But I can see the pool and the house and then the pool yard. There's a tree, and then the pool yard beyond that I can see to the edge, but where the tree is, there's one little section I cannot see."

Still, September could see the tiki lights when they were on and during the daylight hours.

Yet, not one light in the backyard was on as September got ready for work in the second-story room of her home. Not even the overhead dusk-to-dawn light, which is turned off only by a breaker switch or by unplugging it, not a simple on/off switch on the side of a wall somewhere, was lit.

The ECTPD left September Malamon's house with more questions than answers.

In the days to come, a second neighbor, who had been driving by the house at ten thirty-five P.M. on the night Jan was murdered, had also reported that the backyard was completely dark. Two separate witnesses—who did not know each other—making the same exact claim.

"That made a big difference to me," DA Craig Stedman later said. "She (the second witness) also said that the front of the Roseboros' house was dark. This stood out to her. The front of that house was normally well lit up—but *not* that night. There were only two windows in the basement [turned on]."

"Roseboro's story to me was 'I had gone into the house at ten o'clock and left Jan outside . . . with all the lights on,'" Neff said.

In fact, Roseboro said the only reason he went outside to begin with was because he saw that the tiki lights were still burning.

If an intruder had gotten into the backyard and, by some remote chance, killed Jan, why would that intruder light those tiki torches? the detective who had never investigated a murder in his career kept asking himself.

It made no sense.

"Okay," Keith Neff said later, "maybe you can say that

Jan turned off all those lights so she could look at the
stars and planes, as some had told us. But then you'd
have to have a killer walk around and relight torchlights
manually. . . ."

Not a chance in hell.

21

Detective Keith Neff was back at the ECTPD on July 24, 2008, when he received a call from Allan Sodomsky. Working out of the office of Sodomsky and Nigrini in nearby Reading, Pennsylvania, Allan Sodomsky had a reputation as a no-nonsense lawyer who defended those he believed had been wrongly accused and prosecuted, as his choice of profession would make you assume. Part of Sodomsky's reputation had to do with the fees he charged. None of that made much difference to Michael Roseboro, who made upward of $500,000 a year as the funeral director, owner/operator of Roseboro Funeral Home.

"Hi, yeah, I am now representing Michael Roseboro," Sodomsky explained to Neff, "so you cannot speak to him anymore."

This was fairly good timing for Craig Stedman and the DA's office. By then, Stedman later said, "I would have wanted to leave Mr. Roseboro alone, anyway, and begin to interview everyone around him, instead."

The idea was to make Roseboro sweat a little bit. Ratchet up the pressure valve a notch.

Neff said okay. If the ECTPD needed Roseboro for anything, someone from the DA's office or the ECTPD would call Sodomsky first.

Then another call came in—and everything changed.

"I think there might be something going on between Michael Roseboro and Angela Funk," the caller explained.

Angela Funk? Who is that?

It was the first time the ECTPD had heard the name. With a quick check, it was determined that Angela—or Angie—Funk, a married working mother of two daughters (three and five years old), lived a block away from the Roseboro Funeral Home.

How convenient.

Larry Martin called the LCDA's Office and told Kelly Sekula about the call.

"We'll send someone over there to interview her."

The oldest motive for murder in the book had just exposed itself.

County detectives arrived at Angie Funk's downtown home, which literally looked out on the Roseboro Funeral Home's Walnut Street sign, employee entrance, and garage—where Michael Roseboro, in other words, came and went, and where he brought the bodies into the funeral home. Angie could sit on her porch, throw a stone, and hit the side of the building.

To boot, Michael Roseboro's parents lived right next door to Angie.

Small town, indeed.

Angie Funk was rather plain-looking, maybe even tomboyish in her own cute way. Short-cropped hair (Peter Pan–like), which was straight and sandy brown, an average figure, glaring eyes, fair skin, and a bubbly, yet peaceful (some said) demeanor. She seemed to dress conservatively with long skirts and heavy blouses, probably a habit carried over from her days as a Mennonite. By outside appearances, Angie had a homey June Cleaver way about her, and seemed to be nothing more than the ordinary housewife and mother she portrayed herself as. Angie had been a claims adjuster for a local insurance agency, and before that, she had worked in the same industry in various positions.

"Hey," one of the county detectives said as Angie opened the door and, realizing quickly who was at her door, closed it behind her back. "We're here about an affair you possibly had with Michael Roseboro—and we were wondering when that might have ended?"

The only way to put it was directly on the table.

"I wasn't aware that it ended," Angie said right away. Her face was pinched. She looked uncomfortable and scared. Her eyes told the detectives that she didn't want to talk too loud about this subject here on the porch, the door behind her, her children and husband on the opposite side. Apparently, Angie's husband didn't know about this affair that was, by Angie's admission, still going on.

The detectives looked at each other. "Well, we're going to need to talk to you about this," one of them said.

Angie explained that she and her husband, Randall "Randy" Funk, along with their two daughters, were heading down to Ocean City, New Jersey, for a family vacation. Just so happened, they were packing to leave that night.

"We'll be in touch, then."

The detectives didn't tell Angie, but they would be sending a couple of investigators down to Ocean City to talk to her. This situation couldn't wait. It was too important to the investigation into Jan Roseboro's murder.

When Keith Neff heard about this new development, he could, but then couldn't, believe it. "Why hadn't this woman come forward and told us?" Neff wondered. She must have seen that her lover's wife had drowned in her own pool. Why hadn't she stepped up and called?

It was a good (obvious) question. If she was still having an affair with a man whose wife had been murdered, a story well covered in the local press, why hadn't Angie called the ECTPD and told them about the affair? More than that, Angie would soon tell the police that she and Roseboro had planned on getting married. And there was one more surprise that would soon emerge. A bombshell, in fact.

At the least, the appearance of this affair between Angie Funk and Michael Roseboro looked awfully suspicious. Had Angie Funk played a part in Jan's murder? Had she helped Roseboro? Was Roseboro covering for his girlfriend?

These were all fair questions investigators were now asking themselves as they prepared to head east into Ocean City, New Jersey, to interview Angie more in depth about this supposed affair.

BOOK TWO

THE MISTRESS AND THE MORTICIAN

22

It was a family get-together. One of those parties where everyone smiles and says *hello* and *how ya doin'* and acts cordial and friendly. Yet inside, the insults and judgments are buzzing like bats.

Even though he carried the name, Shawn Roseboro had always considered himself an outcast inside the dynamics of the Roseboro clan. Not because twenty-five-year-old Shawn had no interest in the family business (he didn't), or his mother, Michael Roseboro's cousin, was the black sheep (she definitely was). But Shawn Roseboro harbored a secret. And it was at one of those family shindigs that Jan Roseboro pulled the young man aside and asked, "Are you gay, Shawn?" Jan was the only one in the family Shawn felt comfortable confiding in or talking to, not to mention the only family member he viewed as having enough compassion to help him through what were some tough times these days.

As if she didn't know already. Then again, it wasn't necessarily a question, more like an observation. ("Jan wasn't stupid," Shawn said later, "she knew.")

"Of course," Shawn said, answering Jan.

There, he'd gone and said it. The weight of the world. Gone. In an instant.

Well, not really. Didn't work like that.

But it felt good, nonetheless, to admit to someone in the family that he was a homosexual, proud of it, and wanted to live openly *within* the family. No more running from who he was. No more trying to camouflage the obvious. No more lies and stories. No more denials.

Jan shot Shawn a look of compassion that day, acknowledging the eight-hundred-pound gorilla—then gave Shawn a twist of the head and pinch of the face that said, *Come on, how naive do I look? I knew that!* Everybody *knew it.*

They probably did. Still, now it was "official." Shawn could take pride in knowing that Jan knew for certain. Jan had sat down with Shawn and his then-boyfriend not too long after and talked. Shawn was nervous and scared what the family was going to think. What would everyone say?

Jan reassured him. "It's okay, honey," she said. "It's who you are." She squeezed Shawn on the arm gingerly. "You cannot change who you are. It will only hurt you more to hide it."

"Thank you," Shawn said with tears. It had been a rough road: the excessive drinking, partying all night long, stuffing those feelings with booze. He called himself an alcoholic—*ahem*, that is, recovering alcoholic. Shawn was off the sauce now. Getting his life back in order.

"Look," Jan said, "I will always be here for you. Anytime you need to talk, just call me."

Shawn knew that already. In the past, he had picked up the phone from time to time and called Jan and talked to her as though she were his mother. He knew Jan cared. He knew she listened. She was concerned about him. Shawn had always lived under a cloud of disgrace that coming out would somehow tarnish the Roseboro family name. Cause scandal. Not to mention bring up more friction inside the family for him.

Watercoolers would buzz: *Psst . . . there's that Roseboro kid, the gay one.*

"Even now, three years from that day I confided in Jan," Shawn later explained, "when I think about the person that I want to be, I think of Jan."

To Shawn, a certified nurse's aide (CNA) by trade, Jan was the one bright light in his life at a time when coming out seemed to him as though he were committing a grave family sin. But he could confide anything in Jan.

"Jan and I," Shawn said, "we, well, we shared something that I didn't share with anyone else in my family—that being, of course, my lifestyle. My family, I—I could not tell them. They are very unaccepting, in my opinion. Jan was the one person in the family that I could talk to and trust."

Jan was that beacon in Shawn's life who was always willing to sit down and talk about his life, ask how he was doing. There was one day when Shawn shared with Jan the thought that even though he was gay, he still wanted a family. Kids. Lots of them. There would come a time when he settled down with a man. But what would the Roseboros think? Shawn was terrified of the notion that someday he would live as an openly gay man with a family and have the Roseboro surname on his mailbox. Would he have to change his name? Move? Fight insults? These were all things that Shawn was concerned about and had to consider, he later said.

"I'll be here to support you, Shawn," Jan said, placing her arm around Shawn's shoulder, giving him a love squeeze, "and help you with adoption, or even finding someone to help out."

For Shawn, that was a day that truly showed him how deeply devoted Jan was to his life and, moreover, the struggles he faced in the days ahead.

One family member had suggested psychiatric therapy after learning that Shawn had admitted being a homosexual.

Like Shawn, Jan was appalled by this. She couldn't believe it.

It was on days like those, when Shawn would hear "chatter" within the family about his "lifestyle," and how everyone was going to fix him and make him "normal" again, that he'd run to Jan and she'd comfort him. Just the thought that there were open arms there for him changed everything for Shawn.

"Me and the Roseboro side of the family never saw things the same," Shawn said. "Their view of life is based on image." Status too, he added. "Money! Success! Keeping up a good family name. And that stuff never really mattered to me. Being happy mattered to me more than anything else."

Shawn said Jan believed in the same principles. She was a mother of four with a big house. Wife to *the* Michael Roseboro. She had nice things, and could buy just about anything she wanted. But Jan was not the type to let you know that about her, Shawn shared. He envied that about her. She was just as content to walk around town in sweatpants, sneakers, her hair up in a butterfly hairclip, and wearing very little makeup. She didn't talk down to people. Jan understood that life was about relationships and love, compassion and grace—not what money could buy, or what you thought of a person because of who they were. Shawn wasn't saying that all Roseboros were the antithesis of this, but in his opinion a majority were.

"She was an all-around phenomenal woman and mother," Shawn said. "If she had a last dollar in hand, she'd give it to you. Her life was her children, making sure they had what they needed without spoiling them. To me, Jan was more of a friend than family, if that makes sense. I could talk to her as a friend, unlike anyone else in the family."

Jan carried a sense and aura about her that regardless of how much money she and Michael Roseboro had in the bank, and the fact that she didn't need to work, she was a simple person. Someone who believed and valued the plain things in life.

"She didn't care about stuff, like many of the other Roseboros did," Shawn remembered. "I'd run into her in Walmart. She'd be wearing a hoodie."

Michael Roseboro wasn't into flaunting his success as much as other members of the extended family, Shawn claimed. Roseboro was a plain man, in many ways, and although he liked expensive vacations, expensive clothes, and those husky, luxurious SUVs that rule the road, it wasn't Rolex watches for the guy. Roseboro was more into himself: what others—mainly females—could supply him with. He liked to drink. He liked to smoke cigarettes and weed. He loved his job as a mortician. And, of course, his favorite pastime was chasing women. The rule of thumb inside the family was that Michael Roseboro had had a string of mistresses throughout his and Jan's marriage, but, Shawn said, it was never talked about. You kept your mouth shut and curried favor.

Dirty little secrets. Every family has them.

It was even said that Michael Roseboro's father confronted him a few times and told the heir to the throne to back off where those women were concerned, or run the risk of losing his status in the family business, and all the money that came with it. This while another family member, several sources said, would confront Jan from time to time, after she found out Michael had cheated on her again, and tell her to suck it up. "It is the Roseboro way!"

You take it on the right cheek, offer the left, and move on.

"At one time, I actually didn't think that Mike was cheating on Jan," Shawn maintained. But someone, a "very reliable source," Shawn said, "schooled me on what was truly going on." Shawn was told that his cousin Michael Roseboro was known in and around Denver to have scores of girlfriends throughout the years. In fact, he once "had an affair with [a cousin] of his," Shawn was told by that same family member.

"They all know who it is," Shawn said. "[By not the most] reliable source, I have been told that Mike is my father. That was hard. I do resemble Mike a lot. But after twenty-five years of knowing [that source], I don't think it's true. And I don't *want* to know at this point."

There was one afternoon in early June 2008 when Shawn Roseboro got a call to head over to see eighty-nine-year-old E. Louis Roseboro, his ailing great-grandfather. Shawn was told to tell Louie whatever it was he wanted to tell him, because he might not get another chance. Louie was on his deathbed. That white light fast approaching. He was at the Denver Nursing Home, just outside downtown Denver, in Stevens, on Lancaster Avenue. Shawn adored the old man; he was torn up over his imminent death.

"Grandpa Louie was an amazing person," Shawn said. "I called him 'Pa.' I never told him about my lifestyle, but I did introduce him to my partner at the time. He thought the world of [my partner]. In fact, one of the last things he ever said to me was 'You have a good friend there. I think a lot of him.' I was very close to Pa. . . . He was very understanding and was always willing to listen and never judge. I look at my life now that it's somewhat together and I often wish that he could see me."

Pa had lived a long, prosperous life. Everyone in the family was waiting and wondering when that call would come in the middle of the night.

Shawn found the door to the Denver Nursing Home, let himself in, walked down the hallway toward Pa's room. He was energized and saddened. This was going to be it: Shawn had it all planned out—the last words he'd ever get to say to Pa.

He turned the corner and—oh, my goodness— entered Pa's room to a big surprise.

His cousin Mike was standing there, bedside.

Shawn stopped. Not because seeing cousin Mike was a bad thing, or unwelcome. It was the other person in the room with him. Shawn had never seen her before.

There was a woman, she had short-cropped, dark sandy-colored hair, a familiar look, and an awkward presence, as though she didn't belong there. The way she stood next to cousin Mike was as if they were a couple.

Roseboro looked shell-shocked. After all, it was after visiting hours; he had not expected anyone to be stopping by.

"Shawn," he said, "this is, um, ah . . . a neighbor of Pa's."

Mike, Shawn thought as he walked toward Pa's bed, *brought his* girlfriend *up here to see Pa? The freakin' nerve of the guy!*

Indeed, Michael Roseboro stood next to his dying grandfather, with his current mistress, Angela Funk, standing there beside him.

Shawn got on his knees next to Pa's bed and held the old man's hand as Pa's labored breathing grew deeper, slower.

In tears, Shawn told Pa he loved him.

Shawn then turned to see Michael walking backward, pulling Angie out of the room.

"I will never forget," Shawn said later, "how she was just watching me say my good-byes to Pa."

Shawn felt violated. As though someone had snatched that last moment with Pa away from him.

When Shawn left, he saw his cousin again in the hallway.

Angie Funk was gone.

Shawn said good-bye to his cousin.

"It left a sour feeling in me," Shawn said of seeing his

Pa there on that last night with Michael Roseboro's latest girlfriend basically standing over his back. "I still, to this day, will slow down and glare at [Angie] when I pass her house and she's outside. I have a hate for her like no other. Because of her presence on that day, I didn't say a lot of the things I should've said to my great-grandfather."

Shawn never saw Pa alive again.

23

Although many would later dispute her version, according to thirty-eight-year-old Angie Lynn Funk, her extramarital affair with Michael Roseboro began with an innocent smile and a chance meeting near the coffee counter inside a local Turkey Hill convenience store in Denver. Neither she nor Roseboro ever conspired to embark on this adulterous relationship. To Angie (and Roseboro), neither was feeling particularly wanted, important, or loved at home. So when opportunity knocked, they were caught in a weak moment and decided, *What the hell, let's go for it.* Before that day, Angie and Michael had known each other "as acquaintances," Angie later said, "for five years.

"He worked down the street and his parents lived on the same block—well, the next block over," Angie said.

Acquaintance is an open-ended term. Anyone who lived in the same town as Michael Roseboro could call him an acquaintance.

"We'd say hi," Angie said later, maybe hoping to clarify. "You know, small talk here and there."

Prior to their relationship becoming obsessive and overtly sexual, Angie admitted that she knew Michael Roseboro was married and had kids. As it could be safely said that Michael knew the same about Angie, having worked almost directly across the street from the house she lived in with her husband and kids. Randall Funk didn't like to talk much, according to what Angie told police: "Randy is quiet and this causes most of [our] problems." Later, Angie said she always considered Michael Roseboro to be "attractive and . . . nice."

"Angie would sit on her porch," one source told me, "and point at Michael as he was walking into the funeral home or getting out of his car, and say, 'He'll be mine someday.'" This was long before they supposedly bumped into each other at the Turkey Hill.

Angie was a woman who had staked her claim to a man. It was not the first time, other sources said, Angie Funk had done this: stealthily watched a man for a time, baited him, then went after him. Although she framed the scenario as some sort of a joke, Angie herself later said that she and her girlfriend would walk their children down Walnut Street and make note of how "cute" Michael Roseboro was whenever they saw him. "There's your future father-in-law," Angie's friend said one day as Mike's father, Ralph, who lived with Michael Roseboro's mother on the same block, came out of his house and got into his car.

Angie laughed.

One time, about two years before Angie and Michael "hooked up," Angie said to her friend as they were walking, "I would like to be married to him." They were passing the Roseboro Funeral Home. Michael was getting out of his car, waving at the ladies.

It was those times, when they just happened to bump into each other or smile and stare, Angie Funk later suggested, that made the two of them comfortable enough to initiate short conversations. And it was those brief encounters at the local Turkey Hill store, she added, that turned into phone calls, e-mails, text messages, and secret meetings, which were all about the sex and delusional promises of a future that would never be.

On May 29, 2008, after running into each other at the convenience store on several occasions during those mornings leading up to that day—having brief conversations about the weather and the neighborhood regular small talk we all seem to have with our neighbors— Michael Roseboro, according to Angie Funk, called her "out of the blue" for the first time. She was at her house. He was across the street at the funeral home, working. He must have known that Randall, Angie's husband, had left for work.

"Hey," Michael said. He sounded cheery, a hint of adolescent embarrassment in his voice.

"Hi," Angie said. She knew who it was. One would guess by what happened next that Angie was even excited and thrilled about this "surprise" call.

"I cannot stop thinking about you," Michael said, apparently putting it out there to see how she was going to react.

By that time, Roseboro said later, he was officially obsessed with Angie Funk to the point where he literally couldn't do anything without thinking about her.

"Oh," Angie said, casually staggered by the comment, perhaps as part of a strategy.

"Would you like to go to lunch with me?"

It was a strange time for Roseboro to initiate an affair, thus cheating on a wife who had, fewer than two weeks before, lost her mother, Evelyn Binkley. Jan was in the throes of depression and grieving—and here was her husband beginning a relationship with a married mother of two children.

What a guy!

The way Angie later talked about this moment, as if it were *the* moment when things between her and

Roseboro went to the next level, it was as if Roseboro had engineered the entire affair. He was the hunter, she his prey. Yet, when all of the facts were later in, it was absolutely clear that Angie Funk had set a trap for a guy who was, generally speaking, always on the prowl, anyway.

Angie later explained to police that it was only after she had started a new job and began stopping at the Turkey Hill convenience store for her morning coffee that Michael Roseboro found out she was going in there every day and began making himself available.

He was the aggressor, in other words.

Nonetheless, they began to "chitchat," as Angie later put it, during those early mornings before the start of their day. This was in late April, early May. (As with many things, Angie could not recall when, exactly.) They fixed their coffee and talked about work and things going on around town. Michael was all smiles, a glow about him that Angie had never seen before.

A man in his element.

Angie was soon looking forward to those morning meetings, she said, as much as Roseboro.

The call therefore surprised her, Angie explained to police. "Sort of. . . . I wasn't expecting him to call me."

To that request for a lunch date, Angie said, "Yes!"

Ruminating on it after they hung up, however, Angie didn't think it was such a good idea that they "were seen in public" out at lunch around town, or even in a neighboring town. They were adults. Both smart people, in some respects. They knew by making the date that the lunch wasn't going to run along the lines of discussing town budgets and Neighborhood Watch programs. It was, certainly, the beginning of something intimate and sexual.

That next week after Memorial Day, Angie and Michael saw each other at Turkey Hill and discussed the idea that eating lunch in public together probably wasn't a smart move. They needed to make other arrangements to get together.

Roseboro handed Angie his cell phone number. "Call me whenever you like."

She smiled. Stuffed the number into her purse.

In the days that followed, Angie sat outside her house on the postage-stamp front lawn or wraparound porch (while Randall was at work), and she and Michael talked via cell phone. Michael routinely said he could not stop thinking about her, and she reciprocated by saying, "Me too." Lunch out in public was off-limits, they agreed again. But the conversations by phone were not going to be enough. They needed to be together. Alone. Somewhere else.

On a typical day, they talked about how much they enjoyed each other's company and how badly they wanted to be together. Not just sexually, but *together*, together. Inside just a week, mind you, they were discussing leaving their spouses and taking their kids and beginning life together anew somewhere else. This was a fantasy, really (like most extramarital affairs), but both were entirely wrapped up in it. Michael Roseboro was starting another affair, one of two that would later be publicly documented by investigators, but, conservatively speaking, another one of perhaps a dozen over the years that Roseboro was married to Jan. According to one minor, then a fifteen-year-old girl, "Yes," she told me, "Michael and I had more of a sexual relationship than anything. . . ." Roseboro was said to have paid the young girl for sex. Then there was a casual affair he had with a young adult whom he reportedly smoked marijuana with a few times while he rambled on and on about "how he wasn't happy in his marriage. . . ." Although the source never participated in it with him, she confirmed that Roseboro liked to dip marijuana joints in formaldehyde (embalming fluid—angel dust, they call it, "dustin'") before smoking them. And although he never offered her money for sex, and they never slept together, he made it clear to her that he "wanted to have sexual relations." So Michael Roseboro might have *told* Angie he was in love with her, and she was all he ever thought about, but the affair with Angie went right along with who Michael Roseboro was. Lust controlled this man's thinking. Now, apparently, with a bit of obsession sprinkled on for good measure.

"I mean," Angie said later as she talked about those early phone calls with Roseboro as she sat on her porch or lawn like a schoolgirl falling in love for the first time, "we just got to know each other. I mean, as anybody [would]. Like, I didn't know him real well. So we would just talk about how, you know, about things—family, what we liked to do. That kind of thing."

Phone calls quickly turned into text messages— hundreds of them. And e-mails. Again, hundreds. How many per day?

"Forty, fifty . . . I don't know," Angie later said.

For Angie, the first few days after that first phone call from Michael Roseboro in late May—when they were arguably courting—were "just like dating him. . . . It was just like anybody dating somebody—that's how it progressed."

"Anybody dating somebody. . . ."

Well, perhaps if you take into account the man was married and had four kids, and Angie the same, with two kids. Otherwise, this was not a relationship that most people with morals choose to get involved in, or would refer to as "normal."

E-mails as early as June 2, 2008, sent from Michael to Angie, and e-mails she sent back to his account, tell the story of how aggressive and sexual this affair was from the moment it began. It was not anywhere close to "anybody dating somebody." On June 2, for example, at 7:29 P.M., Roseboro sent Angie an e-mail under the subject "Daydreaming." This only a few days, mind you, after that supposed first call. In that e-mail, Michael talked about watching his new target as she walked around on the front porch of her home, and how turned-on he was by the jeans she was wearing earlier that day. He said the "pants should be outlawed." It was clear that Roseboro was infatuated, feeding off the thrill and mystery of not yet bedding Angie down. He said he went "right back to dreaming" after seeing her in the pants, just stopping short of perhaps admitting he had decided to do something nasty that might grow hair on his palms. He told her he couldn't wait to "be alone" with her "and to see you dance for me."

For Angie, with that first e-mail, she started a file at work. After printing each e-mail out on her work computer, she saved all of those e-mails from Roseboro that *were special to* her, *so she would be able to look back at them at a later time,* according to a later police interview transcript.

Reminisce.

Moreover, at the end of every workday, Angie deleted all the e-mails Michael Roseboro had sent her—and just those—on that day.

"I would also empty those files from my 'deleted folder' or 'trash' mail," Angie told police. Police called this "double deleting." She never forwarded any of the e-mails to her home computer and would not give Roseboro her home e-mail address.

"Anybody dating somebody. . . ."

The next morning, June 3, no sooner had Angie got behind her desk at seven fifty-four, did she write back to Roseboro, saying how she didn't think the pants would have that much of an effect, but she'd be more than willing to wear them again. Farther along in the note, she admitted—we're talking fewer than five days *after* the initial call to go out to lunch—that she was having "fantasies" about him and she could not "get them out of" her head, adding that she felt as if she had "known [Roseboro] forever. . . ."

The idea that secrecy was going to become a major

part of the affair was obvious in the way they communicated and the words they chose. Angie explained that her mother was supposed to be "dropping in" later on that afternoon. So if her new lover called her at that time and she "sounded funny," he'd know why. It had nothing to do with him, she went on to say, only that they needed to think about things more thoroughly now and hide everything they did.

Roseboro answered Angie's response e-mail at eleven forty-four that same morning, writing that he didn't want to "pressure" her in any way. He talked about how he hoped her fantasies were "as good as" his. Those fantasies he'd been having left him "weak and smiling." In fact, he dreamt of kissing Angie and holding her and running his "fingers through [her] hair and touching [her] face and lips." Roseboro sounded like a junior-high-school kid who had been promised his first piece of ass. There was desperation and surrealism in the tone of his e-mails. Almost an effeminate quality to them.

Ending that brief note, Roseboro said he was "surprised and flattered" to hear from Angie that she felt the same way about him. He thanked her for making him smile.

They talked about having sex. They talked about passion. They talked about how the romance they both adored and needed, but had been—surprise!—lost in the tedium and boringness of their marriages was now back in full swing—and they loved it. The lust between them grew daily. They viewed it as love and called themselves soul mates. Yet, the expeditious progression and secretive nature of the affair spoke to how it was structured and fueled more by the thrill of *not* being caught and the freshness and contagiousness of it all more than a true love and a desperate need to be with each other. Love at first sight, in other words, was not what this affair was based on; for if that were the case, both would have gone to their spouses and admitted that nothing would stand in the way of this love. But this affair, energized by the sexual charge between them, went from zero to one hundred, it seemed, overnight: from the local Turkey Hill store by the coffeepots to phone calls and e-mails, to meetings and nights of tossing and turning, thinking about each other while lying next to their spouses.

Michael Roseboro soon forgot all about life as he knew it. Everything he did, every thought he had, centered on Angie Funk—and what he was going to do to her once he got her alone, in bed, her clothes scattered about the floor. The guy got up in the morning and e-mailed Angie. Then he texted her. They met at the Turkey Hill store. They looked at each other from across the street, that secret lust hovering there between them, disguising itself as sparks and chemistry. He told Angie repeatedly— in e-mails and calls and texts numbering upward of fifty a day—that he was a simple guy falling in love all over again. That he was grateful for her having shown him how to rediscover love as he had never known it.

But this was a game to Michael Roseboro, one he had played with several other women at various times throughout his marriage. This was an unadulterated ob-session like he had never experienced, a deep-seated desire to bed this woman, to be with her. Angie Funk had done something to Michael Roseboro no other woman had. And yet, studying his behavior, one might gander a speculative thought that Roseboro had turned a corner with his compulsive nature. Because while Roseboro was drooling over Angie in those e-mails and phone calls and text messages, his hormones jumping through the com-puter screen, he was back at home making surprise plans for Jan to renew their wedding vows during an Outer Banks ceremony. He had gone on the Internet and set up a pastor. Looked into rental cottages. Places to have a re-ception. He had talked to friends and family he thought Jan would want there. In addition, Jan and Michael Rose-boro were also planning a family trip to Niagara Falls. It was business as usual for Roseboro back at home. That, or the guy was so infatuated with this new flame and had become so engrossed in the idea of having her, maybe having fixated on her over the years as she walked in and out of her home and sauntered by the funeral home with her friends and children, that everything he did after getting her attention and beginning the affair would now revolve around a master—sinister—plan to be with her. And now he would cancel all plans with Jan. He wouldn't care about causing an uproar inside the Roseboro family dynamic and possibly losing all he, his father, and his grandfather had worked for. There was one source who later said that after Jan found out about an affair Michael had years before Angie had come into the picture, Jan had told her husband that she had no trouble walking out the door with half of everything—*and* the children. Thus, it was clear to Michael Roseboro by the feelings he had for Angie, one would think, that this was not going to be just a fling in the backseat of his SUV, or a few nights at a sleazy hotel. The way he felt about Angie was something more.

Much more.

"You've got a guy," DA Craig Stedman said later, "obsessed with his new girlfriend, thinking about nothing else *but* being with her. *Gotta* be with her! 'We've *got* to be together! We've *gotta* be together *soon!*' . . . But there's a little problem—the man is married and has four kids— and an even bigger problem.

"His wife is alive."

24

On June 5, 2008, Michael Roseboro and Angie Funk met at Turkey Hill that morning as usual. Roseboro gave his new girlfriend a letter he'd written during another of what he said were sleepless nights he'd been having lately, thinking about her. When she got to work a short while later, at 7:50 A.M., Angie sat down at her desk and sent her lover an e-mail. She explained how she had read the letter three times already; it had not been twenty minutes since they had seen each other. She said she "ached" for her new married boyfriend's embrace. His touch. To hear his voice. In the letter, Michael had laid out one of the oldest lines from the *Cheating Husbands Manual,* telling Angie, although he might not be alone at home, it didn't mean he wasn't lonely.

Poor guy.

In her response, Angie said the same back. She ended the short e-mail on an exciting note, saying that "next week" could not "come soon enough."

Their first planned meeting—alone.

My goodness, it was almost here.

In response, nine minutes later, as if he had been sitting at the funeral home behind his desk waiting for

Angie's e-mail, Michael answered, saying how "smitten" and "in love" he was, but "also very confused."

Confused?

Not, mind you, because of the enigmatic situation between them. Or how they would have to carry on in secret, as though they were terrorists, during the coming weeks and months.

Nope.

Instead, Michael was befuddled over what color pants he wanted Angie to wear next.

Decisions, decisions.

Moments later, in another e-mail, Angie said she liked to "hear" that he was in love with her, but longed to, as an alternative, hear him say "it in person," when he could hold her in his arms, cuddle, and whisper in her ear. She concluded this very brief e-mail by saying how she had taken a walk in the rain the previous night and dreamt of "dancing in the rain" with her new married lover.

Michael answered right away, telling Angie how he fell asleep at night thinking of her, then dreaming about her throughout the night, waking in the morning with only—you guessed it—Angie on his mind. His life, he had decided, because of Angie's presence, was now filled with "so much happiness."

According to what Angie later told police, during this early stage of the affair, she laid the law down for Michael Roseboro as it pertained to the price of that *happiness* he had so much enjoyed and believed she could offer him. There were some lifestyle changes in the future for Michael if he wanted to stay with Angie, she insisted. Number one, the cigarette smoking. Angie hated it. She told Michael he'd have to go on the patch and quit.

Or else.

And guess what? Michael went out and bought the patch.

There was one day when Michael told Angie, "Both Jan's side and my side of the family like to drink."

"I don't like someone who drinks all the time," Angie responded.

"I'll drink less," he said.

Yet, the goatee, which wasn't something Roseboro had always worn, Angie said, "she liked."

So Michael Roseboro kept it.

Later that same night, June 5, 2008, the correspondence between them got to an adolescent point, where Roseboro was quoting Bon Jovi songs.

Angie said she loved it, before explaining that she would "always love" him, too, admonishing their current situation, upset at not being able to tell the world how she felt about her man. You know, scream it from the rooftops in Denver. And yet there was nothing, essentially, stopping either of them from leaving their spouses and holding a press conference to announce their undeniable love for each other.

Michael answered tersely by saying how glad he was that she felt that way, how warm and fuzzy it made him feel inside. Then, in an e-mail two minutes later, perhaps rethinking his position on the matter, Michael said Angie had made him "feel more loved" than he had ever felt in his life. Such a bold statement coming from a guy who had stayed married for nearly twenty years to a woman who had given him four kids.

As the e-mails indicated quite candidly, page after page after page (so many, the DA would later refer to the stack as "the e-mail book"), Angie Funk and Michael Roseboro displayed a certain sexual energy and euphoria leading up to what was going to be their first sexual encounter. The buildup was intense and fanatical, almost hypnotic. Their heads were buzzing with fancy and expectation. Yet looking back, one would have to say that, at best, it was more pomp than actual circumstance.

These people didn't know each other, after all. They were locked in some sort of cyber fairy tale that—as competent, intelligent adults, they had to realize—would conclude on a painful, sour note someday. There was no pot of gold here. There was only overblown purple prose saturated in the flight of the imagination between a man, who obviously hated himself and the life he had made, and a woman, who was looking for a way out of a marriage she was obviously unhappy in, but not tough enough to walk away from. So much so, in fact, that one night Angie told Michael, "I want my marriage to dissolve naturally so as not to cause bad feelings with Randy." Later, she said that when she began the affair with Michael Roseboro, "Based on my home life, it was a vulnerable time for me to have an affair. . . . Michael was progressing with the relationship faster than I was," Angie claimed. "I was not ready to leave Randy because my affairs were not in order. I had not figured out everything regarding the custody of my kids, or if Randy would contest the divorce."

But she still played along with Michael Roseboro, not once trying to slow him down. And, some later claimed, it was Angie's plan from the beginning, a continuation of a pattern she'd shown for years. This relationship was much more than a chance encounter that Michael was pushing along at full steam. There was an underlying cause and effect on Angie Funk's part. And that plan, as any solid plan by "the other woman" would have to be, needed to start with the best sex this guy ever had. Angie needed to deliver. Big-time. The buildup had been too intense and heated. The guy was expecting to see stars afterward.

Meanwhile, what was Michael Roseboro planning for the two of them during that first special moment, with all the money the guy had? A day in the Poconos? A five-star hotel in Harrisburg, with rose petals on the floor, champagne on ice, a warm Jacuzzi bubbling away?

Maybe he'd even gone out and bought Angie an expensive red-and-black negligee? Or five dozen red roses? A diamond necklace or bracelet? How would Michael Roseboro and Angie Funk launch their supposed love for each other into a sexual realm?

The first time they slept together, Angie later explained, was in a vacant apartment in Mount Joy, Pennsylvania, about a forty-minute drive east of Denver, heading in the direction of Elizabethtown and Harrisburg. Angie's family owned an apartment complex in town, and Angie managed one of the units, showing the apartments to prospective renters, keeping it clean, etc. It was June 8, 2008, just under ten days before that first call Roseboro had made to Angie, this after scores of e-mails and phone calls, text messages and meetings at Turkey Hill. This wasn't some sort of spontaneous moment of passion. They had planned the rendezvous inside apartment 66. They were together, alone, many miles from home, no chance of anyone catching them. Roseboro made his move. He had even asked Angie a few days before, she later said, if sex was in their immediate future. Not with a Casanova-inspired love poem, or a few lines he had borrowed from Shakespeare.

Uh-uh.

Instead, Michael called Angie on the phone, she explained, and said, "Let's have sex."

Like, *Let's go shopping.* Or, *Let's have chicken salad.*
"Let's have sex."

Angie said she balked at first. "No . . . Mike . . . no." She didn't want their relationship to be about the sex.

But, well, it was, now, wasn't it?

And after Michael kissed Angie inside that unfurnished apartment, just a rug and empty rooms and the dank smell of must and past tenants encircling them like a weather front, she gave in to her passions and allowed Roseboro to enter her.

That affair they had been having through cyberspace,

over the phone, and standing next to each other at the Turkey Hill coffee counter each morning had officially moved to the next stage.

Which would only drive Michael Roseboro, mentally, into a sexually obsessive frenzy.

25

After that first time, when they had sex on the floor of the empty apartment on June 8, committing what would become one of many transgressive acts throughout a short period of time, Angie Funk started to meet her lover inside the funeral home.

"I'd go in the back door," she explained.

Sneak in was probably more like it. Angie Funk's house was down the street from the back of the funeral home—and, wouldn't you know it—Michael Roseboro's parents' house was next door to the Funk house. There can be no doubt that Angie looked both ways before walking into the back door of the funeral home, making certain she was not being seen by anyone.

They'd sit in the office and chat, Angie explained to police.

"It would be nice to have a child together," Angie later said Michael told her during one of those conversations. Regarding the young children he had at home and the state of the affair post Jan finding out: "He said he didn't want to lose his children," Angie reported.

After talking in the office, Angie said, they'd sometimes head into the parlor and continue the conversations as Roseboro did paperwork or perhaps spit-shined a coffin or two. And "once," Angie later admitted, *just one time,* she had sex with Michael Roseboro there in the parlor. Just the undertaker, his Mennonite mistress, and a few dead bodies below. How romantic that must have been. The smell of embalming fluid and rotting flesh wafting up from everywhere, permeating the air. The scent of old flowers mixing with perfume that Angie probably sprayed on herself before heading over. The somber lighting and eerie silence of death balanced pleasantly around them. Everyone can attest to the absolute stale stench of a funeral home. Now, how arousing that must have been for these two lovebirds. Considering what Angie later said, you'd have to believe they couldn't contain their desires. Roseboro *had* to have this woman. *There.* Inside the place where his family had served the dead of Lancaster County for over one hundred years. A funeral home, for crying out loud. What the families of the dead would have thought had they known that while suffering and mourning was taking place inside their hearts, the undertaker—a guy they respected, the same guy who had consoled them and told them he would show their deceased the utmost respect—was having sex with his mistress in the same building where he was preparing their loved ones for viewing and burial.

The other place they met was the Ephrata Cloister, a monastery outside Denver that was founded in 1732 as a Protestant monastic community of celibate brothers and sisters. The order was supported by a married congregation who lived near the settlement. The mostly German immigrant members were in search of spiritual goals rather than earthly rewards.

Not necessarily the most morally correct location to continue an adulterous affair that would gravely affect six kids and two deeply devoted spouses, one of whom ended up in the bottom of a swimming pool, which her husband recently had built for her and their children. They would walk around the grounds, holding hands, her head on his shoulder, discussing the future, Angie told one source. Maybe cuddle on one of the benches. Or just sit in one of their vehicles and contemplate the future.

It was during one of those times, right after they had had sex, that Michael Roseboro said, "I love you, Angie."

"I love you, too," Angie reciprocated, admitting this in a later police interview.

Granted, they had not said this term of endearment, according to Angie Funk, until that day.

Ten days together, and they were madly in love.

"Angela said she absolutely never pressured Michael to get married," Detective Keith Neff later said, explaining one interview he conducted with Angie. "Angela stated that she told Michael that he had to leave Jan first, before she left Randy, because she would have no house to go to." When Neff asked Angie how she truly felt about Roseboro, Angie replied, "I liked the attention from Michael, but also loved him." Furthermore, Angie said, she "had lived in the area [Denver] for ten years and had never heard anything about Michael's [previous] affairs. . . ." That is, until the police knocked on her door that day after Jan's murder and began telling her things about the man she *thought* she knew.

As the middle of June approached and the sex became as routine as Michael Roseboro hiding his drinking and smoking from his new girlfriend, the question kept coming up between them: *What are we going to do?* They were both talking about having found the love of their lives, Roseboro already mentioning that he wanted to marry Angie. But they had spouses to contend with every night at home, spouses to hide this affair from, kids to take care of, and lives away from this fantasy to answer to. This was something they needed to talk about. Angie Funk said she considered this, day after day. They needed to come up with a plan. Soon. This running around when they were clearly in love was not going to cut it much longer.

Yet, Roseboro had other things on his mind.

"Michael told me," Angie said later, "that he wanted me to wear a linen dress and he was looking up dresses online."

Roseboro's idea for their wedding was for them to say their vows on the beach in California. "Or on Turtle Island in Fiji," Angie said. "We were looking into other places, too, like Disney, due to the children—and we expected *all* of our children to be there. This was one of our dreams."

Talk was cheap, as they say. Although she had participated shamelessly in these fairy-tale conversations with Roseboro, Angie later said she had serious problems with all of it.

"Your friends and family, Michael?" Angie mentioned one day. She wondered what they would think of her and asked her lover about it.

The home wrecker. The slut. The *other* woman. These were names no woman wanted to be branded.

"My friends will *love* you!" Roseboro said in response, not mentioning what his family would think.

"I tried to bring him back down to earth," Angie told Keith Neff, "by telling him the kids might not accept me right away." Angie said something about Sam, the oldest, who she claimed knew about the affair after having seen a text from Angie on his father's phone one day while they were out at the pool. "Michael had unrealistic expectations about how easy it would be for us to start a life together. I tried to anchor him down."

"It's going to take some time for your friends to accept me, Michael," Angie said on the night they first talked about getting married.

"My friends are *my* friends—they will like you because of *me*, not Jan!" Roseboro said.

Whatever the case might have been, the plan Michael Roseboro and his new lover made was to be married inside of the next twelve months. If that was the case, their spouses would have to be told. They'd have to break the news that they were in love and their marriages were over. There seemed to be no way around that uncomfortable part of the affair.

Or was there?

26

Although she broke from the traditional teachings of the church later on in life, Angie Funk grew up in a conservative Mennonite family in Quarryville, south of Lancaster, about a four- or five-hour ride by horse and buggy from Denver. Incidentally, Quarryville is the same town popular Olympic figure skater and world champion Johnny Weir was raised in. There is a strong Amish/Mennonite/Pennsylvania Dutch hold in the Quarryville area, as there has been in Lancaster County, some reports claim, since the late 1700s. Outsiders and interlopers might confuse the Amish and Mennonites. Rhoda Janzen, author of *Mennonite in a Little Black Dress,* once cleared up this confusion during an interview. The author was asked what the biggest misconception about the Mennonite community and its people was. "That they are the Amish," Janzen told *USA Today,* adding, "Mennonites look and act and dress like most Americans, although they tend to be conservative in some lifestyle choices."

Angie grew up in a family of hard-line Mennonites; her grandparents, in fact, wore coverings and drove horse and buggy. Her parents did not. Mennonites have Christian values, beliefs, and roots based firmly in what one source said are the "radical wing of the sixteenth-century Protestant Reformation." One estimate puts Mennonite numbers worldwide at 1 million. You ask ten people what the Mennonites in Pennsylvania believe and you get ten versions of nearly the same truth: *Sola scriptura,* Latin for "by scripture alone."

The Bible is *the* Word.

"The Mennonites and Amish," one local told me, "believe the Earth is ten thousand years old, because that's what the Bible says."

Yet, a good portion of the Pennsylvania Mennonites, unlike the Amish, hold firm to earthly values.

"For example," that same man said, "you go up to the [local supermarket] on a Sunday evening and all you see is minivans in the parking lot and Mennonite families swapping kids."

In other words, divorced Mennonite families use the parking lot as a meeting point to exchange their kids after weekend visits. And indeed, the common vehicle for the Mennonites is the soccer mom–approved minivan.

So Angie grew up in a household that, apparently, was grounded in the Bible's Scripture, but was also plagued by an Americanized culture of excess and divorce and ways that are opposite of the Bible's core teachings.

One source in Angie's extended family explained that as a kid, Angie took care of her siblings to a large extent. Angie's father was an over-the-road trucker. Angie's maiden name, the family name, is Rudy. The father was always gone: out and about, on the road. Doing whatever truckers do.

"Angie's mom was well kept," one ex-family member claimed, "and she was always buying things for the kids." Meaning Angie and her two siblings. "Angie ended up a lot of times taking care of [her siblings]."

Looking at Angie's later behavior, one might take a leap and understand that she, like anyone who partakes in the same adulterous lifestyle, learned it somewhere.

For those who cheat on their spouses, something in their lives has made this behavior okay for them, any psychologist will say.

One source said that a roaming eye and adulterous nature was part of the bloodline in Angie's family, which eventually ended up in her veins.

"Angie," said a source inside the family, "and I know this by the stories I heard [from the family *and* from Angie herself], ended up marrying her high-school sweetheart right out of school and they ended up living in Quarryville."

Angie's mother and father ultimately divorced, and her mother remarried. Angie and her first husband lived with her mother and stepfather until it was mutually agreed upon that Angie and her stepfather did not get along well enough to endure life in the same household.

On her own with her new husband, Angie's marriage dissolved. Several people claimed Angie could not stay committed to one man—and took no initiative to end one relationship before she started another.

Her husband divorced Angie. According to those who were around her at the time, Angie got everything—or, at least enough to buy herself a townhome first, then that home in Denver on Walnut Street near the Roseboro Funeral Home. It was next door to the house she later lived in—with Randall Funk—when she began the affair with Roseboro.

Living in Denver, Angie met Michael Roseboro for the first time in 2003 at a town parade. They introduced themselves, seeing that they were, in a sense, neighbors. Michael told Angie that he had seen her around the block. She smiled. Said nice to meet you.

They parted ways.

Not long after that, Michael started driving by Angie's "on a regular basis," waving at her. "On occasion, he would stop and talk," Angie later said. She didn't think then that his behavior was obsessive. Perhaps he was just being a friendly neighbor. (Mind you, Roseboro didn't need to drive by Angie's house to get to work.)

"Michael told me he liked me ever since meeting me at the Denver parade," Angie later told police. "My friend . . . thought he was obsessed with me" from that point on.

With the local undertaker arguably obsessed with her, not long after she had moved into the neighborhood, Angela Lynn Rudy soon met Randall Funk.

"Angie used to visit a local club called Low Places," a former friend said, chuckling mildly at the name of the bar in association with Angie and her behavior. Low Places Country Night Club is located inside the Quality Inn in Lancaster across from the Dutch Wonderland. "She would go dancing there, . . . and she would brag about the fact that she met a forty-year-old [man] at the club and could train him, shape and mold him, into whatever she wanted."

The man in question, Randall Funk, an architect, had money, too, Angie soon found out.

One family member believed that Angie liked married men with money.

In one family member's opinion, part of the thrill for Angie was setting her hooks into these men, and then once she landed them, boredom set in and she moved on. Hence, the wandering eye she'd shown throughout her life.

The other subject Angie often talked about around family was babies.

"She was a master at conception," a former friend and family member both said. "Fertility, the timing, she knows the whole deal on when it's the time to get pregnant."

It was something Angie bragged about over the dinner table.

"She'd know from the *day,* the *night* she had sex even,

how long it would take her. . . . She knew when to go to bed with the guy, when it would happen. . . ."

Family planning. Wasn't hard once a woman knew her body.

There were other women in the family trying to get pregnant, but they couldn't, for whatever reason. Angie would be right there, in their face, family members claimed, doling out advice: "You do this and this and this, and you'll conceive." She made sure whatever the family event—Thanksgiving, Christmas, a kid's birthday party—had to be about her. She was the focus of it all. And generally speaking, one of the main topics of conversation she routinely partook in was her knowledge and know-how of conception.

There came a time shortly before she hooked up with Michael Roseboro and had sex with him when Angie stopped bringing Randall to those family gatherings. She just didn't see the point anymore, she told family.

During those family functions, or maybe just during a normal day at work or at home, after she and Roseboro were an item, Angie would step outside by herself and call her new lover.

"In the past," Angie told police, "I have left Michael phone messages, easily longer than two minutes, on his cell phone. I would say things like, 'I love you. . . . I want to be with you.'"

And now she was.

27

During the second week of June, the affair Angie Funk and Michael Roseboro had initiated on May 29, 2008, was in overdrive. The calls, the e-mails, and the text messages were riddled with adolescent puppy love and schmaltzy diatribes that both would probably look back on some day and wonder what in the heck they were thinking. They were meeting at various places and having sex. They were still seeing each other each weekday morning at the Turkey Hill. And yet, throughout it all, Roseboro maintained his family life back home as loving father and husband. Granted, he and Jan were not taking sunset walks, holding hands, or hitting the town for candlelight dinners. But they were a married couple in a brand-new house, spending time together poolside, playing cards with the kids, hundreds of thousands of dollars in the bank, and all the suburban perks and accessories to go along with it. Contrary to what he was telling Angie, Michael was not trying to find a way to let Jan down easy. Instead, Roseboro was working hard at planning their marriage vows renewal vacation in the Outer Banks as a surprise to Jan *and* a weekend trip to Niagara Falls, New York, with the kids and a few friends of the family, to celebrate Sam's high-school graduation.

"The entire family went to Niagara Falls," DA Craig Stedman later told me. "As did some extended family. Angie was not happy about this. . . . It was my position that Angie would *not* have tolerated the upcoming North Carolina trip. Thus, he never told her. Thus, his time window to juggle both women was closing fast."

Angie knew about Niagara, but Roseboro never told her about the Outer Banks.

A vise, as it were, was closing in on Michael Roseboro. In letting Angie know about the trip to Niagara—and the fallout he endured after revealing that information—Roseboro had learned a lesson.

There were plenty of e-mail exchanges between Angie and Michael during the first few weeks of June. But a later computer forensic search could only come up with bits and pieces of those e-mails, fragments of text, if you will. An *I love you* here. A *your body* there. Maybe a line or two from a gushy love poem. Or a *how beautiful you are* and a *why would you love me* type of exchange. Angie later said that although she printed out "some of the e-mails," she deleted the original e-mails into her trash bin and emptied her trash bin on occasion (when she was actually doing this on a daily basis for the most part). Law enforcement, however, could not find any trace of those same e-mails in Michael Roseboro's work computer.

"Remember," Craig Stedman later observed, "many of the e-mails [Angie] printed out were deleted and not recoverable from the computers for whatever reason, but she voluntarily *gave* those to us—many of which we would never have had but for her choosing to turn them over. Mr. Roseboro gave us nothing and cleaned his computer [out] as much as he could."

The first complete e-mail that law enforcement picked up on, again following those e-mails in the early

part of June, was written under the subject "YOU." As it
turned out, it was the beginning of an exchange that
would bring about the first major problem of the affair,
positioning a dark cloud over Michael Roseboro's forthcoming trip to Niagara with his wife, children, and
friends.

Roseboro's e-mail address, beginning with *morty*, was
an obvious play on his job as a mortician. Angie said she
and her lover never gave each other nicknames. But
on June 17, a Tuesday, *afunk* wrote to *morty*, at 10:20
A.M., reminding him that he was leaving at the end of
the week for that Niagara trip. After an opening address
of "sweetheart" and "I love you so much," Angie said she
had totally forgotten about his leaving that Friday. It
had slipped her mind that this was the week he was
going away with Jan and the kids. She encouraged
him—although not before acknowledging that it was
going to "hurt" to say it—to have a good time, pointing
out that she meant "with the kids *only*." She said it would
feel like an "eternity" while he was gone, despite it being
just a three-day weekend. She gave Roseboro some
advice about sightseeing, having gone to Niagara herself in the past, ending with what had become a familiar
sign-off between them: that she would be missing him
and thinking of him always.

Michael wasted little time responding, darting off a
short e-mail, noting that his "good times" would be only
with the kids, certainly not with Jan. Beyond telling
Angie he was staying one hundred yards away from
Horseshoe Falls, at the Embassy Suites, Michael ended
the e-mail, assuring his lover that he was going on the
trip only out of obligation to his kids.

Angie must have been waiting for the reply, because
she answered right away, laying what was the first guilt
trip of the relationship on her boyfriend. She mentioned that her biggest fear was that Roseboro was
going up north, into the romance capital of the

northeast, to "rekindle" his "relationship" with Jan, noting how great a place Niagara Falls would be to do that. She said how much she loved Michael and that she was "scared to death of losing" him back to Jan, before admitting that anxiety was the likely cause of her insecurities—that it was nothing Roseboro had done or said. It's clear Angie was jealous of Jan going on the trip, and quite upset that he was going to be alone with Jan. Wasn't he supposed to be breaking it off with her? Instead, it seemed as though Michael was doing the opposite.

Angie concluded her e-mail by saying that perhaps all she needed to do was close her eyes and dream of her lover holding her, telling her that everything would be okay. Maybe that was all she needed, a picture in her mind of Michael Roseboro coming to the rescue, wearing his love on his sleeve.

In his haste to send Angie a response that would possibly curtail her insecurities, Michael horribly botched the first sentence of the next e-mail he sent. He told Angie to "rest assured that there is *a chance*"—my emphasis—that he and Jan were going to rekindle their relationship. He said how it took "two to tango" and he wasn't going to be the one doing any dancing with Jan. Then he made a promise that he would "be right here" and "do whatever it takes to make you my wife." From there, he talked about how he had just gone out to see Grandpa Louie, and the old man was completely out of it. Michael forecasted that Grandpa Louie wouldn't make it through the rest of the week. After mentioning that, perhaps trying to drum up a bit of sympathy from his mistress, he talked about how many kids were going on the trip with him and Jan, and that the weekend would be anything but romantic because of the amount of teenagers tagging along. He said he "didn't have a romantic bone left in" his body until two and a half weeks ago. Ending the e-mail, Michael broke into one of his

"It's only you that I . . ." signatures he now commonly used to sign off an e-mail. Substitute any word of desire for the ellipses and you get the picture. It's only you that I *adore* . . . and so on.

Angie sent a quick one-sentence e-mail in return, indicating the potential mistake Michael had made in forgetting that one word in the first sentence of his previous e-mail, reminding him that he had "better read" the e-mail again.

Roseboro was quick to correct the record, explaining he meant "*no* chance of any relationship" (again, emphasis mine) being rekindled while he and Jan were in Niagara. Looking at the fact that not only had Roseboro planned this trip to Niagara Falls but was, at the same time, putting the final touches on his wedding vows renewal trip, one would gather that the first time he wrote the sentence, he had made a Freudian slip.

Angie came back with a heartfelt message for her lover. When taken into context later, it would seem to put an awful amount of pressure on Roseboro to break it off with Jan as soon as possible. Angie said she wanted to be "Mrs. Roseboro" so bad that "it hurts." She had never felt this way, she claimed, about anyone else. She added that "true happiness" would only be when she was standing next to Roseboro saying "I do" while "looking into" his eyes. Her life would be "complete," she said, when that day came.

That response sparked an idea from Michael Roseboro. He mentioned to Angie in his return e-mail that he had been thinking about it seriously lately: He wanted to write their vows. Why? Well, because "expressing my love for you," he said, came "easily and effortlessly." Then he set the scene, noting how on the day they married, the "sun will be setting," and when it was over, he would be "the luckiest man alive."

Angie wrote back saying she had "never written vows" before—that is, for any of her two marriages. Putting words on paper was not one of her strong points, Angie admitted. Then she asked Roseboro if he had given any thought to where they might get married, before noting that it was almost time—twenty-two minutes—for her to make her daily noon call to him, a moment she could hardly wait for.

Roseboro dashed off his response a minute later, saying that his plan included "a pure white beach" in Carmel, California. He wrote of the day as if he were penning a scene in a Harlequin romance, some bare-chested Fabio look-alike, bouncing up and down on a bareback horse on the cover. He said the waves would "softly" fold "at our feet" while the breeze blew your "white linen dress" in the air. "The beauty of it all," Roseboro added, would actually pale "in comparison to the woman" standing there by his side on the beach that day.

Before sending the e-mail, Roseboro corrected Angie's time on the noon call, signing off that it was now only nineteen minutes away.

28

There are a multitude of underlying causes and character defects—both nurture and nature affiliated—that fuel an obsessive personality, the most common being "emotional addiction and the need for control," one psychologist told me. Michael Roseboro was sensing—right about now—that the control he had been managing in both relationships, although it had slipped from underneath him earlier in the day when Angie Funk questioned his intentions regarding the trip to Niagara, was back. All it took on Michael's part was some sweet talk about a beach and the love of his life standing next to him and their children as they recited wedding vows he had written, and he had Angie once again eating out of the palm of his hand. And make no mistake about it, for Roseboro, it was all about control and maintaining a balance between his life at home and his secrets.

Any e-mails sent on June 18, 2008, were not recorded on either computer. In many of the e-mails leading up to this day, both had spoken often about their anticipation of an upcoming rendezvous that day. Anytime they got together in a place where they could be alone, you could bet on it that they had their clothes off, scattered around them, moments later.

There had been one e-mail where Roseboro claimed to have driven by Angie's house "a hundred times a day," just to catch a glimpse of her. This was before they had hooked up, when he was clandestinely obsessing over being with her. Angie said she couldn't sign off on one hundred times—that was a little much. "It depended," she added, "on whether I was outside or not. That was the only time I would see him, if I was outside." And yet, if it wasn't a hundred, "some days it was one or two" times that she saw Roseboro drive by. "Some days it was, you know, ten or fifteen. It all depended on whatever."

Isn't "ten or fifteen" excessive enough?

On June 19, they were back to e-mailing, darting off the electronic missives of the same sentimental mishmash and longing they had for the past few weeks. In one e-mail, Roseboro said how great it made him feel that Angie considered him good-looking, a role he had never seen himself in, adding that he would look a lot better once she was on his arm all the time.

There was a complete shutdown of e-mail communication between Angie and Michael after he left for Niagara Falls on June 20 and returned June 23. There were phone calls, however—twenty-five altogether. Five made by Roseboro on Friday, June 20; eight made between the both of them on Saturday, June 21; nine on Sunday, June 22; and by Monday, June 23, when Michael was back in town, they spoke on three separate occasions and met that morning at Turkey Hill.

Those four days she didn't see her lover tore Angie Funk apart, a feeling that was entirely apparent in the e-mails she sent Roseboro early that morning, June 23, after she saw him briefly at Turkey Hill. This new thread of e-mails fell under the subject "I MISS YOU." Part of the first e-mail has been lost to cyberspace, or Angie's work hard drive, because computer forensics was able to recover only part of the original e-mail. And yet the one paragraph forensic technicians pulled from her computer explained a lot. Angie said it was "fantastic to be with" him, knowing that any time she spent with her man was a time in her life she cherished with all her "heart." In one instance, she said, "I ache for you, baby" . . . "so badly." Beyond "not being able to talk" to her lover whenever she wanted, or e-mail, see, touch, or kiss him anytime she wanted, due to their sneaking around, what Angie had trouble with the most was not "being with [him] physically." She called Roseboro the "most amazing man on earth" for the umpteenth time, before listing a host of adjectives she had used in past e-mails. Roseboro was "everything" and "strong." Angie could not wait until he was able to take her as his wife, which, she said, was going to be the "happiest day of all my life."

After what must have been reunion sex that night when they met up, Roseboro e-mailed Angie early the following morning, June 24, 2008. The first e-mail of this new day came into her computer at 3:49 A.M. It was not a joyful moment, however, for Michael Roseboro, at least not initially. The subject line of the e-mail, "my inspiration," Roseboro said, he had gotten from the Peter Cetera song, "You're the Inspiration." Although the subject might have indicated a different manner of feeling for him, Michael had some bad news to share. He had made the prediction himself the previous week, and here it was coming true. In fact, it was the reason why he was up so early.

His grandfather Louie had died. Roseboro said "we"—he and his father, three generations of Roseboros there in the embalming room—just finished preparing his grandfather's body at 3:35 A.M., not fifteen minutes before he sat down at his work desk to send an e-mail to the woman he loved.

His *inspiration*.

Roseboro said there were crazy thoughts and emotions running through him as he worked on the old man. It was hard to prepare Pa's body, he explained, but thinking of Angie and how wonderful life was now that she was in it had gotten him through it all.

He said he found himself stopping during the process before "I say or do something," with only one thought on his mind: *"What would Angela say or do?"*

He talked about a "profound respect" he now had for Angie because of this revelation. There was an "unimaginable love" he had found within himself for her—and that was his sole *inspiration* for life now.

Roseboro then talked about the drive home from Niagara the previous day, when he heard the Aerosmith song "I Don't Want to Miss a Thing" on the SUV's stereo system. He said how true the lyrics of the song were, especially now that he could view them in the light of Angie's place in his life.

What disrespect he showed here. Roseboro was driving home from Niagara Falls, Jan likely dozing off by his side, his kids in the backseat, maybe playing video games, texting friends, or snoozing, and he was up front listening to Aerosmith, fawning over his mistress. Even in terms of husbands cheating on their wives, this subtle lack of respect showed how much Roseboro did not care for Jan and/or her feelings.

Roseboro mentioned next how "deep" and "pure" his love for Angie was, and how he had realized this during what was the terrible tragedy of Grandpa Louie's death. So much so, Michael added, that he was e-mailing Angie, mainly, to invite her to Pa's funeral, saying that he completely understood if she couldn't make it. After all, he didn't want his lover "to be uncomfortable in any way" while mingling among his family members.

In proving how much it meant to him that Angie share in this moment of grief, Roseboro relayed a brief

story to Angie about one of the last conversations he'd
had with Pa.

"I've found the love of my life, Pa," Michael had told
the old man while the Roseboro patriarch lay on his
deathbed. "I am going to marry her!"

Roseboro told Angie that Pa smiled after hearing him
say this. It was a memory, he now wanted to share, that
he'd "hold on to for the rest of [his] life."

From there, Roseboro explained how much he had
missed Angie. They had a planned meeting, apparently,
at noon that day (where, neither of them said). He
couldn't wait to hold her "so tightly." He wanted so
badly to kiss Angie, he said, before again indicating how
much he loved her, finally thanking Angie for *loving*
him back. But "most importantly," Roseboro added
before signing off, "thank you for being you."

When Angie got into work, she logged onto her computer, printed the e-mail, and stuck it into what was a
growing file of heartfelt e-mails from her lover. Then she
sat down and tapped out her first response of the day.

Angie thanked her man for loving her uncondition-
ally. She called Roseboro the "strength and the love of
my life." She knew true happiness only when she was
talking to and spending time with her man, she said.
And this made her feel alive again.

She would try to get to the funeral. She said she
wanted to be there for her man, and would do everything in her power to make it happen. One of the only
things holding her back, she mentioned, wasn't necessarily being seen by the family or any awkwardness she
might feel, but a time.

Why?

Because Angie needed a babysitter for her kids. The
viewing was on that Thursday night between the hours
of six and eight P.M. The funeral, however, was on Friday,
11:00 A.M., at the Faith United Evangelical Lutheran
Church, right down the block from Angie's house on

Walnut Street, with interment to follow at Fairview Cemetery, on the opposite side of town.

Randall would be at work during those times.

At the end of the short e-mail, Angie reminded Michael how much she loved him, adding that she was willing to "go to the ends of the earth" for him.

Seven minutes later, Michael sent Angie an e-mail describing a letter she had written him. He must have just found it, because he said that after he finished reading it (just then), he was able to type only "after wiping the tears" from his eyes that the letter had brought upon him. That letter, he said, expressed exactly what he was feeling: that they "completed" each other. He didn't mention, one way or another, if they had recently watched *Jerry Maguire,* that 1996 Tom Cruise–Renée Zellweger movie, whereby that sappy line, "You complete me," had made the movie a pop culture phenom. Or if Angie had mentioned the scene in the letter. But from the gist of Roseboro's response, it was clear this was an inside joke between them.

Roseboro called Angie his "fountain of youth" for making him feel so alive and open and free to love once again. He made the inference that Jan had never been able to bring this out of him; the love he and Jan once might have shared had long ago dried up. This "alive" description was to become a theme both would go back to quite frequently in the coming weeks. For the first time, they both claimed in their numerous e-mails, both Angie and Michael felt as though they were living, as if the floodgates to what once provided happiness had been unleashed, and a resurgence of romance had been rekindled by this particular affair.

Eleven minutes went by, and Angie returned the e-mail by saying how she wanted to keep Michael happy for the rest of his life, before breaking into the familiar "grow old with you" line that many lovers use. She ended the e-mail with the idea that her life's passion had now evolved into being by Roseboro's side forever—being his wife.

Angie wrote how this would happen, "no matter what."

Answering that, Michael said if Angie ever tried to leave his side, he would "superglue" her to his hip.

In return, Angie said she wanted "to be Mrs. Angela Lynn Roseboro more than anything else. . . ."

Anything.

Roseboro said they could forget about superglue (Angie had suggested he wouldn't need it, anyway, because she was all his), but that maybe "some oil" would be nice. He then mentioned how he had been thinking about the marriage a lot lately, and how he wanted to have their kids present for the ceremony.

Angie agreed, adding that it would be a blessing to show the kids how much a couple could love each other, before asking Roseboro if he was "being naughty" by mentioning oil. If he was, she said, she "would love that," but there would have to be a shower involved and Michael would have to wipe the oil off her wet body.

It was a strange set of comments, considering that they were sandwiched between such serious talk about the kids and how Angie wanted them to "feel the love we have" between "us." She began the e-mail by speaking of their children; went into that "naughty" talk of oils and showering together; and ended with more talk of how much they needed to show the kids that they loved each other. It was as if that "love" they described, over and over, was centered around the sexual attraction they had for each other and the different things they wanted to do in the bedroom to satisfy such an unquenchable thirst for sex.

Family values. Sex. Love. Family values.

A strange way to look at beginning a new life together.

Michael took the bait and admitted that he was indeed being naughty, blaming Angie for bringing "out that side" of him. He warned her that if they had to shower, it "would start the whole cycle over again."

It had been only a few hours since Roseboro had described how terrible he was feeling at having to embalm Grandpa Louie. Yet, here he was, on that same morning, undoubtedly preparing for the old man's wake later that day, talking about rubbing oil all over his lover and then taking showers with her and showing their children how a *real* love worked by having them present at their wedding. The line between fantasy and reality was blurring for Michael Roseboro. He and Angie Funk were deeply locked inside this pipe dream of an alternate reality; yet neither was doing anything to make it actually come true.

At Fairview Cemetery, eighty-nine-year-old E. Louis Roseboro, a church organist for forty years, on top of being a mortician, and a fifty-year member of Ephrata Lodge #665, was laid to rest on Friday morning, June 27, 2008. Pa left behind two sons, Harry, husband of Marian (Gockley) Roseboro, and Ralph, husband of Ann (Myer) Roseboro, along with five grandchildren, Daniel, David, Melissa Voler (Michael Roseboro's sister), Erik Snyder, and Michael Roseboro, along with thirteen great-grandchildren.

He was preceded in death, said the obituary Michael Roseboro likely wrote, *by a daughter, Mary Ann Snyder.*

Angie Funk made it. There she stood, graveside, taking part in the ceremony. When asked about her attendance later, "I knew his grandfather," she said under oath, as if they had been old friends.

As the proceedings went forward, Angie became incensed when she saw Jan kiss Michael, but she could do nothing about it. That kiss upset her deeply, she said later, and also made her jealous.

Nonetheless, after the ceremony, Angie walked away without saying anything.

For the next several days, heading toward the end of June, Angie and Michael kept up the sexual pressure on the relationship, meeting to have sex, talking dirty on the cell phone, texting each other what was dozens of times per day, and meeting again inside the funeral home. (She never mentioned "the kiss" to Roseboro in any of her e-mails.)

On June 30, a Monday, Angie e-mailed Michael, saying how glad she was that "we had [last] Saturday." The "whole world disappears," Angie explained, when she was with her man. The relationship was steaming along at breakneck speed now; the sex the best Michael had apparently ever had. What had been a former mark, a piece of prey, was now an obsession he could have whenever the opportunity presented itself.

Roseboro returned the e-mail, which was more of the same "I cannot live without you; I adore the air you breathe; you make life worth living" gushy spew they had been sharing with each other now for over a month. The sugary compliments seeped out of Michael—the tight pants Angie wore, the way she kept her hair, the perfume she sprayed on her neck, the cards she sent. It was as if anything she did was perfect. They used the word "love" as commonly as a conjunction or pronoun. To them, love was passion. Love was lust. Love was the intense euphoria they felt while either talking about having sex or actually committing the act.

In the following e-mails—on that same day—you could almost feel the desperation in Michael Roseboro's tone as he extolled the need to be with Angie all the time. It was beginning to be too much for him to bear. He couldn't work. Certainly couldn't sleep or think. Drive. Walk. Eat. He could do nothing—without Angie slipping into his thoughts. He was so consumed with desire that it was all he could do not to run across the street, grab Angie, take her in his arms, and have her there on the front lawn or foyer inside her house. The way he described his feelings was almost like a Bogie and Bacall film he had just seen on cable. Yet, the longing was the driving, motivating factor behind whatever Roseboro now said or did. One would have to ask how long this overly sentimental talk between them could go on *if* they left their spouses and actually moved in together?

In an e-mail at 8:22 A.M. on June 30, 2008, Michael Roseboro made a direct promise to Angie Funk. He said he would always take care of her and her girls—that he would love them, as if they were his own.

Angie darted an e-mail back saying she had wanted the same things. Yes. She had been thinking about this, too. How perfect was this? The both of them concerned with their children, and her new man now willing to take care of them. She couldn't imagine life without him, Angie said after glorifying his willingness to include her children in their future. He was her "world," her "heart and soul." It was getting hard, Angie said halfway through her response, to have to wait around for *something* to happen. What, indeed, were they waiting for, actually? Was there a plan?

Michael Roseboro said he didn't "want to wait" anymore. He then described the "deep need and desire" he had within him to be with Angie.

It was almost "unbearable to hold inside" anymore, Roseboro explained.

29

Sometime after Jan Roseboro's death, Angie Funk shared a letter with police. Michael Roseboro had scribed the missive on the night of his and Angie's one-month anniversary, which would have been somewhere around June 30, 2008.

My Dearest Angela . . . , the letter began. The previous night had been another round of sleepless hours of darkness, Roseboro explained, which he had gotten all too used to by that point. His life—every aspect of it— was now consumed with the thought of being with this woman, having sex with her, sharing his life with her, and marrying Angie inside the next year. Michael could not get the idea of marrying Angie from his mind, he admitted in this letter.

Looking back on the relationship, studying every nuance of it, a part of it all seemed as though Roseboro had a terrible lack of personal insight: He never saw who he was as a father and/or husband (to Jan and his children). And yet none of that mattered anymore. He could not rationally take a look at his life and see that Angie Funk, an object of his desire, represented a fantasy and surrealism. She was a *thing* he had sought out to conquer, a woman he'd had his eye on for what was years, by some estimates. Now that he finally had a taste, he needed to take it to the next level in order to justify the amount of time and thought she had taken from him. And that's what it came down to for Roseboro: *more.* Running around town wasn't enough. Meeting and having sex wasn't doing it. Talking to Angie on the phone dozens of times per day, sending dozens of text messages and scores of e-mails wasn't satisfying this man's gargantuan thirst for this woman.

He was now convinced that only marriage could put the kibosh on such a ravenous appetite.

For every obsession, there is a consequence for the obsessed. There has to be. It makes it all worth it. A fan becomes infatuated with a celebrity. Those feelings fester inside him for weeks, months, years. Finally, overcome with emotion and confusion, not to mention an inconceivable amount of desire to gain control of the situation and a fear of losing her, he suddenly realizes one day he'll never have her (maybe he steps into reality for a moment) and lashes out, shooting or stabbing her to death.

If I cannot have you, no one . . .

This letter Michael Roseboro wrote in late June was the first time he had ever discussed "how far" the relationship had come in such a short period of time. He called his love for Angie—again—"immeasurable." He said he would never let Angie down—ever—and placed that promise at "the depth of [his] soul." He admitted that Angie was now his "dreams," "passion," "longing," "laughter," "tears," "hopes," "future," and "love." She was *everything.* His entire being—Roseboro said in not so many words—was built around this unassuming, average-looking, five-foot-five, part-time insurance consultant, wife, and mother of two— a woman across the street from his work he had watched and groveled over. And now she was all his.

In that handwritten letter, Roseboro acknowledged he would "go to any length to show" Angie how much he adored and loved her.

Any length.

Still, while Roseboro was saying all of these things to his most current obsession, he was back at home on the computer, searching for pastors and beach resorts in the Outer Banks to renew his marriage vows to Jan. In fact, Michael had even set a date: August 13, 2008, now just six weeks away. He was forced into marking the calendar, because he wanted many of Jan's friends and family there to share in the celebration and surprise.

"He doesn't tell [Angie] about his plans to renew his wedding vows with his wife," DA Craig Stedman said, "because he's telling [Angie], of course, all along [that] 'my wife doesn't mean anything to me, our relationship is nothing, there's no love there, we're not really together, we're only in the same house.' That's what he's telling [Angie].

"Lies."

Many would later ask: *What in the world was Michael Roseboro up to?* Two worlds—of which he was actively participating in—were on a collision course. He had to know this.

"What he's doing," Stedman added, "is carrying on an affair in secret. Secret sexual encounters. Secret e-mails. Secret from the whole world, from anybody in his world, but him and his girlfriend. Secret texts. E-mails that are so full of obsession that you actually probably [cannot] believe the content. . . ."

As the month of July beckoned, Roseboro was "a man who's living on borrowed time," Stedman said. Roseboro's cell phone bill was $688 for that one month he had been with Angie, all because of the text messages and phone calls. The bill itself looked like a teletype readout for a list of someone's assets, with Angie Funk's number coming up repeatedly, page after page after page, as if misprinted.

"So he's . . . running out of his ability to carry on two relationships," Stedman concluded, describing Roseboro's state of mind as he headed into the month of July—"and to plan *two* weddings at the same time."

30

Jan Roseboro knew about Michael's affair, one source told me. Not that she knew her husband was running around the county, having sex with Angela Funk inside vacant apartments, his SUV, and the funeral home. But Jan *knew* when her husband was stepping out. He had done it before, plenty enough times, and Jan had caught him. Add to this something Jan had said to a friend weeks before her death: "Mike has an awful lot of paperwork to do at the funeral home lately. . . ."

Jan was not some naive housewife.

She damn well knew.

Few women can deny that feeling, no matter how much they try to repress, stuff, or ignore it. It might be the way he acts. The fact that he wants to have *more* sex—doubling up, if you will. Or that he brings home flowers for no apparent reason, out of character. Maybe he likes to minimize the computer screen when his wife walks into the room. Or hang up his cell phone quickly when the Mrs. comes around, and rushes to get the mail on certain days. A wife's intuition cannot be stifled; it is too strong an emotion. And Jan was a smart woman. If her husband had done it once before, was it so hard to believe he would do it again?

Susan Van Zant, a family consumer science teacher during the time of Jan's murder, had been working for the Cocalico School District since 1974. Jan's sister was well known around town. She had kids of her own. She had even grown up in the original house on Main Street in Reinholds/Denver that Michael and Jan Roseboro had converted into that U-shaped "estate," if you'll permit the term, which now took up the corner lot.

Jan and Suzie were close, and they had lived about three miles from each other, or in the same house, for what was forever. Being the older sibling, Suzie viewed Jan, she later said, "like a daughter."

Jan had grown into the person Suzie had envisioned when they were kids. Down-to-earth. Kindhearted. Easy to get along with. Modest. Cheerful. And, for the most part, happy. Jan was so at ease with life that she owned a cell phone, but, Suzie later said, she "never checked her messages," or even used it if she didn't have to. And that was Jan. She'd just as well sit outside, enjoy her new pool and the kids, and leave the darn cell phone inside, where it belonged. That, or hang out with her dogs, whom she loved greatly. Whenever Jan was outside by the pool or hanging around, maybe weeding the garden, walking around the land, her dogs went with her.

When the pool was officially opened on the weekend of July 4, 2008, Jan was the first one to call and tell Suzie she could use it anytime she wanted.

Jan and Michael Roseboro had invited Suzie, her fiancé, Gary Frees, and her family to North Carolina that summer, and Suzie accepted. There were other family members going, too, Suzie said later. Cousins and brothers and friends. The group, including Michael and Jan and their kids, was large.

"It was a huge house," Suzie explained, describing the place where they were supposed to stay at the Outer Banks. "It was a very, very *huge* house. Everybody had a suite with a Jacuzzi and a fireplace. . . ."

Her brother-in-law, Michael Roseboro, Suzie recalled, had even pulled her aside one day and mentioned his plans. Michael said he "planned on renewing his vows with Jan down there and he was making arrangements to do so. . . ." He said it was going "to be on the beach." Apparently, like Angie Funk, Jan was a big fan of the ocean. She adored the feeling of sand between her toes, the warm breeze and constant hum of the water crashing into the shoreline. This would have fit well into her ideal day on the beach: renewing her wedding vows, making new promises of love, hanging out with friends and family. To Jan, it might have meant that her husband was taking their life together seriously once again.

Or maybe Jan would have decided not to go through with it at all.

"That will make her very happy," Michael told Suzie, meaning the beach setting.

Suzie agreed.

Brian Binkley, Jan's brother, had been close to his sister throughout the years. Living in Pittsburgh, Brian, a twenty-two-year CPA by trade, enjoyed those times with Jan, his nieces, nephews, and brother-in-law. They got along well. Yet living far away from Denver, not seeing everyone as much as he would have liked, afforded Brian the opportunity to view the changes in family members perhaps more objectively than those involved on a daily basis could. Brian noticed things whenever he got together with his sister and her family.

"I think we had a great relationship," Brian recalled. "I can tell you the first part of 2008, everybody really enjoyed moving into the new house. Everybody was happy. We had a lot of celebrations there." And if work hadn't called him out, Michael Roseboro was at every one of those parties and get-togethers, generally manning the bar, cracking jokes, drinking, and smoking cigarettes.

The consummate dad and husband.

It was June, Brian explained later, during a trip he took to see his sister and her family, that Brian noticed a considerable change in his brother-in-law.

"I started seeing a difference in some of the characteristics of Mike," Brian recalled. "There were just some changes, some changes that I saw in terms of discussing things with him and Jan, and raising the children, things in terms of behaviors with the dogs."

There was a certain "possessiveness," Brian shared, on his brother-in-law's part, he had noticed. It stood out. Knowing Michael Roseboro for more than twenty years, Brian said he had never seen him act that way before.

"There were changes in his personality."

Brian Binkley recalled one instance that took place. Brian couldn't say exactly what he had been talking to his brother-in-law about, but at some point during the conversation, Michael shouted, "This is *my* house!" in a voice Brian was unfamiliar with.

"It was a possessiveness I had never seen in Mike before."

Pressure. Roseboro's two lives were closing in on him and he was flying off the handle at the slightest thing.

Some in town who knew Michael Roseboro were struck when, in late June and early July, Roseboro's SUV was seen parked at the downtown neighborhood bar. It was one of those local joints—some might call it a "dive"—that working men go to get their drunk on and talk about what's going on in town. But there was Roseboro, the local wealthy undertaker, a new goatee, a smile from ear to ear, a cocky nervousness about him few could ever recall him exhibiting, bellied up to the bar, ordering beers, stubbing out cigarettes, mixing it up with the locals as if he belonged there.

"The type of person he was," Richard Pope later said, "that was *not* the type of bar you'd expect Mike to go to. It was just odd. That's all. I had never seen that before."

"Jan walked in on him one time," Angie Funk later told police, "when we were on the phone and Michael immediately hung up."

Angie asked him about the incident a day later.

"Jan was not upset," Roseboro insisted to his lover, as if it were business as usual.

Sometime later, Angie asked, "Does anyone ever hit on you?"

It was a question rooted in jealousy. The two of them were cheating on their spouses with each other, and Angie was insecure, believing that Michael might or might not be cheating on her with someone else?

"Some woman hit my leg on an airplane once," Roseboro said, explaining that he took it as an invitation to a conversation.

"But he has never admitted to me," Angie told police, "that he had other affairs."

As the relationship between Michael Roseboro and Angie Funk took on this insecure dynamic near the end of June, Angie and Michael talked, she later confirmed to police, about their spouses.

"I figured Jan would find out about the affair," Angie recalled to Keith Neff, "due to the phone records. But I never talked to Michael about what we would do when our spouses found out."

Sneaking around, Angie admitted, was "hard on my home life." She said she never discussed with Roseboro what would happen to the funeral home or custody of his children *after* he left Jan and married her.

"I assumed he would leave the house to Jan," Angie said.

On the morning of June 30, 2008, Angie Funk sat at her work computer composing yet another string of e-mails to her lover. The first e-mail was more of the same promises to love and cherish you and your kids for the rest of my life.

Flirtatious gibberish.

Mike Roseboro responded with another one of his quirky, adolescent turns of phrase, telling Angie how there was "no 'I' in love." He mentioned the shower again, before telling Angie it was becoming increasingly hard on him to be away from her for one minute. When they were together, he said, she'd be there working with him, playing, sleeping. They'd spend every second of every day together.

In return, Angie said she knew she was going to have to wait, and the thought of having him to herself one day kept her going.

Michael said in response that he didn't want to wait any longer. Something needed to be done—and fast. He admitted that she had turned him "into a babbling and giddy teenager. . . ."

They made plans in the next series of e-mails to meet at the Cloister later that day.

Roseboro said he was "smiling just thinking about" the rendezvous.

On July 1, Mike Roseboro e-mailed first, telling Angie how seeing her in the morning at Turkey Hill was the highlight of his day. He carried on about how beautiful she was and how he could never, at this point, "live without" her. It wasn't going to be possible to go on without having Angie Funk by his side.

It seemed the strain weighed on Roseboro to do something in the order of moving his relationship with Angie to the next level.

Angie, in turn, ratcheted things up by telling Michael in her response that she needed to wake up next to him and go to sleep by his side. That she couldn't "wait to be Mrs. Roseboro" and "share *everything*."

Roseboro said he would never squander an "opportunity to make love" to Angie when they were together. He explained that she would never have to worry about him "being in the mood" because just a gentle kiss from her aroused him. Either they spent a night together—although no record of it exists—or Roseboro watched as Angie went out to get the morning newspaper, because he told Angie how gorgeous she was in her pajamas, her "hair undone, no makeup at all." He called Angie the most "beautiful woman in the world" and professed that he was going to be her husband, no matter what stood in their way.

31

Angie Funk fell deeper and deeper for the fantasy Michael Roseboro described, both in his daily e-mail dispatches and the conversations they had in person. For Angie Lynn Funk, Roseboro represented a man out of her league. Although she had fixated on and dreamed of being with him, she thought she would never get him. She told Roseboro that "in a million years" she would have never "thought" of being with him, especially not in the capacity their relationship had grown to between June and July (talking about getting married and raising a *Brady Bunch*–type family). Still, whenever she saw Roseboro, maybe around town or during her daily walks throughout the years, Angie said she had felt there was some sort of "connection" between them, beyond a general attraction. And here she was, now writing in e-mails to the same man she had fantasized about and had viewed as a catch beyond her means.

It *was* like a dream.

Roseboro later admitted that he was intimidated by Angie Funk from the first moment they had met at the Denver Parade many years before he had made the first phone call. It was a day both Angie and Mike had gone back to in their e-mails from time to time.

* * *

"I'm Michael Roseboro," the distinguished undertaker said, sticking out his hand that day of the parade.
As he stared at Angie, Roseboro later admitted, he was
thinking what it would feel like to kiss her and get to
know her better. He had seen Angie around town. He
had noticed that when they stared at each other, both
had given that second look, a slight moment of hesitation in the eyes as they turned away. He said thinking
about being with Angie back then (five years prior to
their hooking up) was a "dream"—and he never imag-
ined he would one day "act on" his "impulses." From
that moment, Roseboro explained, whenever he saw
Angie, either walking into the Turkey Hill store alone
(or with her friend), or just around the neighborhood
(even with her husband), his "palms would get sweaty"
and his "heart would race. . . ."

He *had* to have her.

They had come so far since those days of playing
games. From meeting at a parade, to "flirtatious fun," as
Angie put it, to that lunch invitation Roseboro had
made on May 29, 2008, to having sex.

From motionless to mach one in just weeks.

Before Angie had kids with Randall Funk, she and
her husband traveled a lot, former family members and
friends said, taking cruises and visiting other touristy
spots throughout the globe. Angie Funk was not a
person who talked all that much about her dreams,
goals, and what she wanted out of life beyond the
normal material stuff most of us cling to. Instead, Angie
was into talking about sports, the Pittsburgh Steelers—
her favorite sports team by far—in particular. The other
thing Angie never mentioned was sex. "I never heard
her once talk about it," said a former friend. It was

either something that wasn't on her mind, or something she'd rather do than talk about. But it was clear to many around Angie as she grew up and into her early years of being married to her first husband that she was definitely into the romance part of relationships. The long walks, arm in arm. Candlelight dinners. Expensive trips to exotic locales. Naughty talk.

"Big wedding person," said two sources. "Angie was into planning weddings and having extravagant weddings herself." And when she planned a wedding with a friend or family member, Angie took over. "She liked being in control."

Even demanded it.

There came a time in early July when Michael Roseboro mentioned to his lover that he was going to be gone for a week in August. He had to bring it up. Face the fact of disappearing with his wife and family. He and Jan and the gang were going. He couldn't back out of the trip. Angie Funk needed to know.

But how much would Casanova divulge?

"We're going for a week," Roseboro explained. "I won't get to talk to you or anything. It's a family trip. It's no big deal, really." He further added that "everybody in his (and Jan's) family" was going with them on the trip. He talked it down, Angie later implied, as though it wasn't anything special. A family obligation he was being forced to fulfill. It was nothing. Same as Niagara. There would be scores of kids and others around. Angie had no need to worry about anything.

Had she known that the trip to the Outer Banks was actually being planned around her boyfriend renewing his vows with his wife, Angie later said, "I would not have got involved." But she was involved—in a big way. The main reason, Angie said, was because Roseboro had repeatedly told her that he and Jan were together only for the kids' sake. Nothing else.

"There was no love there," Angie told police.

Two ships . . .

A couple staying married to raise a family.

Still, the trip was on the calendar, and although "it created some anxiety" for Angie, "there was nothing," Angie later said, "that [I] could do about it."

The topic of what Jan would do when she found out about the affair came up between Roseboro and Angie a few times, she claimed. Angie was no dummy. She was a woman. She knew women thought about those sorts of things. Plus, with four kids on the line, a huge house, all that money, a family business. Running around with Angie and ultimately leaving Jan, Angie realized, Michael Roseboro was looking at potentially losing a lot. The question became: was he willing to risk it all?

"If she finds out about us, she's going to take the kids and everything," Angie told Roseboro one night, reminding her lover how much was at stake. "A woman scorned usually, you know, especially a wife, can hurt you pretty bad sometimes. Bleed you dry."

Roseboro thought about this. He was concerned about the family business, sure. So much so, he responded to Angie, "I am going to see about putting the funeral home in my dad's name—that way she cannot touch it."

Five years prior to the affair with Angie Funk (and presumably many other women in between), while Michael Roseboro was having an affair with Liz Cannon (pseudonym), whom he would text and talk to by cell, same as he was with Angie, Jan found out about the affair after going through the cell phone bills one day. When Roseboro told Cannon about Jan uncovering their little ongoing tryst, he *discussed the financial consequences of getting a divorce from Jan,* a 2009 court stipulation reported. More than that, Roseboro's father found out—and he wasn't happy about it. "My father explained to me," Roseboro told Cannon, "that if I continued the affair . . . he was going to divide the funeral business into quarters between himself, my mother, my sister, Melissa, and me!" Considering he was married to Jan and a divorce might split that quarter into an eighth, Roseboro expressed to Cannon that "one half of one fourth is *not* enough to live on." Another woman Roseboro knew years before he met Cannon, according to a second stipulation (both of which Roseboro ultimately signed, thus inserting his stamp of validity on each document), heard him bemoan the fact that he "could not get a divorce from [Jan] because he would 'lose his kids.'"

So Roseboro had some trepidation regarding the stakes of committing adultery and getting caught; he knew damn well that, in his case, he stood to lose just about everything he had.

On Tuesday, July 1, 2008, Angie e-mailed her lover. As the morning wore on, they became engaged in an e-conversation about how the relationship had developed over the course of the past several weeks. Angie said Roseboro had "composed himself really well" during that period when he was stealthily watching her from afar. She called him a "gentleman." She said it was still hard for her to imagine that *the* Michael Alan Roseboro actually loved her. And now that they were actually together, the thought of it all was something she was having a tough time wrapping her brain around.

Roseboro responded with one of the longer e-mails he would ever send to Angie Funk. He talked about "a journey" his "heart" was taking him on—one he thought he could never have expected in his lifetime. He said it was a "ride that [he] never wanted to see end." Part of the allure driving the relationship, he added, was to "see what the future holds for us." He couldn't wait to see what it was; nor could he wait to "roll over," as he put it, each morning and tell Angie how much he loved her. "I know it is going to happen," he added, before saying how Angie "rocked" his "world" and that he was in "awe" of her.

They saw each other the following morning at Turkey Hill. Roseboro explained in an e-mail later on that morning how he "could cry every time" Angie smiled at him inside that tiny convenience store with the dirty floors and coffee-stained counters. She had always looked "so perfect" in the mornings, he said. Farther along in the e-mail, Roseboro gave Angie the website URL for a resort in Turtle Island, Fiji. He said he could have never seen himself horseback riding along the beach in Fiji, but Angie had brought that romantic, free-spirited side out of him, and he now looked *forward* to it. He sketched out how great it was going to be to ride horses side by side along the shoreline, the water crashing at the hooves of their horses, the two of them holding hands as the horses walked slowly behind them.

The next series of e-mails were a combination of the transparency most adulterous affairs brought out of those involved, not to mention the utter disregard for the shame Roseboro had. He carried on and on, for example, about how he had never felt loved and how his love for Angie had no limitations. He never considered that making love to a woman "could be so consuming" and "passionate" and "tender" and "gentle" and "wonderful." He never thought it would be possible to work with his wife, but now that he knew Angie's love, that idea was not only a possibility, it was going to be a reality: apparently, Angie was going to become part of the family business as soon as he dumped Jan and married her.

Beyond that, Roseboro said he was feeling emotions he had never experienced in his marriage with Jan.

Near the end of the e-mail, if he had to, Roseboro said, he would "die for" Angie.

That last e-mail had made Angie fight back tears of emotion while at work, according to what Roseboro wrote on the morning of July 3. Angie was so overcome by the tenderness and love Roseboro had shared, it took everything she had not to cry in front of the girls and guys in her office.

In response, Michael Roseboro said he couldn't help himself. He wanted to be "completely open and honest with" her. No matter what. And if there was ever a doubt in her mind about the love he felt, Roseboro wrote that he would gladly give up "everything I have if that's what it" took to be "your husband."

This sparked some anxiety on Angie's part. She didn't want to, obviously, hold that much power over someone's existence. In saying this, it would appear that Angie Funk was grounded more in reality than her smitten lover. She said she would never ask him to give up everything, because sooner or later he would resent her for doing it. There would come a day, Angie was certain, when Roseboro would throw it all back in her face. She didn't want their relationship to begin with this dark cloud hovering over it. She was glad she made Roseboro happy, Angie wrote, but "I am not the only thing that makes you happy." She assumed his kids provided a warm feeling in his heart that she could never hold a candle to.

Michael Roseboro never answered the e-mail with any sort of antidotal response to her trepidation and concern.

July Fourth weekend came. On Saturday afternoon, Angie Funk and Michael Roseboro met and had sex. By Monday morning, Roseboro was giddy again, talking about how much fun he was having with Angie, sneaking around and hanging out together. There's no doubt that part of the thrill for Roseboro was in running around town, hiding from their spouses and friends: that double-life scenario he had been living for a decade or more. There was one time when Roseboro met Angie at a local Costco shopping mart in Lancaster County. They were frolicking around the megastore like an old married couple shopping for their family, when Roseboro spotted somebody he knew, and Angie conspicuously slipped away from him so as not to be noticed, later having the audacity to tell DA Craig Stedman, downplaying the moment, "I went on my way . . . [because] I had shopping to do and I wanted to get home."

From the hundreds of pages of e-mails left behind by Roseboro and Angie, considering how fast the relationship progressed and how immature and terribly lust-struck Michael Roseboro sounded during this period, it's quite clear he was having the time of his life, screwing Angie Funk any chance he got, while maintaining that family man image at home. In his mind, Roseboro had the best of both worlds. He wrote Angie that he had never thought of ever looking forward to Mondays, but because he could see her at the store, talk on the phone, text and e-mail all day long, Mondays were now well worth getting up for. That "Saturday afternooner," he added, coining a phrase in an e-mail on Monday morning, "didn't hurt either."

Wink-wink.

What Roseboro didn't know was that a turn of events was about to take place in his life with Angie that would change everything. Long before Jan Roseboro was murdered, a set of circumstances began in Michael Roseboro's life with Angie, placing a tremendous burden on the man, with the potential to cause a great crisis, or scandal, not to mention embarrassment.

This, mind you, beyond the affair with Angie being exposed.

While Angie was beginning to show signs that all of the lust-filled, teenage-inspired romantic e-chitchat was fun and sounded good, her mind raced. This as Roseboro sent her messages that included gems of prose to the tune of, "You have unleashed the lion in me. . . ."

Angie wrote and asked Michael Roseboro what time he was leaving for his first funeral that morning. She wanted to know if it was at a church or the funeral home? Apparently, Angie Funk wanted to attend. She needed to see her man.

It sounded urgent.

32

Every problem that came between Michael Roseboro and Angie Funk, the undertaker quickly learned, could be resolved with another overstated, oversexed e-mail, perhaps opening with a scene of them holding hands and running into the sunset along the shoreline while dolphins crested on the horizon. Michael kept sketching the image of the dream Angie now believed in, without letting up. On July 7, for instance, the obsession of the day became Angie's face. It was "so beautiful," Michael said in the beginning of his first e-mail. He felt the love she had for him in every smile, adding that her "eyes sparkle," even though, he said, he could "see the naughty side coming out" of that surprisingly subtle twinkle. Angie was "magnificent" this morning. His "dream come true." She was "every tear that" he shed. Just a simple touch by this woman sent a shiver down Roseboro's spine.

Angie never documented or later talked about why she wanted to see her lover so urgently that morning. Maybe she just wanted to be with him. Or perhaps ask Michael Roseboro what was going on at home: was he making any progress with that little problem of having a wife and four kids?

But the following morning, July 8, a day both Angie and Roseboro would have trouble forgetting in the weeks, months, and even years to come, Roseboro had sex on his mind. When he saw Angie at Turkey Hill, he said an hour later in an e-mail, he had pictured her not wearing any panties. He felt so lucky, he claimed, standing there, mixing his coffee, chatting with townies, watching Angie waltz in, knowing that someday she was going to be his wife—and that later on that afternoon, she was going to be servicing him with that killer body.

Michael kept feeding Angie little nuggets to keep her going. Here, this morning, he said that when the time was "right, my love for you will be a secret to nobody." Beyond telling Angie that every kiss was something born out of a deep passion he had never felt in life before meeting her, he said it made him "weak in the knees" to touch her lips with his—"literally." He was speechless, he added, but obviously that was just a turn of phrase, because Roseboro couldn't stop writing, texting, or talking on the phone to Angie. He couldn't wait, he said, until their lives became "one life." Near the end of that over-the-top e-mail, he said pointedly, "I am going to marry you. . . ."

Angie bought it all.

Hook. Line. Sinker.

Any worry or fear she had could always be wiped away by a few morning e-mails from her lover. Michael Roseboro, the accomplished cheater, had a way of making everything sound so perfect.

Angie wrote back explaining how she had "read that e-mail you sent several times. . . ." She called it "beautiful," same as the love they shared for each other. There were times, Angie Funk continued, when it was overwhelming to believe that "you are so in love with me." Here, in this e-mail, she admitted to having been "attracted" to Michael Roseboro "for years."

With words alone, Roseboro had turned Angie back

around and kept her focused not on the future, the next day, next hour, or the Outer Banks, but now.

The moment.

Writing back at 8:29 A.M., Michael Roseboro broke into a diatribe about what the term "soul mates" meant to him. It was so exaggerated, he must have felt a pang of childish volatility in him as he wrote it. He used every cliché associated with love imaginable, not sparing a word.

They made plans to meet for sex that afternoon.

"Yeah," Angie later said, "July eighth, somewhere in that time frame," speaking of an afternoon sexual romp she would be forced to remember.

How was it that Angie Funk was so sure it was *that* day she had gotten pregnant with Michael Roseboro's child?

"Because that's the only time when the condom broke," she later said in court.

Broke?

Well, she added next, "Yeah. Or came off."

Angie wasn't sure which. She explained that when that mistake happened, she and Michael discussed it, but she could not recall any details about their conversation.

Others later speculated, based on knowing Angie, that she became impatient and made sure the condom didn't work the way that it should have. Or told Michael to forget about the condom altogether.

A source close to Angie believed that Angie "needed this baby."

Before the affair with Michael started, Angie would give subtle hints within the family that she had her eye on someone in particular—this, mind you, while still married to Randall Funk. "There's this guy," she said once to a family member. "We've had coffee. . . . He's really nice."

That same source later observed, "I never put two and

two together until later. It was the way she said it. She made it seem like they were 'friends.'"

It was right around the time that the affair with Michael Roseboro started, some friends and family later speculated, when Angie began to say things like, "I want him (Randy) out! I cannot take him anymore. I want a divorce!" These were things Angie had never said in the past during family get-togethers. All of a sudden, without warning, she stopped bringing Randy around, and she spoke as if she hated him.

"This was all a setup on her part. There were neighbors in that vacant apartment Angie and Michael met in that said it would get a little loud in there at times, if you know what I mean."

If there was the least bit of concern about the condom malfunction, and the slightest chance Angie Funk was going to become pregnant, neither Michael Roseboro nor his mistress expressed any fear in the e-mails they wrote after that particular sexual event. In fact, quite to the contrary, the e-mails post–July 8 were even more foolish and slapstick lovey-dovey nonsense than anything either had written previously. It was not a simple "good morning" any longer for her lover. Instead, "my love" was plastered on everything Angie wrote after that condom malfunction, with a "madly and deeply" tossed in from time to time.

By now, they were meeting just about every day at lunchtime.

"I can't get enough of you . . . ," Angie said, repeating the same phrase in all caps at the end of the same e-mail.

Michael expressed his own amount of redundancy in his next e-mail by repeating the word "sexy" (in describing Angie) eight times—that is, before calling her an "angel sent from heaven." He talked about how Angie had been placed here, on earth, apparently, to "rescue" him from the life he had been living with Jan.

Was he insinuating that being with Jan and the kids was his version of hell? It would seem so, considering how the overly dramatized romance was becoming so natural for Michael Roseboro. It seemed every hour of every day was dedicated to Angie Funk.

Still, neither of them had the one thing Angie was beginning to get a little impatient with: freedom from their spouses.

Thus, the countdown started.

July 14, 2008

*Eight days before
Jan Roseboro's murder*

33

On that Monday, after another wild weekend of what must have been, at least by their estimation, crazy-wild sex, Michael Roseboro told Angie Funk she didn't need to thank him for anything he did for her ". . . but I do appreciate what your love has done for me." He must have bought Angie some sort of extravagant gift, because she was whimsical and blissful over that "thing" he had done.

Because of this new life he had with Angie, Michael admitted, he had found himself stopping to take in the simple things in life: singing birds, the rising and setting of the sun, the stars, flowers. Those godly creations he had taken for granted all these years. He was a changed man, Roseboro said. Yet the "sweetest thing" in the universe to Roseboro now, despite all that newfound bliss, was the sound of Angie's voice. He said he "lived" for Angie's telephone calls, along with her messages, texts, and e-mails. Yes, indeed, by July 14, 2008, Roseboro was "living each day and not simply existing" any longer. He knew what life was about. The secret. He felt alive and joyous. The sky was bluer. The air smelled fresher. Each song on the radio sounded better.

All because of Angie Funk.

A few hours after sending each other several additional e-mails (which have been lost or destroyed), Roseboro wrote Angie a poem and e-mailed it. He called it "My Heaven." The woman had inspired him to begin writing poetry. He was truly caught now in the daze of desire and—one could argue after reading the poem—humiliation. The poem was something you'd likely see from a tenth-grade English class. It is full of lines such as the following: *I feel your need against my thigh.*

July 15, 2008

*Seven days before
Jan Roseboro's murder*

34

Michael Roseboro was still locked in that drunken sexual smog he had obsessively mistaken for love. The urgent nature of being with Angie Funk all the time, replete in the e-mails he sent to her all morning long, energized each sentence. You can feel the anxiety and need Roseboro had to be with this woman sexually anytime he desired. He couldn't get enough of what she was giving him. He talked about never having been a "cuddler" in all the years he was married. But that was all he thought about now: cuddling night after night with his future wife. He admitted that the affair had "ignited a flame" that had "burned inside of him" for Angie over the past five years as he stealthily watched her from afar after meeting at the parade. That "flame" became the metaphor that he so embarrassingly used throughout the remainder of the e-mail to explain how much he loved Angie. That flame, Roseboro said, had now met "oxygen," and had begun to burn "out of control"; it was a flame, in fact, that was "consuming" him. After seeing her for the first time, after the initial phone call on May 29, he realized that as the flame grew, he could one day "internally combust." He said he needed to make Angie his wife.

That "fire," he explained, "will never, never go out. . . ."

Angie was, Roseboro concluded, his "eternal flame."

Again, although she later handed over to police several of these e-mails from Roseboro, Angie's responses for that day do not exist.

July 17, 2008

*Five days before
Jan Roseboro's murder*

35

On Thursday, two days after the so-called flame died down, Angie Funk was back to being "baby" in Michael Roseboro's "good morning" e-mail. He had seen her at Turkey Hill. He said his days were complete before they actually started because he was able to catch a glimpse of the woman he loved. On this day, he told Angie how "hot" she looked while standing inside the convenience store. He said that while he was scoping her out, he had wanted her "soooooooo badly."

Next, Roseboro explained a party idea he had for Angie's fortieth birthday, which was over five months away (Angie was a Christmas Eve baby). It was something special. Something extravagant. An event to end all events. There was plenty enough time, Roseboro explained, considering that he knew when Angie's birthday was; he had that covered, anyway, he added, because he didn't want to give the love of his life a birthday party on or near her actual birthday—that would be too typical. Instead, he wanted it to be a surprise, at a time when she "least expected it." He laid out the scenario he saw himself actively involved in as though he was some sort of party planner. He told Angie how he would call her mother so she could give him all the names and numbers of Angie's friends and family. He had sat and mused, he said, about what type of food to serve, adding that he "loved thinking about the future" because it was going to be their "reality soon."

He said all this, however, without giving Angie—at least in any of the e-mails left behind—a carefully scripted plan for how and when he was going to divorce Jan.

Looking at the immense amount of communication between Angie and Michael, considering what he wrote and how often, it was as if to Michael Roseboro (and this is a very important point), Jan was already gone. The mother of his children, his wife for two decades, did not exist. He had entirely cropped Jan out of his life. In Michael's world, Jan Roseboro was a memory.

Already dead.

Next, Michael told Angie how he would "love to teach" her girls "how to swim," along with Angie, too, of course. He said this while describing the image of bringing them all to the park one day so they could take a walk and play on the jungle gym sets, like a normal family out for a day of fun. Afterward, they could stop by Turkey Hill and get Slushies, "extra large."

In the next series of e-mails, Michael sent Angie to several websites—JCPenney and a Hawaiian shop among them—to look at wedding dresses that he was thinking about buying for her. He made it clear that he was paying for the gown. No matter what it cost.

"This was nothing new—he had sent a few of his *other* mistresses to those same websites," a source in the family later told me.

Only fragments of Angie's e-mail responses to the wedding dress questions remain. In one, Angie said how it flattered her that Michael was browsing the Internet, looking for a wedding gown, but she should be the one doing those sorts of things. Nonetheless, she told Michael he was an "amazing" man for going to such extremes. With him looking into wedding dresses, she sensed now this was not bedroom talk, a pipe dream, or figment of his incredible imagination. The guy was actually hunting down wedding dresses and sending her the links.

He was serious.

Michael wrote and told Angie to forget about JCPenney; the dresses he saw on the site paled in comparison to those on the Hawaiian site.

They discussed how a long dress with a train wasn't going to suit their needs because it would drag along the beach and get ruined by the sand and surf.

Touché, touché.

In another fragmented e-mail later uncovered by a computer forensic search, Angie agreed that the dresses on that Hawaiian website were far superior to JCPenney's.

The fact that Roseboro was going to all this trouble fed into Angie's belief that he was planning on leaving Jan, a sentiment implicit in the way she answered. "It means so much to me . . . ," she said, talking about him "looking." She said there was no way they could go out together—or she alone, for that matter—in or around Denver, shopping for dresses. How would she ever explain searching for a wedding dress when she was married already?

Michael ignored her fear of getting caught shopping and instead came back with an e-mail affirming his dreams of marrying her and how he could not wait to make her his wife.

For the next few e-mails they talked about how Angie Funk would wear her hair—Michael Roseboro suggesting it would be great if the sea breeze could dry it as they waited to say their vows on the beach—and how he would wear his. Like a pair of twentysomethings getting married for the first time, they grappled over the idea that their hair needed to be perfect, but that none of it mattered as long as they were together, holding hands, reciting their vows.

By 11:00 A.M., they were anticipating seeing each other within the hour, a near daily meeting by this point in the relationship that included a quickie, if they could fit it in.

July 21, 2008

*Twenty-seven hours before
Jan Roseboro's murder*

36

The day before Jan Roseboro was beaten, strangled, and drowned, Michael Roseboro was in his element. In the e-mails extracted from his computer, it seemed as though Michael was experiencing a euphoric high, maybe like a runner after a marathon. An endorphin rush. There was a sense of ease in his writing style and narrative voice. Urgency too. He needed to be with Angie Funk all the time. And nothing, it appeared, was going to stop him or get in his way.

Every morning that he saw Angie walk into the convenience store, Michael wrote at 7:53 A.M., was like seeing her for the first time. The absolute compulsive nature of Roseboro not being able to get a handle on his emotions—constantly thinking about this woman, constantly fantasizing about having sex with her and one day marrying her—had overtaken him by this point. He could no longer contain his desires, separate reality from fantasy, or restrain himself with the slightest bit of maturity in what he was writing. This conclusion is based not only on the words Roseboro chose to use over the next twenty-four hours, but in the fact that he repeated phrases over and over, as if the redundancy would somehow make what he had to say more genuine, meaningful, and important. Because the truth of the matter remained: Michael Roseboro was scared to death of losing everything he had worked so hard for. There was no way he was going to allow his wife to take his four kids, that massive addition they had put on Jan's childhood home, and certainly not part of a business his late grandfather and father had built from the ground up. And yet inside of that fantastic bubble of wanting it all, there was Angie Funk, a woman he had no intention of walking away from. Michael Roseboro needed desperately to have everything: status, lifestyle, money, kids—*and* his lover. The only person not in his skewed image of a world he so much wanted was Jan.

"When you see . . . the e-mails," Craig Stedman later said, speaking about those days leading up to Jan's murder, "just the e-mails that we have—and we don't have them all—you'll see from the content that it is clear to this man that losing his girlfriend is *not* an option."

The Roseboro Funeral Home, for which Michael Roseboro was now 95 percent owner, had been estimated at over $3 million. Michael had joined the business as a formal partner in June 1990, when the local press rolled out the red carpet for the family, proclaiming to its Lancaster County audience the handing off of the torch. Michael was the great-grandson of the founder of the business, Harry Mellinger. He was the only son of Ralph Roseboro and, of course, the grandson of Louis "Pa" Roseboro, who owned the business from 1959 to 1972, when Ralph had taken over. So engrained in the culture and societal hierarchy of Denver, the headline on June 4, 1990, announcing that another Roseboro was stepping in to fill the shoes of his forefathers, said it all: ROSEBORO FUNERAL HOME EXTENDS THE FAMILY TRADE. The subhead elaborated: FOURTH GENERATION BEGINS WORK AT PROSPEROUS DENVER BUSINESS. Three years after this headline ran, in March 1993, Roseboro was elected president of the Lancaster County Funeral Directors Association.

The man's star was on the rise.

On top of losing such a profitable family business, a staple in Denver, Michael Roseboro had just moved into that new home with nearly three-quarters of a million dollars' worth of additions and renovations.

There was a lot at stake here.

"He likes being rich," Stedman added. "He likes nice things. This man . . . is kind of a big deal in his town, in his area."

Michael Roseboro was well aware of the risks he was taking bedding down Angie Funk.

"In an attempt," Stedman concluded, "to keep all this and keep both worlds"—Angie Funk and his home—"together, I guess, for him to keep it all up . . . [he] lies. He lies, essentially, to everyone in the summer of 2008. He lives a life of lies. He lies to his friends. He lies to his girlfriend. . . . He lies to his family. And, of course, he *lies* to his wife."

Yet, in looking at Michael Roseboro's e-mails to Angie Funk on this day, he sounded as if he had the world at his fingertips, and everything under complete control. When, in reality, his life was nothing but a house of cards, about to collapse, leaving Roseboro backed into the corner of even more lies.

On that morning, July 21, 2008, the day before Jan Roseboro was murdered, her husband told his lover he wanted to be with her every minute of every day.

Angie's response to this and any other e-mail both of them sent throughout that day were never recovered. The fact that Michael Roseboro and Angie Funk talked on the phone thirty-four different times throughout this day, sent thirty text messages to each other and four e-mails, which are known of, certainly shows that the relationship was heading into a different realm, a different stratosphere, with different needs and far different expectations on Michael's part.

To say the pressure was on Michael Roseboro—and being turned up as each moment passed—would be the understatement of the relationship.

July 22, 2008

The morning before
Jan Roseboro's murder

37

The day Michael Roseboro murdered his wife dawned as a gorgeous midsummer morning. At six fifty-three, it was 70 degrees, humid as a sauna at 97 percent, clear, a 5.9mph WNW wind grazing the ridge of mountains surrounding downtown Denver, no doubt gently blowing the midseason crops from side to side like algae. The roads running in throughout the Denver/Reinholds region of Lancaster County are wispy and winding. There is farmland for as far as the eye can see. In the fall, on these same roads, you can drive for miles through what is a literal maze of cornfields, at times not knowing where you are or what's around the corner, due to the ten-foot-high stalks walled all around you. On certain sections of the road, one encounters a muddle of "road apples"—some squished by hooves and car tires, others fully intact—from the Amish and Mennonite horse and buggies that travel along these parts all day (and sometimes night) long. The bridges spanning the creeks and rivers around town—most of them, anyway—can fit only one car (or a horse and buggy) at a time. Motorists, both locals and those passing through, are tolerant and patient of one another and of the Amish, who never look you in the eye. With their blue shirts, black pants and suspenders, straw hats, straight as ribbon hair cropped bowl-shaped around the ears and forehead, an alarming number with the same piercing glacier-blue eyes, the Amish go about their business as if only they exist, not talking or gesturing to anyone outside the sect. It is a simple way of life: one that the locals don't pay much attention to anymore; one where forgiveness is the key to living in God's wondrous world.

Roseboro began his workday inside the funeral home after seeing Angie Funk, as usual, at Turkey Hill just minutes before. He was at his desk, scribing his first e-mail of the day to Angie by 7:49 A.M. In what appeared to be twenty-four–size font, Roseboro began the electronic missive with "WOW," followed by twenty-nine exclamation points. Something that Angie did had obviously flipped his boat that morning.

The wow was a reaction to the skirt Angie had on that day. Roseboro had seen her wearing it at Turkey Hill. By now, he was so preoccupied with the clothes this woman wore, he was commenting on them daily. It seemed he was enthralled by the element of anticipation, wondering as he drove to Turkey Hill what his love would be sauntering into the store wearing on any day. And yet, in retrospect, it wouldn't matter what Angie had on: Roseboro was going to go wild for it, anyway.

After the "wow," Michael told Angie she was "incredible" and "the most beautiful woman" he had ever laid eyes on. He said his heart "fluttered" and "pounded" whenever he saw her. Not from what she wore, it turned out, but "what's inside of the outfit," he was now convinced, had done it for him.

He then talked about a "deep desire" he had never felt before in all of his forty-one years. Angie had brought it out of him. He never knew it was there, perhaps hibernating, waiting for the right woman to come around and summon.

After that, he launched into the same old, tiring story

of never having experienced a love like this, how lucky he was, and how much he appreciated Angie loving him.

Ending the e-mail, he said, simply (for once), "I adore you," then repeated the phrase by adding "completely" to it.

Only one minute later, their e-mails nearly crossing paths in cyberspace, Angie tapped out her response. She called Michael her "world" (only three exclamation points). He was now, according to Angie, the sole reason why she "got up in the morning." Not to take care of her two kids, or go to work to support her family. But the reason why Angie Funk existed in this world was because of Michael Roseboro. Again, the urgency in this set of e-mails jumps off the page, with all the exclamation points and repeated phrases and words. It was as if a decision had been made—a silent agreement between them.

Angie said she could not wait any longer to be in Roseboro's arms every morning when she awoke and every night she went to bed, adding that, oh yeah, lest they forget about "that afternoon," as they had made plans to meet and have sex in the vacant apartment she managed in Mount Joy.

Ending her response, Angie mentioned how she couldn't wait until all their dreams came "true, baby, all your dreams!" (Angie wrote "all" in upper-case lettering, and finished her proclamation with eight exclamation points!)

In the back of her mind, Angie Funk later said, when she sent that particular e-mail, she "knew" that Jan was going to find out about the affair sooner rather than later—because it was the time of the month in the Roseboro household when Jan did the household bills; and in the past, after studying his cell phone bill, she had caught her husband cheating.

Six minutes later, Michael typed a response. He made Angie a promise from his heart, letting her know that he was never going to let her go. He said, "I need to be your husband," adding how he needed her to be his "wife."

Before they started e-mailing at seven-fifty that morning, Michael had called Angie seven times, beginning at five thirty-six. He dialed from his cell, from home, and from the fax machine at the funeral parlor. In all, between 5:36 and 7:49 A.M. on the day he would murder his wife, Roseboro had spoken to either Angie's cell phone voice mail or Angie herself for a total of thirty minutes.

Angie's response at 8:09 A.M. was a bit pleading. She opened by commenting on the dream portion of Roseboro's previous e-mail, saying that all of her dreams would come true when he took her as his "wife and we go home TOGETHER!!"

Pressure.

She then said she had always wondered what life would be like being Mrs. Angela Lynn Roseboro, saying she wasn't going to have "to wonder much longer."

(Whatever *that* meant.)

At 8:20 A.M., Angie wrote to say she would be home until nine, when she was going to have to leave for an appointment. She asked Roseboro how long he was going to be at the parlor that morning.

He responded by telling Angie a vile joke about a nun and a priest in the desert whose camel falls suddenly ill and dies. After giving her the raunchy, blasphemous punch line, Roseboro said he "liked that one" and "missed you, baby." He couldn't wait to see her in what he said was only five and a half hours.

Angie responded by saying she liked the joke. Then she explained the rest of her morning. After that appointment, she was leaving work at 11:45 A.M. to pick up the girls at her friend's house. Then she was driving straight up to Mount Joy—where the vacant apartment she managed was located—to drop off the girls at, of all places, her mother-in-law's, who lived close by. From there, she was scheduled to head over to the apartment. She needed to be there by 1:00 P.M. to show the place to a potential renter. She knew Roseboro had a doctor's appointment in Lancaster and told him to call her before he left, so she could go out and get them some lunch, ending the e-mail by professing how much she loved "taking care" of her man.

Michael called Angie from the funeral parlor fax machine phone at 8:42 A.M., staying on the line for forty-eight seconds, one would presume, leaving her a voice mail message. She called right back. They talked for exactly one minute. An hour later, Angie sent her lover a text message. At 9:17 A.M., Roseboro sent Angie an e-mail, indicating he would call her when he left for Lancaster, concluding that he was "drooling, thinking about" her "in that outfit" she had promised to wear.

Angie sent a return e-mail moments later. This one was written in all italics to either suggest a softness or importance. She talked about how fantastic it was going to be to see her man later on that day. In fact, any time she spent with him she would always "cherish." After that, she carried on with more of the same yearning they had been spewing to each other over the past few days—that same gushy, adolescent lovespeak they had repeated ad nauseam.

They texted each other five separate times between 10:08 and 10:26 A.M. Angie wrote another e-mail—again in italics—at 11:01 A.M., telling Roseboro how much she missed him and how much she was looking forward to holding him and touching him and being with him that day.

It was as if they had not seen each other for weeks.

They texted each other five additional times between 11:02 and 11:49 A.M., when Angie called Michael on his cell phone. Then, between 12:26 and 1:40 P.M., they spoke a total of eight times via cell phone, for a total of thirty-one minutes and change.

Since Michael Roseboro had woken up at 5:36 A.M. and called Angie that first time, they had communicated via phone, text, or e-mail thirty-eight times.

And it was only 1:40 P.M.

July 22, 2008

*The afternoon before
Jan Roseboro's murder*

38

If you look at a simple computer-generated chart (maybe Excel, something like that) listing the times Michael Roseboro and Angie Funk communicated on July 22, 2008, there is not an hour without several calls, e-mails, or texts—that is, with the exception of 1:40 to 4:59 P.M., when the electronic contact between them came to a complete halt.

Why?

Because they were inside that Mount Joy apartment spending the afternoon and early evening together. When later asked about the nearly three and a half hours they spent alone that day, Angie had a hard time recalling any details—imagine that? The things she did remember, however, tell a story.

"I had gotten lunch before he came over [to the apartment]," Angie said, trying to recall the events of that day for Detective Keith Neff, "and we ate lunch together and then . . . then we just hung out for a few hours."

Hung out.

The apartment, she explained further, was in transition. It wasn't totally empty, nor was it completely furnished. There was a couple "in the process," Angie said, "of moving their things out."

And so, to their advantage, Angie and Michael had a table and a sofa to use on this particular day. They wouldn't have to worry about rug burn or rolling around on a soiled carpet. They could use the table or the couch—maybe both, maybe neither.

Angie was later asked what things she had talked about with Roseboro that day, considering they had spent so much time together; and when they weren't in the same room, they had been e-mailing, texting, or talking.

"Oh," she said rather defensively, "I have no idea. I honestly don't know. It was just talk. I can't honestly remember *what* we talked about."

Angie was then asked if she could recall "just one thing" she talked about that day with her lover.

"I . . . honestly, I really don't know," she offered. "I really don't remember. It was probably all small talk or getting to know each other. I don't know. I don't remember."

"Getting to know each other."

They had been intimate and had seen each other every day during weekdays for the past forty-nine days. By this point, one could safely say that Angie and Michael knew each other well enough. Between the previous morning, July 21, and this time on July 22, they had communicated over one hundred times. Yet, Angie Funk said she could not recall anything they discussed.

She was asked if she recalled having sex with Michael Roseboro on that day, in those hours before Roseboro drove home and murdered his wife.

That, Angie Funk remembered: "Yes," she said brazenly, without hesitation.

More than any of this, however, Angie was later asked about scratches on Michael Roseboro's face and if she had seen any that afternoon. One could take a leap in assuming that being with him for that time, being close enough to kiss him and have sex, she would have seen scratches on his face. If they were there.

"He did not have any scratches on his face," Angie told police.

July 22, 2008

*The evening of
Jan Roseboro's murder*

Surrounding the Roseboros' Denver/Reinholds, Pennsylvania, home, in and around Lancaster County, the Amish still hold true to the values of their ancestors. *(Author's collection)*

Some call Lancaster County "God's Chosen Land," where the rolling hills collide with fairy-tale sunsets. *(Author's collection)*

The Roseboro family called Denver home. *(Author's collection)*

Pretty and intelligent, Jan Roseboro was the ideal mother, neighbor, friend, and wife. *(Courtesy of Shawn Roseboro)*

Jan liked to dress down. Here she is heading into Fulton Bank on July 22, 2008, unaware that a murderer was planning her death for that same night. *(Courtesy of the East Cocalico Township Police Department)*

East Cocalico Township PD Detective Keith Neff, who had never investigated a murder, was determined to find Jan Roseboro's killer. *(Author's collection)*

Detective Sergeant Larry Martin knew Jan Roseboro's husband, funeral director Michael Roseboro. *(Author's collection)*

Jan's husband, Michael, took over the family funeral business from his father. *(Courtesy of Shawn Roseboro)*

The Roseboro Funeral Home has been a staple in Denver, Pennsylvania, for over a century. *(Author's collection)*

Angela Funk became the center of Michael Roseboro's affection and obsession in the weeks before Jan's murder.

Angela Funk lived directly across the street from the Roseboro Funeral Home. She and Michael exchanged hundreds of emails, over one thousand phone calls and hundreds of text messages in the seven weeks of their adulterous affair.
(Author's collection)

Angela Funk came from a conservative Mennonite background.
(Author's collection)

Fulton Bank Reinholds   07/22/2008 12:14:15.44

Jan Roseboro walked into Fulton Bank, in Denver, wearing the same clothes she was later found murdered in. Note that Jan is not wearing any jewelry—a fact that would help convict her killer. (*Courtesy of the East Cocalico Township Police Department*)

Fulton Bank Reinholds   07/22/2008 12:11:39.96

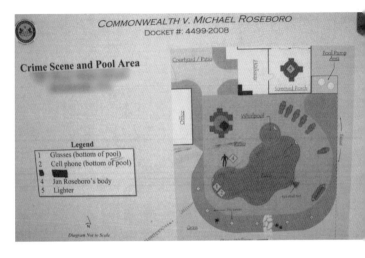

Crime Scene and Pool Area

Courtyard / Patio

Screened Porch

Pool Pump Area

Office

Whirlpool

Patio

Legend

1 Glasses (bottom of pool)
2 Cell phone (bottom of pool)
4 Jan Roseboro's body
5 Lighter

N

Diagram Not to Scale

This diagram shows the Roseboros' in-ground pool. It seems unlikely that an intruder would have murdered Jan and then lit five tiki torches (below) before fleeing the scene. (*Courtesy of the East Cocalico Township Police Department*)

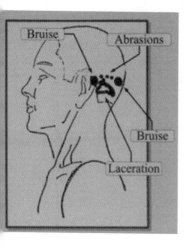

This diagram shows the "circular puncture-type wound with an L-shaped marking" that Jan Roseboro sustained to the back of her left ear. The deep gash went all the way to her skull. (*Courtesy of the East Cocalico Township Police Department*)

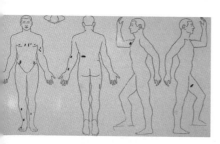

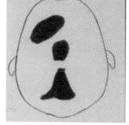

This series of diagrams show the number of injuries Jan Roseboro sustained on her body and head during the attack that ultimately killed her. (*Courtesy of the East Cocalico Township Police Department*)

This aerial photograph shows how many lights an intruder would have needed to turn on after murdering Jan but before fleeing the scene. (*Courtesy of the East Cocalico Township Police Department*)

In this aerial photo, it's clear how unobstructed a view each neighbor had into the Roseboros' backyard. (*Courtesy of the East Cocalico Township Police Department*)

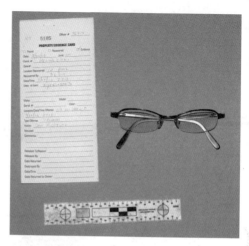

Jan's glasses (above) were found in the bottom of the swimming pool alongside her cell phone and two stones. (*Courtesy of the East Cocalico Township Police Department*)

A close-up of Jan's cell phone found on the bottom of the pool. (*Courtesy of the East Cocalico Township Police Department*)

Forensics checked Michael Roseboro's swimming trunks for blood, but found no trace. Still, Jan Roseboro's husband claimed to have worn these shorts—soaking wet—to bed on the night Jan was murdered. (*Courtesy of the East Cocalico Township Police Department*)

Jan was found unconscious and not breathing in the deep end of the in-ground pool, wearing the same sweatshirt she was photographed in at Fulton Bank earlier that day. (*Courtesy of the East Cocalico Township Police Department*)

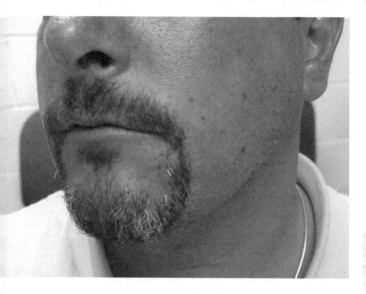

Michael Roseboro had three scratches on his face, one witness testified, which were "oozing" on the night of Jan's murder. (*Courtesy of the East Cocalico Township Police Department*)

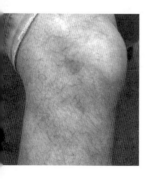

Michael Roseboro also had fresh bruising on both his knees. (*Courtesy of the East Cocalico Township Police Department*)

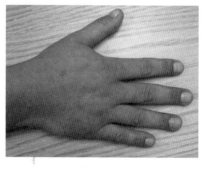

This photo of Michael Roseboro's right hand shows a bruise and slight cut just below the thumb line and to the left of the top knuckle. (*Courtesy of the East Cocalico Township Police Department*)

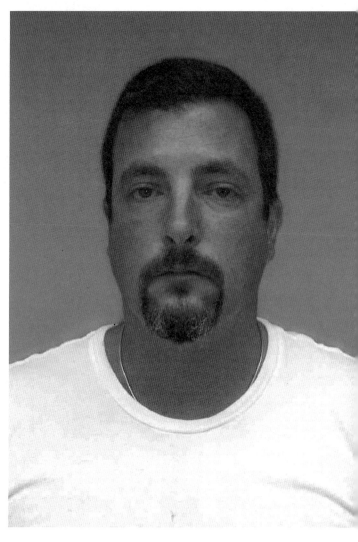

Ten days after his wife was brutally strangled, beaten and drowned to death in the family's in-ground swimming pool, Michael Roseboro was booked and processed on first-degree murder charges. (*Courtesy of the East Cocalico Township Police Department*)

Downtown Lancaster has not lost its flair for deep Puritan roots. *(Author's collection)*

Michael Roseboro's trial was the subject of widespread rumor and gossip in Lancaster County during the summer of 2009. *(Author's collection)*

The entrance boasts of a castle-like structure, but Lancaster County Prison, where Michael Roseboro was held, provides anything but fairy tale endings. *(Author's collection)*

After living the plush life of status, wealth, taking whatever he wanted, building a dream home he saw himself in during his retirement years, former undertaker Michael Roseboro now calls a lonely prison cell home. *(Author's collection)*

39

They had arrived in separate vehicles. After the fun-loving afternoon came to an end, they left in separate vehicles. The drive back to town for the lovebirds took about forty-five minutes. Angie Funk probably stopped to pick up her children at her mother-in-law's—this, after having adulterous sex all afternoon with her lover—although she never mentioned this in her play-by-play of the day later on.

No sooner had they left Mount Joy did Angie call Michael Roseboro. That first call at 4:59 P.M., as they trekked down Interstate 283 toward Lancaster, lasted two minutes; but the next, at 5:05 P.M., went on for thirty-six minutes.

Later prompted by law enforcement to recall *anything* said during those thirty-six minutes, Angie could not remember a single word, saying in court a little over one year after the events, "I have no idea. I mean, it was conversation, you know. I don't . . . I don't know the specifics. . . ."

"Getting to know each other."

For the next forty minutes after that call, there was no communication between them. Then Michael called

Angie's cell phone from his home phone at 5:45 P.M., a call that lasted twenty-six seconds.

Eleven minutes later, Angie sent Michael a text.

He responded one minute later.

Two minutes after that, Angie sent a text back.

Three minutes later, Michael responded.

Then, at 6:01 P.M., Angie answered him.

He did not reply.

Angie sent another at 6:46 P.M.

Again, Michael failed to respond.

What was wrong?

Roseboro called Angie's cell number from his house at 7:19 P.M.; they talked for seven minutes. At 8:42 P.M., Roseboro called her back—a call that lasted seventeen minutes. Of that seventeen-minute call, when asked, Angie could recall only that her lover said, "I'm tired. . . . I'm going to bed," adding, "That's really all I remember. I'm sure we talked about the day."

And what a day it had been.

"Well," Angie said, thinking back, "it was the most time we ever spent together. So, yeah, I guess you could say [it was a big day]."

When pestered to recall what she talked about during that 8:42 P.M. call, Angie admitted that they shared "how much we loved each other and that we planned to leave our spouses."

This was an important revelation. On the night of Jan Roseboro's murder, Jan's husband and his lover discussed divorcing their spouses. It appeared that this was something Angie was beginning to wonder about as their relationship carried on in such a holding pattern.

Yet, there was more, according to what Angie had said in September 2008, a little over two months after the day in question.

"Like," she said, talking about the content of the 8:42 P.M. call, "getting married and all that stuff. . . . I mean,

I just said that, you know . . . [Jan] could probably take him for a lot if she found out about us."

Pressure.

They also discussed the fact that Michael Roseboro, if Jan ever found out about Angie Funk, could lose the funeral home in a nasty divorce.

"That he didn't *want* to lose it," Angie said. Once again, she and Roseboro talked about him putting the funeral home in his father's name until the divorce was finalized. "Then put it back in [Mike's] name or whatever." The reason for that, Angie said they discussed, was so "she [Jan] couldn't touch it."

Michael had spent more time with his lover that afternoon than he ever had. They ate lunch together. Had sex all afternoon. Talked marriage and wedding dresses and beaches and all things Mike and Angie. But now, as the strain of Jan at home wore on him, Roseboro was feeling it somewhere near 9:00 P.M. Jan was outside at the pool. Roseboro was, undoubtedly, wondering what he was going to do about a wife he was certain would take him to the cleaners in a divorce.

Tell her and lose everything?

Or kill Jan and try to make it look like an accident?

Regarding this so-called wedding, Angie Funk told Michael Roseboro one day when they were discussing getting married, she wanted him to "grow his hair longer for the wedding."

"It'll become curly," Roseboro said.

"Do it now," she demanded, "so I can see what it will look like for the wedding."

Like listening to country music now—when before meeting Angie, he had despised it. Roseboro agreed to grow his locks out.

The wedding was scheduled "soon," Angie later said during a police interview. They had never set a particular date other than, she agreed, within a year's time. Yet, Angie would later refute her own words, saying, "I'm not denying that I said that, but I don't—there's no way we could have been married within a year." She went on to say she didn't think she could have divorced Randy and resolved all of her personal affairs in twelve months. "I'm just saying it would not be possible for me to be married within a year. . . ."

As they talked some more about being married and their life together, the subject of affairs came up. Angie was obviously worried about Michael continuing to do in the future what he was doing to Jan.

Roseboro said he'd never had an affair before Angie. But the conversation had somehow sparked a memory in Roseboro, which he shared. And this was where Roseboro utilized his best manipulation skills: dodge the hardball questions by dredging up some sympathy. Get Angie to focus on something else.

"What is it?" she asked. Roseboro looked dismayed.

Roseboro explained that someone close to him "has had affairs." He paused. "I don't want to be like [that person]."

In recalling this conversation to police, Angie said, "I was fooled by Michael. If I confronted him about things, he would just explain them away.

"He was a good liar."

Those last two phone calls Angie Funk made to Michael Roseboro on the night of July 22, 2008, must have been important. For two people who had communicated throughout a day with what Craig Stedman later called "an extremely unusual amount of contact," back and forth, the final calls of that long day of communication would have been significant. Between 9:37 and 10:14 P.M., cutting it close to the time that Jan Roseboro was murdered, Angie called her man three

times and sent one text message. At 9:37 P.M., Angie
called Roseboro's cell phone and left him a five-minute
voice mail, something she later noted that, besides the
time on that night, was not unusual for her to do. Then
at 9:43 P.M., a minute after hanging up from the previous call, she left a three-minute voice mail; then, at
10:08 P.M., another five-minute voice mail. Finally, on
her last communication of that busy day, Angie Funk
sent Michael Roseboro a text message at 10:14 P.M.

He never responded to any of the calls or the text.

When asked later what she had said, and why she kept
calling back, Angie could not recall.

"I just don't know."

Had Angie Funk told her lover that she was carrying
his child—and had that information sent Michael Roseboro over the edge, to the point that he did not want to
talk to her? According to Roseboro, he was wide awake
during those times, save for maybe that last text at 10:14
P.M. In fact, Roseboro was inside the house with the
young kids, he claimed, while Jan was still outside.
Couldn't he have slipped away from the children (like
he had so many times before) and, at the least, answered the text, or walked to another part of that large
house and called Angie back?

If you asked Angie, she'd say, no way. She had not told
him she was pregnant during any of those voice mails.
Craig Stedman posed this question to Angie: "When did
you find out that you were pregnant?"

"July," Angie answered without hesitation. But then
she seemed to think about it and said: "Or no! August
first."

"Was it July or August?" Stedman wondered.

"It was August first."

July 22, 2008

*The night Jan Roseboro
was murdered*

40

What happened in the hours after that last phone call between Angie Funk and Michael Roseboro? What were Jan Roseboro's final moments like?

Only Michael Roseboro knows for sure—and he refuses to admit that he had anything to do with the murder of his wife.

From the evidence left behind, however, including all the testimony and the interviews conducted by the ECTPD, the pathologist's report and the autopsy, those initial reports from the hospital where Jan was taken, the findings and experience of several of the detectives and the Lancaster County DA's thoughts, all indicators point to the murder having taken place near the Roseboros' inground pool. All the lights were out—several neighbors reported this. Michael might have told Jan he wanted to look at the stars with her ("Like the creepy schmoozer he was," someone in law enforcement told me), which would allow him the excuse to go around and turn off all the lights. Roseboro even made mention of this in his first statement to police and to some of his family members who came to the house that night and the next day.

The evidence the pathologist uncovered pointed to

Jan's murderer having begun by putting her in a carotid neck choke hold. In cutting off blood and oxygen to the brain via Jan's carotid arteries, those two main veins on each side of the neck that throb under stressful conditions or from a tight necktie, Jan would have passed out quickly. This would have allowed Jan's killer to fake the drowning then, which everyone agreed was Roseboro's plan from the start.

Likely, as Jan struggled with her killer inside the pool, she scratched him on the face by reaching behind herself as he continued to strangle her. (This theory lines up with the scream Cassandra Pope heard that night, which, she said, came from that area of the yard at about this time, ten-thirty.)

The scream indicated Jan was confronted and murdered outside the home, as opposed to down in the basement, or in a section of the house near the pool deck. No one could have heard her scream if Michael Roseboro accosted his wife in the basement. On top of that, the deep gash on Jan's head behind her ear was likely caused by her head hitting the corner of one of the large planters next to the pool as she struggled and/or fell backward, or was simply bashed over the head with some sort of weapon never recovered.

With Jan bleeding and perhaps unconscious, Michael needed to get her into the pool so he could call 911 and put that accident theory into motion. As Jan was tossed into the water, there's an indication she "came to" while in the water. She was definitely alive and breathing while in the water; the soapy liquid released from her lungs during the autopsy proved that.

The question became, then: did Jan Roseboro wake up entirely, or was she partially awake and unable to fight off her attacker?

The minor bruising found all over Jan's body indicated a struggle. Or at least a partial fight on Jan's part.

No doubt about it: Jan Roseboro wanted to live.

She fought for her life until the end.

With blood all over the deck of the pool, one would have to ask why no blood was found when the CSI Unit sprayed luminol, or when the first responders took a walk around and looked for evidence of an accident or a struggle.

How had Michael Roseboro gotten rid of all the blood?

Being a funeral director, a person who dealt with blood on a daily basis while embalming bodies, Roseboro was well schooled in how to clean up blood.

Why weren't any traces of chemicals found, the same chemicals he had access to at the funeral home? All that rain, and a crime scene that the ECTPD didn't get to until nearly a day after Jan Roseboro was murdered.

41

Angie Funk was worried when she didn't hear from Michael Roseboro on the morning of July 23, 2008. Roseboro had always called, every morning during the week, near five forty-five, as soon as Randall Funk left for work.

Not hearing from him, Angie dialed Michael's cell phone.

It went straight to voice mail. Michael had his phone turned off.

As the morning wore on, and a hazy sun burned off the cloud cover, Angie called her lover twice, she admitted, between nine-thirty and ten forty-five.

She was unable to reach him.

"I hadn't heard anything [from him]," Angie later testified, "and I was starting to get a little worried, 'cause it wasn't like him not to call me."

Interestingly enough, Angie got into her car and drove by the Roseboro home out on West Main Street. Moving slowly by the house, looking at all the cars and people roaming around, Angie became even more concerned, she later said.

"I was trying to get in touch with Michael," Angie told police, "because I knew something was wrong."

She drove back home and called the funeral home. When he wasn't at the funeral home, Roseboro would roll the calls over to his home phone.

"Hello?" Michael said, picking up the phone call at his home.

"What's going on?" Angie asked breathlessly.

"I cannot talk. Jan died. It was a drowning," he said. Angie was "in shock." She had never heard Roseboro sound so static, flatlined. The guy was generally upbeat and drooling when they spoke, making jokes about what she would wear, how she smelled, what time they were to meet up.

But not today. Michael Roseboro had his hands full.

During an interview with Detective Keith Neff, Angie said her first thought, after hearing that Jan had (conveniently) died, was, *"Oh, crap!"* Then: "I did not want to be a full-time mother of six children. I did not want any more children."

At the time that she was thinking about having just been saddled with Jan's kids, Angie Funk was carrying Roseboro's fifth child.

"What happened?" Angie asked Michael, wondering how Jan had died.

Roseboro gave Angie that familiar mantra he had been repeating to everyone in law enforcement, along with anyone else who asked: "I woke up," he told Angie on that morning, "saw a light on, went outside, and saw Jan in the pool."

"He did not go into detail," Angie explained during that interview with Neff. "He was never 'broken up' about what happened, but he sounded upset when I first talked to him."

Speaking to Michael during those days right after the murder, Angie said that she just assumed he had told police about their affair (and that's why, she seemed to suggest, she never came forward). And yet as the ECTPD and Detective Jan Walters, of the LCDA's Office, split up and began interviewing friends and family connected to Jan and Michael Roseboro, not one person reported the affair. Even after Angie Funk's name was brought into the discourse of the case, Roseboro still held firm and told people that any suggestion of an affair was a lie. A terrible misunderstanding. Roseboro had told family and friends that Angie was nothing more than a woman helping him plan the renewal of his marital vows to the woman he truly loved, Jan.

Later on that day after Jan's murder, Michael called Angie.

"Hey . . ."

"Michael."

"I just wanted to hear your voice," he said.

"Okay."

"I need more time," he stated.

Angie presumed he was saying this because Jan had died such a tragic death—and he needed to be with his family. She completely understood. No pressure.

"Yes," Angie responded.

"I just need to be in your arms," Roseboro said. "I love you."

"I love you, too, Michael."

42

Shawn Roseboro had just lost his house and his job. Times were tough on the kid. Much of it, Shawn later said, he had brought on himself with his drinking. But still, there seemed to be a "bad luck" vibe all around him during the summer of 2008. He could feel it, and it was making his own selfish behavior worse.

On the day after Jan Roseboro was murdered, Shawn was alone. His sister and her family had gone to the beach. He was staying at her house. The phone rang. It was his dad.

"Mike found Jan in the pool, and she's dead."

Was there really any other way to put it?

Shawn recalled that he "hit the floor before the phone did—I lost it at that point."

After picking himself up off the ground, Shawn let his anger go and punched a hole through the door.

"I didn't know what to do with my emotions at that point."

With no one to lean on, Shawn said, he logged onto Lancaster Online, a local blog, that afternoon, just to see what was being said about Jan's death. While reading and thinking and reminiscing about Jan, Shawn started drinking.

Heavily.

It was one of the only ways to deaden all the pain. Shawn lost Pa just a month prior, he said, which was devastating enough, even though the guy had lived a long life. Now the only person in the family who "totally got" who he was and understood his feelings was gone.

What am I going to do?

"When Pa died, it was at the peak of everything going on in my life, and I was, like, completely *numb*. Jan dying on top of that—well, everything just clicked in at once."

In his heart, Shawn said, he questioned it a little: Jan's death, that is—the way she had died. Over and over, he asked himself: *How could Jan drown?*

It seemed so illogical. So impossible. So . . . unreal.

"But I never thought anything else."

No one did—at least in those early days when Michael Roseboro was being questioned by Keith Neff, Larry Martin, and now Jan Walters—and the secret of Angie Funk was still being kept under wraps.

Jan and Shawn had lost touch for about a month before her death, making the impact of it even that much more overwhelming for him. Two days before Jan died, Shawn had sent Sam, Jan's oldest son, a MySpace message, telling him to give his new phone number to Jan and to have her call him.

"So that was—that was," Shawn recalled, choking up as the memory came back, "very hard on me. Jan was gone. I didn't know what to do."

When Charlotte Moyer, Jan's married-into-the-family cousin, showed up at the house that morning after Jan's death, she walked in and spied Sam crying. He looked terribly upset. And why wouldn't he be? His mother . . .

Vanished like dust.

They sat on the ottoman at first and talked. Charlotte

wanted to be there for the child as much as she could. She had known Jan since Jan came into the world. Charlotte was married into the family by the time Jan was born in 1963. Charlotte had watched Jan grow from an infant into a wonderful adult with a family of her own.

After speaking with Sam, Charlotte walked into the sunroom. She sat, shaking her head, wondering.

Michael came into the room after seeing Charlotte sitting there.

He sat down.

"We were just sitting out there by the pool," Michael said after a moment of silence between them. "I wasn't feeling well. I went into the house. I had asked Jan if I should turn off the tiki lights, you know, put them out. Jan said no. She said she was going to stay out there a little while longer."

Several parts of this conversation, as Charlotte remembered it, were far different from what Roseboro had told police. For one, he said Jan was sick. Two, he never told the police that Jan said she wanted the tiki lights left lit.

Charlotte asked Michael what happened next.

"I went to bed, and a bit later, I got up and the tiki lights were still on and the kitchen light was on."

He'd never mentioned this to police.

Charlotte thought he was going to end the conversation there, but Michael said one other thing. "She had probably fallen into the pool and drowned," he told Charlotte. Then, "She had a contusion on the left back of her head."

That word, Charlotte said later, "stuck in my mind. . . ."

"*Contusion.*"

What's more, after saying this, Roseboro just up and walked out of the room, abruptly ending the conversation.

Thinking about it later, Charlotte considered his

demeanor to be "very matter-of-fact, not any kind of emotion. . . ."

Later that morning, with everyone roaming about the grounds of the house and inside, Charlotte and Michael passed each other. They were walking down the hallway. Michael Roseboro stopped for a brief moment as Charlotte got close to him.

"Nice haircut," he said, complimenting her.

43

By noon on July 23, 2008, word had worked its way through town that Jan Roseboro was dead. An improbable accident in the pool was the story being shouted back and forth across fuel pumps and from behind coffee counters. But grinding in the grist of the town gossip and rumor mills was a far different scenario.

Cassandra Pope called her mother, Marcia, who, with her husband, had been friends and neighbors of Jan and Michael Roseboro's for years when they all lived next to one another on the opposite end of town.

"Jan's dead," Cassie said. "Suzie said she hit her head maybe, but they weren't really sure."

Suzie's husband had died of a heart attack at a young age. Cassie said that Suzie mentioned she thought maybe the same thing might have happened to Jan.

Heart attack . . . a slip, fall, and then she drowned?

They just didn't know.

Marcia got on the phone and called a neighbor, who had also known Jan rather well.

"Oh, my God . . . ," the neighbor said.

They talked for a few moments.

Two hours later, Marcia's neighbor called back. "It just hit online that Jan was murdered!"

"Murdered? You're kidding," Marcia said. "Oh, my goodness—Mike did it!"

Where had that come from?

It was the first thought she had, Marcia later said, after hearing Jan might have been murdered. The Michael Roseboro whom Marcia had known all those years—the guy she had seen around the neighborhood, helping newly appointed widows and widowers deal with the loss of their spouses, that same guy who liked to be the bartender at all the neighborhood parties— had murdered his sweet wife, a good friend of hers. She was certain of it, for some strange reason. This was how the town reacted during those early moments, Marcia and her husband later said. The women in town were all under the impression that Michael had done it; while the men gave Michael the benefit of the doubt. For those who truly knew Michael and Jan, his reputation for sleeping with anything he could get his hands on was old news. So killing Jan *now* didn't make sense in terms of an affair as motive. The guy, after all, had cheated on the woman for years.

"When you talk about small town," Marcia, a romance novelist by trade, said, "you have to talk about Denver being part of Reinholds, because they are connected. Even though the Roseboros' new home was in Reinholds, everyone called it Denver. Jan and Mike were . . . Well, let's say I have never seen them as 'the perfect couple.'"

"But they appeared to be the 'perfect couple,'" Cassandra Pope remarked. From her point of view, as a child watching Jan and Michael from afar, the Roseboros seemed to have it all together. Living next door, renting from Jan, Cassie had watched them build the new house. She recalled Michael and Jan from family and neighborhood gatherings, cookouts and block parties. They appeared to be in love. Later, though, Cassie saw something different. They had grown apart. A couple who had their individual roles inside the family rubric, played the part, but lived separate lives.

"Everyone knew that Mike was running around on Jan," Marcia added. "Jan was the mother figure, the Earth Mother. She wasn't out gardening with a big hat and gloves, but she did plant a garden the year she died and she was very excited about it. Jan enjoyed being a mother. She lived for those kids. That's the horrible part. She loved kids. When Cassandra had her baby, Jan was right there. She went out and got Toys 'Я' Us gift cards for the baby, and she was positive it was a girl. After Cassandra had her, whenever Jan saw Cassandra outside with the baby, she'd run over and hold her and play with her."

Michael Roseboro was never around. Always at work. Or "out."

"It seemed to me," Cassie's husband, Richard Pope, said, "during those months leading up to her death, when Jan was home, Mike was gone. And when Mike was home, Jan wasn't around. I don't know if it was planned to be that way or it just worked out. But that's what I saw while living next door."

Being home with her new baby during those days after Jan was murdered, Cassie saw much more, she later said. And now that Jan was dead, Cassie was scared to death of this enigma of a man next door whom she knew only from childhood and from what she remembered. Roseboro now seemed to be this dark figure, the undertaker who possibly murdered his wife. And as the hours passed and rumors buzzed, Cassie and Richard watched the house, where Michael Roseboro, they said, was acting strange.

Looking out their window one morning, Cassie and Richard looked on as Michael, who was bent over inside Jan's garden, stood there as though he was pulling weeds. He had a bunch of grass in his hands. This, while a man Cassie presumed to be one of his lawyers snapped digital photographs of him. After the photo op concluded, Roseboro righted himself, brushed off his hands, and then walked into the house, Cassie and Richard said.

What in the heck are they doing? Cassie asked herself.

Richard said something similar.

"They have a gardener," Cassie recalled. "I don't know why he would be out there pulling weeds!"

The Roseboros' next-door neighbors were a little uneasy, anyway, considering that they believed a murder had taken place not one hundred yards from Cassie and her newborn. There were cops in unmarked cars sitting in their driveway, watching the Roseboro house at times. There also was a cop roaming around the neighborhood. Detectives had been by to take a statement, and Cassie and Richard had told them things. Cassie had described that scream she heard the night Jan died.

What would Roseboro do, Cassie wondered, *if he knew I was talking to the police?*

44

Jan's best friend, Rebecca Donahue, was sitting outside on the little patio by the pool with Michael Roseboro and his father, Ralph. It was one of those shake-the-head-and-wonder-what-the-hell-happened moments. You turn on CNN and see that some boyfriend beat the snot out of a little baby and the child died. You shake your head. You hear that some dude dressed like a science teacher walked into a building and mowed down ten people with an automatic rifle because he lost his job. You shake your head. You find out your best friend, a woman you knew to be a fairly decent swimmer, drowned in her own pool. You cry first; then, like Rebecca Donahue, you shake your head and wonder, *How in the heck did* this *happen?*

Rebecca was in a state of shock, to say the least. Her friend was here yesterday. Today she was dead. It made little sense. Jan was the sweetest person in the world. One of those women who comes along and changes your life for the better. Someone who cared about her community, having volunteered and supported various causes that truly helped people.

Michael was staring at the ground. Ralph and Rebecca sat, speechless. Then, finally, Michael spoke up. "We were going to renew our vows," he said, "on the beach while on vacation."

Rebecca wanted to cry.

"Jan had always wanted to get married on the beach," Michael added.

This was the first Rebecca had heard of Jan and Michael renewing their vows. Jan had not mentioned it to her.

One of the reasons why this subject had come up was that Michael Roseboro was scrambling around, trying to devise a good excuse as to why Angie Funk was contacting him. Angie had called the Roseboro house that morning—and several people in the house had seen her number and name appear on the caller ID. The unspoken word inside the Roseboro camp that morning: *who is this woman?* Roseboro was telling everyone Angie had contacted him because her sister was a wedding planner he had been using to help arrange the Outer Banks trip. She had called to inquire about it.

Why *Angie* and not her sister? some wondered.

If Michael Roseboro was so consumed with pain over not being able to renew his vows, he seemed to be over it. Twenty-year navy man Robert Bachman, who went on to get his Ph.D. in behavioral psychology from Penn State after serving in the military, was Jan's cousin. "One of fifteen," Robert later said, "on my mother's side. I'm the oldest one, Jan [was] the youngest. . . ."

After Jan's dad passed away in 2003, Robert explained, he became more of a father figure to Jan. "She seemed like a daughter to me."

Robert and Jan "talked frequently." So much, in fact, that rarely two days went by when they didn't see each other or speak over the telephone. "Anytime something came up," Robert said, "I'd just call Jan and say, 'Now what do I do?'"

Robert had a name for Jan: "Miss Yellow Pages." She knew everyone.

Through that relationship with Jan, Robert got to know Michael Roseboro "really well," he later explained in court. It was about a month prior to Jan's murder that he and Michael got to talking about the trip to renew the couple's wedding vows. Michael had told Robert about it, saying, "Jan and I are going to be renewing our vows and we'd like you [and your wife] to come."

"Oh," Robert said, "that's nice."

Robert and his wife got the call about Jan's death and rushed over to the house. They got there about nine o'clock the morning after. It was somewhere just after noon, perhaps not long after Michael Roseboro had spoken with Rebecca Donahue and his dad, that Robert Bachman had a chance to sit down with his cousin's husband and chat. They were, once again, in what would become Michael's chosen place to hold family court, poolside, sitting at a patio sofa not ten yards from where Jan's body had been pulled from the water fewer than fourteen hours before.

Michael had that look on his face. The one that nearly everyone around him—save for his immediate family, mother, father, sister—later described as empty and flat. Not sad. Not immensely burdened by the melancholy one would guess the death of a wife would bring. But an even keel, like the undertaker he was.

"We were sitting out here," Michael told Robert, referring to the night before. "Just talking about various things."

Robert didn't know what to say.

"Jan said she was so glad that we had built this pool," Michael continued. "The kids had such a good time in it yesterday afternoon." Of course, Robert didn't know this yet, but Michael had made what would turn out to be one of several bizarre comments, especially when put into the context of coming from a man who had spent the entire afternoon and part of the early evening with his lover—not his kids—having sex and talking of their future wedding plans. Michael said, "Jan was not so in favor of building the pool. But she said, 'Pop would have liked it.'" Meaning her dead father.

Robert was taken aback by these words. He had never heard anyone express an opinion that Jan was opposed to the pool. To the contrary, Jan was all for the pool. What was Michael trying to do here? What was he saying?

"And the conversation," Robert later explained, talking about that day he sat with his dead cousin's husband, "was a conversation as though nothing had happened. There was no indication that Jan was dead. There was no expression on his face like grief or anything else. It was just *casual* conversation."

And then, when Robert got to a point where he believed their little chitchat could not get any more uncomfortable, Jan's husband—simply sitting there, talking to Robert as though Jan were still alive—came out with what Robert later referred to as "an off-color joke."

This was very disturbing to Robert. Michael Roseboro had lost his wife hours earlier and here he was, sitting yards from where she had died, telling a racist joke.

How peculiar.

45

The next day, a Thursday morning, July 24, Angie Funk "found out from the media," she later claimed in a police interview, that Jan Roseboro's death was being classified a homicide. The local newspapers were calling it the first murder in West Cocalico Township history. One article said: *A 45-year-old Reinholds woman was severely beaten before she drowned in her own swimming pool. . . .* Another, this in the form of a headline, tried to push the case into the overhyped and salacious television talk show—tank that crime TV media sharks routinely swim in: MURDER HOUSE YIELDS EVIDENCE: BLOODY TISSUES, DISINFECTANT SEIZED. Online, message boards fed the media-frenzy flame as comments speculated that Jan and Michael's son Sam was behind the murder, and Michael Roseboro had helped the boy cover it up.

Nonsense. All of it.

That disinfectant, in fact, was from the cleaning bucket sitting near the screen door. Keith Neff later said that Suzie Van Zant had told the ECTPD that she had been cleaning the screens with the bucket. That bloody tissue was a mere snot rag with a spot of blood on it that could have come from a child's cut, a bloody nose, or perhaps a couple of oozing scratches on someone's face.

Still, DA Craig Stedman came out swinging in the morning's newspapers, his opinions particularly lucid, explaining to residents of Lancaster County that there was "no possibility" of Jan's death being "accidental." Stedman said Jan suffered a "significant beating," telling reporters that "someone murdered her, and that person is at large in the community."

Sobering words of alarm from a man who was, behind the scenes, going after Michael Roseboro with all of the law enforcement and investigatory muscle he had at his disposal, Stedman had his man in his sights. He was willing, though, to give Roseboro the benefit of the doubt. At least publicly, for the time being.

A retrospective look at the crime scene showed that the Roseboros' house and the pool patio, where Jan was murdered, were so spotless that that was one of the reasons why law enforcement was focused on Michael Roseboro.

"There should have been a lot of blood with Jan's head injury," Detective Keith Neff told me later, "and we found none—and with the amount of trauma Jan's body sustained, it is likely there was a struggle. So this goes along with there being *no* signs of a struggle."

If you're a cop, you have to take a serious look at this information and ask yourself why.

Nonetheless, whether she got the homicide information *after* or before sending an e-mail to Michael that morning, the first e-mail of the day that Angie wrote to her lover would later tell law enforcement a lot about the affair.

Angie began the e-mail—this one written in italics— by telling her lover how sorry she was for what had happened. She said her "thoughts and prayers" were with Roseboro and his kids. (Kind of ironic that murder would bring such sentiments out of the same woman who, fewer than forty-eight hours before, was having sex with this dead woman's husband, the father of those same kids she was now praying for and thinking about.)

Next, Angie told Michael she would do everything in her power to help. Whatever it was. Just ask. She understood her man needed "time," and she "totally" got the fact that they were going to be apart for some time. It was going to "hurt like hell," she explained, meaning that when the death of his wife hit him, Michael was going to whither and cave in emotionally (or at least one would think that onslaught of grief was coming), regardless of what had been going on. Angie said she was prepared to give Michael "all the time" he needed to work through this obvious painful period of his life. She told Michael he was still the love of her life, and she was willing to "go to the ends of the earth" for him—and that was her "promise." She said she would also be there for his kids, whom she said she loved already without even knowing them.

Michael's response to this e-mail—if he sent one—does not exist.

"I went in to talk with police," Michael told Angie during a phone call near this time. Angie, who admitted to "a lot of phone calls" with Roseboro after Jan's murder, could not recall when, exactly, this particular call took place. "Gary Frees came with me," he said. Then: "We'll still be together, baby—I still believe in our dreams."

"I love you," Angie said.

There was a phone call later that day Michael made from his sister's house to Angie. He mentioned that the police were accusing him of the murder, adding in defiance, "I did not do this!"

"If anyone needed to believe you," Angie responded, "it would have to be me."

Apparently, in making such a bold statement, Angie was stating that she was standing behind her man and did not believe he was capable of murdering his wife, nor did she think he did it.

Sentiments that, in due time, were about to change for Angie.

Then there was the little surprise Angie Funk had for her lover.

The baby.

BOOK THREE

MORBID CURIOSITY

46

Putting it simply, death was a part of his life, Michael Roseboro, then a twenty-six-year-old, full of piss and vinegar, said back in 1993. And death, on any level, terrified him. The eager-to-please, newly married mortician was interviewed by Doug Wenrich for a business article in the *Lancaster New Era* not long after he took over the family business. The future for Michael then was paved in gold. Here he was in his midtwenties and he had total control over the family business, which was already turning hundreds of thousands of dollars of annual profits.

Michael began his mortician career in high school, he explained to Wenrich—the hubris he would exude like vapor in the years to come not anywhere present in his tone. His chores were "mainly washing the hearse, setting up folding chairs, and doing other odd jobs." Michael Roseboro graduated from Cocalico High School. From there, the heir to the undertaker's throne studied mortuary science at Northampton County Area Community College, where he earned his associate's, finally passing the state and national boards in 1989.

Before the murder of his wife became a burdensome

narrative playing out in his daily life, putting the kibosh on the family business for the moment, Michael Roseboro had not been in trouble with law enforcement.

In that 1993 interview, Michael said he had always been frightened of death. "The whole idea of it," he told Wenrich, "just scared me. The finality of it scared me."

It wasn't until he began talking to families in mourning that Michael said he realized his job as a funeral director wasn't about embalming, putting makeup on corpses, or even burying or cremating the dead; it was about consoling the living. Making sure those who had lost loved ones were not taken advantage of, or made to feel worse by an undertaker out to sell them the most expensive burial package in his catalogue. The art of dealing with mourning families was in taking care of every detail for them, being certain they did not have to deal with anything other than grief and tears.

The funeral itself was "not really about mourning the dead," Michael had said to Wenrich, but more ". . . about celebrating that person and [his or her] life."

In total contrast to the way he was acting since his wife had been beaten, strangled, and drowned, Michael Roseboro, married to Jan by then, added, "I honestly believe people are helped by getting it out, by talking about it and letting their emotions go."

So far, no one in Michael Roseboro's family or circle of friends had reported that he had shown any sort of serious emotional reaction to Jan's death. Instead of wiping tears and walking around with drooped shoulders and a sullen, withdrawn look on his face, Michael was bouncing from friends to family, selling that same story he had told police. It was a story that law enforcement, at the moment, was punching holes in.

Investigators were anxious, for one, to speak with Angie Funk in a more official capacity, maybe in a more

comfortable space. That short talk on her front porch—
Angie shielding her kids and husband from the conversation with a closed door to her back—was a warning, per
se, letting Angie know that she still had some explaining
to do. Her life with Michael was, quite possibly, the key to
solving Jan Roseboro's murder. She was not going to be
able to walk away from this without telling the cops all she
knew. Angie had said she, her husband, and her kids were
going on a little vacation, and that would give her time to
explain to Randall what was going on.

Law enforcement had given her that space—two
days ago.

Now it was time to own up to her responsibilities.

While investigators were on their way to Ocean City,
New Jersey, Angie took a phone call from Michael on
her cell. She must have spied the number on the LCD
screen, grabbed the phone, and snuck away from Randy
Funk and their kids.

The noose was tightening. Michael could sense it. His
voice indicated as much. There was a certain tone in
what he said, indicating that the heat of the investigation was being ratcheted up a few notches and possibly
getting to him.

"Things are not going so good," the embattled mortician, now the sole suspect in his wife's murder, told
Angie, according to an interview Angie gave a few weeks
after the call. "They think I did it."

"If you did not do anything, Michael, you have *nothing*
to worry about," Angie responded.

"She was not able to remember anything else about
this conversation," Detective Keith Neff's report of the
interview said. Neff had asked Angie if she confronted
Roseboro with "why the police" had felt he had done it.

She said no, she never asked him that.

It was here, Angie said later, that she began to think
"about how their dreams of being together were gone,
and how Michael threw [them] away."

The matter of her lover being accused of murdering his wife wasn't much on Angie's mind as Roseboro faced a tough road in the days ahead.

"Those issues of his," she said, "were the least of my worries because I [had] my *own* issues to deal with."

Boy, did she ever.

47

Ocean City, New Jersey, is a 130-mile, two-hour-plus ride from Denver, Pennsylvania. If you're a cop in a cruiser, lights spinning, siren blaring, probably a little less.

Investigators met Angie Funk at the Ocean City, New Jersey, Police Department on Central Avenue, downtown. Angie appeared tired, a bit nervous, and quite defiant in her own way. She was definitely a bit shellshocked by all of this, no doubt pondering the notion that all those e-mails she and Michael Roseboro had shared were going to become public knowledge sooner or later. Yet, as soon as Angie started talking, out came what would become *her* signature response: that uncooperative tone in her voice that would drive law enforcement crazy over the course of the next year. Many in law enforcement who spoke to Angie said, in not so many words, that getting straightforward information from her—just the facts—was harder than sucking peanut butter through a straw. The more you pushed Angie, the more she resisted, or beat around the bush, leaning heavily on the phrase I don't recall/remember.

"Another interesting thing with Angie," one law enforcement source said, "is, things that possibly no person could forget, she would *conveniently* forget."

This was the first time law enforcement had the chance to talk to Angie in a professional manner. She wore a tank top and shorts. She sat in an interrogation room, with two detectives, one on each side.

At first, they asked Angie questions about the affair: how she and Roseboro met, where they met, how they communicated, how the relationship progressed, did her husband and Jan know about the affair, details about the sex.

Softballs, you could say. All questions Angie could answer in any way she wanted to, perhaps.

For whatever the reason, getting Angie to dole out information with any profundity was indeed like the two sides were speaking different languages. Angie was all about holding her cards close.

Were she and Roseboro in love? "Yes."

Did they have sex? "Yes."

Did she know he was married? "Yes."

Did he ever mention harming Jan? "No."

Did he ever say anything about being scared that Jan was murdered? "No."

Was he in fear for his children's lives since Jan's death? "No."

It seemed that if Roseboro had not murdered Jan, then someone had walked onto the property—an intruder, in other words—and not only had murdered Jan by beating and drowning her, but had cleaned up the crime scene and turned all the lights on before leaving. If that insanely ridiculous theory had actually played out, a murderer was roaming around Denver—and one would think Michael Roseboro would be standing in front of his kids with a shotgun, protecting them from the same fate his wife had suffered. Remarkable as it sounded, however, Michael's kids were spread out at various family residences. He wasn't even with them most of the time.

"Yes," she answered. He was still telling Angie that

he loved her, and they were going to ride off into the sunset once this situation settled down.

At some point, investigators told Angie that the man she had fallen in love with, Michael Alan Roseboro, her knight in shining armor, the love of her life, was, in fact, a serial adulterer—that he'd had many affairs throughout his marriage and was perhaps involved with other women while sleeping with Angie.

Indeed, Roseboro was a "playa," in every sense of the urban word.

Angie's demeanor changed after law enforcement gave her that news. Her face dropped. She was particularly shaken by this information. No doubt she had thought she knew Michael better than anyone, and now she realized that perhaps what they had was nothing more than another one of Michael Roseboro's conquests. She was one more in a line of mistresses. A mark. A lick of his thumb, turn of the page. Someone for whom he had tossed the charm on, like rose petals, lied to, and taken for quite the ride—in more ways than one.

If Angie had any doubt about what they were telling her, the two investigators explained how they had spoken to some of those "other women" in Michael Roseboro's life.

If she didn't buy that, they gave Angie a few names. Asked her if she recognized them.

After the impact of this revelation settled on Angie, they gave her various details regarding the manner of Jan Roseboro's death, specifically that Jan had been savagely beaten. This fact was not yet made public.

Angie didn't seem too upset by this. She was still back at the accusations of the other affairs. Later, she was asked "why it appeared she was more upset . . . about learning of the affairs than about Jan's death."

"I never met Jan . . . ," Angie responded to that question.

The tears for Jan would come later, she claimed,

when she sat and thought about the entire situation from Jan and Jan's kids' points of view.

There was a method to the investigators' decision to give Angie exclusive details from their investigation. They wanted Angie to place a call to Michael Roseboro. Right then and there. In front of them. The interview with Angie was being videotaped. They wanted Angie to make the call and confront Michael on the phone about his other affairs. See what he had to say. They gave Angie the name of a woman with whom Michael had carried on an affair.

"Did he ever tell you that he was going to hurt Jan?" one investigator asked Angie at some point during the interview.

"No," Angie said, shaking her head.

Angie dialed Michael's number from her cell. She sounded subdued and preoccupied. The investigators could hear only her side of the conversation. But there was no doubt Michael had asked Angie what was wrong. Maybe even, "You okay, baby?"

There were a lot of *yeah, no, I don't know* statements from Angie in that vein.

Then, at one point, Angie confronted her boyfriend about his affairs. She gave him the name of the woman.

"No," Angie later said Michael told her on the phone that day. "I did not have an affair with [her]. She has been stalking me," he said.

Angie didn't respond right away.

"Look, I have text messages from her!" Michael said, according to Angie's later recollection. "I have *never* sent [her] text messages—you *have* to believe me!"

Then, during the conversation, as investigators sat and listened, there was an extended pause. Michael was doing all of the talking.

What was he saying?

The only part of that long pause Angie Funk later

recalled was when Michael said, "The only time I ever touched Jan was when I pulled her out of the pool."

Later, during an interview with the ECTPD, Angie was told, "Michael Roseboro clearly said a lot more than that [during the long pause]. What more can you tell us?"

"I cannot remember what he said," Angie answered.

The investigation had hit another major roadblock: Roseboro's family was tight-lipped. They were not speaking to detectives or investigators. No one, in fact.

"We tried every avenue," one law enforcement source later told me, "to get them to speak to us—Ralph and Ann Roseboro, and Mike's sister and brother-in-law—and we were pretty much shut down."

There was one time outside of Michael's sister and brother-in-law's house, in the driveway. Keith Neff walked up to Ralph Roseboro. "We need your help, Ralph. Can you tell us anything?"

Ralph wouldn't talk.

Neff went to Roseboro's sister.

Same thing.

The family spokesperson, the Roseboros' pastor, was telling Neff and his team that the family was grieving. They were in mourning. And needed to be left alone.

"Well, we understood that," DA Craig Stedman said, "but wait a minute, if what the family believes is true—that Michael is innocent—then that means there's a murderer on the loose—and wouldn't you want to do everything in your power to help catch that person?"

"Yeah," Neff reiterated. "They—the Roseboro family—would not tell us anything!"

To the contrary, Suzie Van Zant and Jan's side of the family were suffering a terrible loss, the life sucked out of them by the murder, and they were willing to help.

"They (Jan's family) talked more than Mike's, but they, too, were tight-lipped. It was hard for us in the beginning," a law enforcement source told me, "to get any information out of *anyone*."

Getting to know Michael Roseboro through his family was going to be crucial. But even more than that, if the guy had nothing to hide, why wouldn't his family support the idea that his name needed to be cleared so the real killer could be found?

Neff and Jan Walters were frustrated. They needed to do something to get the families to open up.

"Can you say something to the press?" Walters suggested to Craig Stedman.

"We have to solve this case . . . yeah. That's a good idea."

"Funny," Neff said, "Roseboro's not calling us, asking how the investigation is coming along, if we have any leads. He has not called *once*."

So a decision was made. Craig Stedman talked it over with ADA Kelly Sekula and Jan Walters, and they came to the conclusion that there was only one thing left to do at this point.

Stedman called a press conference.

The case was becoming bigger than anyone could have anticipated, judging from the amount of calls Stedman's office was receiving. Scores of calls, at all hours, were flooding into the DA's office.

"I don't ever remember as many calls," Stedman remarked later. "I said, 'We're going to do *one* press conference—and that's it.'"

To his credit, Stedman didn't want to spend half of his days talking to the press. One press conference and he could get back to investigating the case.

That's what he had hoped, anyway.

48

A memorial service for Jan Roseboro was held on Saturday, July 26, at the Roseboro Funeral Home. This after the coroner released her body (so it could be autopsied for a second time by doctors whom Roseboro had hired). It was a large crowd. In the hundreds, the local newspapers reported. The mass of people had been expected, considering how many lives Jan had touched, and how many people felt compelled to pay their respects to a woman who seemed not to have an enemy among them. A plainclothes police officer walked around. The guy happened to be a neighbor of Jan and Michael Roseboro's. Mixing and mingling, he made sure things stayed in order and, additionally, maybe get a feel for how Roseboro was handling what was such an enormously tragic, sad event.

For Michael, it was business as usual. He was in presentation mode. He had done this hundreds (maybe thousands) of times. Here, today, however, he allowed people to console him, rap him on the shoulder and share their condolences, maybe a kiss on the cheek from those family members who were close enough. In light of the police breathing down his back, it had to be a walking-on-eggshells moment for the undertaker. Rumors were abounding, buzzing. People in town were like chicken hawks, swooping in, whispering about the fact that law enforcement had come out in the morning papers with some fairly scurrilous accusations. It was no secret that the one suspect the LCDA's Office was focusing on happened to be the guy in charge of burying his wife.

Craig Stedman had said there was a possibility that a murderer was on the loose in the community, and the DA's office needed the public's help in finding him. Then Larry Martin told reporters outside the doors of the ECTPD that his team believed evidence had been cleaned up from the crime scene (the Roseboros' pool and patio, perhaps inside the house) in an effort to make the murder look like an accidental drowning, adding that police noticed scratches on someone's face during an interview that the ECTPD conducted on the night of Jan's death.

To townsfolk, this could only mean one thing: the "person of interest" was a popular undertaker no one was naming just yet.

Reporters had gotten hold of the search warrant Larry Martin had written for the Roseboro home, which was full of incriminating speculation about Michael Roseboro.

According to what he told police, Michael wrote Jan's obituary that appeared online, on the Roseboro Funeral Home website, and the hard copy published in the newspapers. How many times, one might consider, has a suspected murderer written an obituary for his victim and provided burial services? If Michael had killed Jan, as the ECTPD officers were now completely convinced, the creepy thought of him sitting down and penning Jan's final biography was just one more strange occurrence in what seemed to be a murder mystery that was getting more interesting and convoluted with each passing day.

In that obituary, Roseboro wrote that his wife had *entered into rest unexpectedly*. He said Jan was a member of the Faith United Evangelical Lutheran Church in Denver. She had been treasurer of Cocalico Creek Watershed Association (where the family had asked donations be sent in lieu of flowers) and was past president of the East Cocalico Swim Team.

With the service at the Roseboro Funeral Home concluded—there was no viewing—a second service at the Swamp Evangelical Lutheran Church in Reinholds commenced. (Jan and Michael Roseboro were raised in different Lutheran churches and maintained relationships with both throughout the course of their marriage.) After that, Roseboro told police, Jan's body would be autopsied and cremated.

Ashes to ashes.

The Reverend Larry G. Hummer, who was given the distinction of being the Roseboro family spokesperson, aptly referred to Jan's death as an "immeasurable tragedy." Swamp Lutheran Church pastor Dennis Trout, who had been at the Roseboro house the night before, consoling family and friends, was present for the memorial service. Trout didn't know it yet, but Michael had lied to him about Angie the day after Jan's death. It was somewhere around 2:00 A.M. on July 23 when the two men spoke, merely hours after Jan's death. Trout and Roseboro were sitting down. It seemed during those wee hours after Jan's death, Michael made the rounds, being sure to sit and chat with everyone he could, setting in place his padded story.

"I had made arrangements," Michael had told Trout that night, "for Jan and me to renew our marriage vows when we went on vacation. I wanted to surprise Jan. She had always wanted to be married on the beach." Michael had framed the comment with that now-it's-never-going-to-happen tone he was getting pretty good at feigning.

Being a pastor for some four decades, Trout was a good listener during times of what seemed to be an unbearable heartbreak for a husband. Jan and Mike, the pastor surmised, were supposed to grow old together and bounce grandkids off their knees. Here it was, the prime of their lives, and Jan was a murder victim.

In speaking about the clergy person he had chosen to renew their vows, Michael Roseboro had told Trout, "I made arrangements with a woman down the street"—Trout learned later during the conversation that Roseboro was referring to Angie Funk—"who has a relative . . . who's a minister. . . ."

The Reverend Larry Hummer did much of the talking during the service. As he would soon become extremely vocal about DA Craig Stedman's public outcry that the Roseboro family was not doing everything in its power to aid the investigation and cooperate with authorities.

"We grieve the all-too-short life of this wonderful woman," Hummer told the distressed throng of mourners. "Jan was gracious and giving. She had a zest for life! Jan will be remembered for the example she set."

There were gorgeous, fragrant white lilies on the altar. On their way in, mourners had been given remembrance cards. There was a photo of Jan on the front, the popular "Footprints in the Sand" poem on the back. To many of those there, Jan was walking with Jesus now, having lunch and dinner with Saint Peter. She was safe. At peace.

Home.

"Some family members," Stedman had told a reporter, a statement published on the morning of the services, "have been uncooperative."

Shawn Roseboro, Jan's cousin, had spoken out on Talk-Back, a local online forum, after reading what Stedman and the ECTPD were saying about Michael Roseboro and his family. Shawn believed the media had "missed some aspects of the story." He said the papers had not covered the fact that Michael Roseboro had been there for his children:

> Nobody looked at how close the family is and how difficult it is to be under a cloud of suspicion in such a close community. I just wish people would put themselves in the Roseboros' shoes.

He concluded his comments by writing: the dramatic nature of the crime is potentially damaging to the family's funeral business and reputation.

Shawn told me that he regretted those comments the moment after he posted them. He believes Michael Roseboro to be a rat fink murderer and philanderer, who used "and abused" his wife for most of the time they were together.

While Jan Roseboro was being formally remembered, the ECTPD was in the process of getting a warrant to go into the funeral home and conduct a search. For the most part, investigators wanted the company computers, same as those at Angie Funk's work and home. It was important to get into the computers and take a look at the electronic trail the affair left behind. By now, the investigation had yielded many interesting bits and pieces of that night Jan was murdered—the most promising being, according to several of Jan and Michael's neighbors who had been interviewed, no lights were on in the backyard on the night Jan was murdered. This was in stark contrast to Roseboro's story: *"I got up, went to the bathroom, saw the lights on outside, went to shut them off, saw Jan in the pool."*

Now the investigation had unearthed opposing views of what was going on in the backyard that night.

More evidence that Michael Roseboro was lying.

Michael's story, as Larry Martin, Jan Walters, and Keith Neff had suspected all along, was crumbling.

Motive (the affair) and opportunity (he was home and the lights were *off*) are the two biggest factors in determining if a suspect could have committed a crime. In this case, as Neff and Martin exchanged information with investigators from the LCDA's Office and members of the Major Crimes Unit, it appeared that Michael Roseboro was the only person who could have murdered his wife.

Either that, or he was covering for someone else.

But Craig Stedman issued a warning to everyone working the case: Don't get ahead of yourselves. We need much more before an arrest warrant can be issued. And with Michael Roseboro lawyered-up with the likes of Allan Sodomsky—beyond motive and opportunity— obtaining hard evidence was essential.

Stedman faced another serious problem, however. Reports from his investigators were coming in regarding Michael Roseboro's behavior. The guy was acting erratic, his actions borderline unpredictable. One source had claimed that only five days after Jan's death, Michael came down the stairs with a rifle in his hands. He headed into the dining area of the house, where a group of family members had gathered for breakfast. "This is custom made for me," he announced proudly, displaying the weapon. It was "unusual," said a family member who was there. The guy's wife had been murdered and there he was showing off a gun, for no apparent reason. Bragging about it.

Michael's drinking was on the rise, too. He had a squirrelly, nervous look to him. Craig Stedman was concerned that if he had killed his wife and now felt the vise of law enforcement tightening, Roseboro might do what so many others had done when facing the same situation: take out his kids and then himself.

Was this what Michael was trying to say by flaunting that rifle? Was it a cry for help?

What no one in law enforcement knew then, despite all the innuendo and rumor flying around town, was that Michael Roseboro's lawyer was about to unload a bombshell on Keith Neff, trying to close the gap of his client's guilt, thus offering an alternative theory for the murder.

49

When investigators interviewed Angie Funk briefly on her front porch during the afternoon of July 24, they had asked her not to contact Michael Roseboro again. She said she would abide by that request. No problem. She was leaving, anyway, on that vacation—what timing—to Ocean City, New Jersey. On Sunday, July 27, as Keith Neff and Larry Martin were busy working on those new search warrants, Angie, still in Ocean City (reportedly returning to Denver later that night), was interviewed over the telephone by one of the lieutenants working with the MCU.

"At that time," one of the investigators later said, "Funk stated that Roseboro has corresponded with her via e-mail at her place of employment in excess of twenty times from the Roseboro Funeral Home."

Twenty times? That was probably the understatement of the investigation so far. Nonetheless, this declaration by Angie—added to mounting evidence against Roseboro—was enough to convince a judge that the Roseboro Funeral Home needed to be searched.

As investigators were getting the warrant signed, Reverend Larry Hummer fired back at Craig Stedman. The cleric said on Sunday night that he realized police had jobs to do, but Jan Roseboro's family was deeply disturbed by Jan's death, as expected, and all of them were "struggling to cope with [the] loss," concluding that both families were in "a state of shock."

Later on, Hummer called Stedman's fingerpointing "reprehensible," saying that the Roseboro family wanted to "cooperate" but at this time "they can't."

In response, Stedman asked the Roseboro family to reconsider, "reach out to investigators" and help them find out who killed Jan. It was frustrating for the prosecutor. He could understand their pain—Stedman had dealt with murder victims' families for years—but he also wondered if there were additional motivating factors. Why wouldn't those who loved Jan want to see her killer behind bars as soon as possible?

On Monday, July 28, investigators confiscated several items from the Roseboro Funeral Home: computers, fax machines, four Maxwell CD-Rs with cases, some paperwork, and other potential pieces of evidence.

Throughout the day, investigators read e-mail after e-mail—those that weren't double deleted and needed to be recovered via computer forensics. In just about every e-mail either Angie Funk or Michael Roseboro sent, that blazing, obsessive nature of their affair became evident. This gave the team a clear indication that Angie and Michael were much more than mere casual sexual partners. From the e-mails, it was apparent they were planning a life together.

Angie turned over several e-mails she had printed and stuffed in a file at work—the remainder they uncovered from her computer during a forensic search.

Meanwhile, Craig Stedman and Kelly Sekula discovered a vital piece of information that would fit congenially into the matrix of circumstantial evidence they were busy weighing. In speaking with Brian Binkley,

Jan's brother, it was discovered Binkley had learned that Jan had been *murdered* after he arrived on scene at the house a day after Jan's death. Brian was talking to a police officer he knew. But Jan's brother had kept this fact to himself for a time. What struck Brian as odd as the week progressed was that his brother-in-law never—not once—mentioned this fact to anyone in the family: the idea that police believed Jan had been murdered and had not drowned accidentally. Many found out via the media. Michael Roseboro had known about it at least twenty-four hours before anyone. Why wouldn't he go running to family members bemoaning the shocking revelation that his wife had not died accidentally but had, in fact, been murdered? Why wouldn't Roseboro be enraged by this information?

"One of the conclusions we came to based on that information," Stedman said later, "was that Mr. Roseboro had murdered his wife. But this was not super significant. It was one more piece of circumstantial evidence."

Late afternoon or early evening, Monday, July 28, Angie Funk went out for a walk in the Walnut Street neighborhood near Sixth Street. As she sauntered down the block, Michael Roseboro phoned her.

"Hey."

"Hi." A car drove by speedily as Angie answered. She was just down the road from the funeral home.

"Was that a car in the background?" Roseboro asked. "Where are you?"

"Just a few blocks from the funeral home," she explained.

"Can you meet me real quick out back? . . ."

There was an alcove in back of the funeral home, a place to slip into without being seen—perfect if you're two people embroiled in a murder investigation and really shouldn't be spotted together. How would it look, after all, Michael Roseboro and his mistress embracing days after his wife had been murdered?

Angie walked toward the back parking lot of the funeral home. Roseboro was standing there in the alcove. He looked "upset," she said, "scared."

They hugged tightly. "I love you," he said.

"I love you, too."

Then they kissed.

Beyond that, Angie and her selective memory could not recall what was said or what happened. All she could tell police was that the meeting between them did not last long.

That night, Angie got a call from Michael, a conversation well documented in her testimony a year later and in several interviews she gave to the ECTPD in August 2008. It was one of fifty-nine calls and 165 text messages Angie and her lover would share between July 23, the day after Jan's murder, and August 2, 2008, a coming day that both would not forget.

"I'm leaving . . . going out to Pittsburgh, where Jan's brother Brian [Binkley] is," Michael told Angie. "I need to get away."

Angie said later, "I just thought he wanted to get away from everything."

Continuing, Michael added, "We're [he and Brian] going to try and find out who really killed Jan." Next, he said something about hiring a private investigator. "I noticed the jewelry Jan wore was missing."

Pittsburgh was an awfully long way from Denver to go in search of a killer—a 250-mile, four-and-a-half-hour ride, to be more exact. Sounded like Michael Roseboro was running from something more than helping the investigation.

"Jewelry?" It was the first Angie had heard about this jewelry. Where was this coming from?

"Yeah, I looked for it (that jewelry)," he explained,

"where she normally kept it, and it wasn't there after her death." He mentioned nothing about Jan *wearing* the jewelry on the day she died. The fact of the matter: if Jan had been wearing it, why would he feel the need to look for it where it was normally kept? This statement would make no sense when placed under a microscope next to a claim Roseboro would make about this jewelry in the days to come.

"Michael, I saw in the news," Angie asked more in the vein of a question, "that they said you had scratches on your face?"

"Oh, that," he answered. "My youngest daughter did that while we were playing in the pool."

They talked about other things, Angie said, but she had a hard time recalling what. At some point, she asked him again: "Did you have any prior affairs, Michael?"

"No. No."

"What about [that woman the investigators told me about—who you claimed was stalking you and your family]?"

"No," Michael reiterated. "That's not true."

The fact that Angie Funk asked this question, however, was an indication that she was beginning to look at Michael Roseboro in a different light.

Michael Roseboro spent much of Wednesday, July 30, over at his sister and brother-in-law's spacious home in the affluent Mustang Trail neighborhood in Reinholds. He and friends and family sat poolside; they had food and drinks over conversation. Later that day, a few of them went over to one of Roseboro's good friends' home and continued the party in her dining room.

"And every time we always got together," that friend recalled later, "before Jan passed away, we would always play Catch Phrase," a board game.

As they all sat around the dining table, Michael said, "Let's play Catch Phrase!"

They all looked at each other.

A moment later, they were playing the game (which would last about three hours).

Roseboro's wife was dead—murdered—and the cops were breathing down his back like vampires, ready to draw first blood. According to Michael, he hadn't killed Jan. So that meant there was a killer on the loose. He had told Angie Funk he was looking into the missing jewelry and working with Brian Binkley to find Jan's killer. But on this day, Roseboro was more interested in sitting poolside with drinks, smoking cigarettes, and playing board games. The idea that he was worried about a killer, or was out there running around like a private eye, trying to catch a killer, flew in the face of credibility for anyone who later learned what he had been doing.

At some point, this same friend had a conversation with Michael about the investigation. Roseboro said the cops had been asking him about "a woman he was calling."

Angie.

But he did not say her name on that night.

"Who is she?" the friend asked.

"Just the person who is planning . . . renewing . . . making plans to renew our vows."

For Michael Roseboro's friends and family, all of whom were eager and ready to believe whatever it was he had to say, this had been enough of an explanation for some. But for this one particular friend, who had known Jan and loved her dearly, something wasn't quite adding up. She sensed a bit of hesitation in his voice.

As the conversation between them became more serious, Michael said he needed to say something.

Jan's friend was all ears. What is it?

He wanted to warn her that, on the following morning, the newspapers were going to be saying that he'd had an affair with someone named Angela Funk. It was all going to come out, Michael explained. He wanted to let Jan's friend know ahead of time. But he also had a favor to ask of her.

"I need you to tell everyone," Roseboro pled, "that it is *not* true. I wasn't having an affair with her. . . ."

"Mike, are you *having* an affair with Angela Funk?" the friend asked.

"No. You know I've had problems in the past, but I swear to God," Michael said, "I'm *not* having an affair with Angela Funk."

The friend didn't know how to respond to such frankness and what seemed like genuine sincerity.

"Look," Roseboro continued, "they are even going to say that I was having sex with Angela Funk on the day Jan died."

"Well, were you?"

"No, no, no. I had a doctor's appointment in Lancaster that day. . . ."

"Well, then, you shouldn't have any problem—because they can prove where you were."

Michael Roseboro didn't respond to that particular statement. Instead, he repeated a previous point, adding, "Just please tell everyone that I was absolutely *not* having an affair with this woman. She is this woman who walks her little kids [in the neighborhood], and I was friendly with her. . . . She was planning our renewal thing."

50

Keith Neff was in his office on Thursday, July 31, when a call from Allan Sodomsky, Michael Roseboro's attorney, came in. It was a message from the lawyer that would soon raise the stakes for investigators, a continuation of the same idea that Roseboro had planted in Angie Funk's mind two days before.

"Listen, Jan was wearing some jewelry that night she died . . . valued at approximately forty thousand dollars," Sodomsky said.

Neff was stunned by this disclosure. Jan had put on jewelry worth twice as much as the car Neff drove? Just to go out to the pool? And this was the first time the ECTPD was hearing about it, nine days after her death?

Sodomsky read from a list of what Jan had been wearing: emerald-cut diamond earrings (two carats), platinum wedding band with six diamonds, a David Yurman bracelet (silver and gold), a one-carat diamond-studded earring, and a necklace of "minimal value."

News to Neff.

But there was more. The punch line of the call was that Sodomsky was now informing the ECTPD that when the family picked up the body *after* the coroner released it, Jan wasn't wearing any of this jewelry. Nor had anyone claimed to have returned it to them from the hospital, or anywhere else.

It was gone.

Was Roseboro providing an alternative motive for murder? Were they putting it out there—this *after* reports in the newspapers had clearly stated that the Lancaster County district attorney had repeatedly said there was no evidence of a robbery in the case of Jan's death—to provide a second scenario and maybe take the heat off Michael Roseboro? Others wondered after the news broke, if Roseboro was reaching for those same stars that he had insisted his wife had been watching on the night of her murder.

Or, was Michael Roseboro lying to Allan Sodomsky?

One of the investigators told Sodomsky they needed photographs of the jewelry, if any were available. Receipts too, if Roseboro could produce them. If he was claiming the jewelry had been stolen, an official report needed to be filed.

The following day, Roseboro's brother-in-law showed up at the ECTPD with photographs of Jan wearing the jewelry. Roseboro was telling his lawyer that anyone who knew Jan could testify to the fact that she loved to wear jewelry and was hardly seen without it.

The investigator at the ECTPD told Roseboro's brother-in-law that they needed Michael himself to come down and report the jewelry missing. "We'll need to ask him a few questions."

The brother-in-law left.

Michael would never walk into the station house or call to report the jewelry missing.

The tipping point here was that Michael Roseboro had not reported Jan wearing any jewelry on the night he pulled her out of the pool. And he never mentioned it at any time after. Why now? Why come forward *now* and say that she had been wearing expensive jewelry and that it was gone?

51

Laurie Sauder had known Jan Roseboro since their days in high school together. They had been friends ever since. Sauder had also worked for Fulton Bank, which Jan's family had been connected to professionally up until Jan's dad sold his business—Denver National Bank—to Fulton. Sauder was one of Fulton's assistant managers. She worked at both the Cocalico and Reinholds offices, splitting her time. On July 22, 2008, Sauder had been working at the Reinholds branch.

Jan had happened to do some banking on that day and Laurie ran into her inside the building.

When Laurie saw Jan at one of the teller's booths, she walked over.

"There was a conversation between the teller . . . and me and Jan," Sauder said later. "She (Jan) made a deposit or payment or something."

Laurie stood within breathing distance of her high-school friend. Laurie adored Jan. Had nothing but great things to say about her. And there was Jan, dressed down, as usual, in a sweatshirt—the same one she would later be found dead in—and flip-flops and black shorts.

"She was not wearing any jewelry," Laurie Sauder later said. Laurie knew this because it was more than a chance meeting. They spoke for ten to fifteen minutes. Laurie knew Jan well enough, and like many other friends of Jan's later recalled, she was not about flaunting what she had and wearing flashy clothes and pricey jewelry around town. Okay, she drove a Range Rover, but that was about where it ended for Jan. It just wasn't part of her DNA to wear what was later reported to be $40,000 worth of jewelry to the bank at lunchtime to take care of her financials. Same as it wasn't part of who she was to go home after an afternoon of errands and dress up like Cleopatra in bulky jewelry to hang out at her pool. If anything, she would have taken the jewelry *off* before she got settled outside. Chlorine wreaks havoc on jewelry.

If Sauder's memory wasn't good enough, however, she called Keith Neff and explained that the bank took surveillance video daily of its customers coming and going. It would have video of Jan at the counter and walking into the bank.

Neff interviewed Laurie Sauder.

"She was the first person I interviewed who actually broke down and cried for Jan," Neff said later.

Nevertheless, that information had to give Keith Neff a warm feeling. Here might be proof, beyond witness testimony, of what Jan Roseboro was wearing on the day of her murder.

Cassandra Pope was in her apartment tending to her baby. Richard, her husband, was at work. Cassie was alone.

And terrified.

"Mom," she said, calling her mother, Marcia Evanick, Jan and Mike's old neighbors, "I see his [SUV] over there." She was referring to Michael Roseboro's vehicle. "What do I do?"

"What . . . ," Marcia said. "He's not going to *do* anything to you."

"Mom!"

"Is your door locked? Look, if you don't want to say hi to him, don't go outside while he's there."

Cassie probably knew this, but hearing it from her mom felt good. It wasn't that she was concerned Michael was going to barge into her apartment and try to kill her—that was a bit absurd and an overreaction.

Nonetheless, she was "creeped out," Cassie said, "by his mere presence."

Cassie watched her neighbor, along with the ebb and flow of the house, as the days went on and Michael was still a free man. Sometimes she'd look out the window and see Michael Roseboro sitting by the pool, alone, staring into the water, chain-smoking, drinking beers.

"He just sat there and stared at that water."

And that, she said, was horrifying to watch.

52

All she had to do was walk across the street. It was not hard to see when his big black Denali was parked out back. The cops had told Angie Funk to stay away from Michael Roseboro. She herself, maybe without realizing it, by asking him certain questions, was beginning to have second thoughts about their love and their future. But Angie couldn't stay away. She still loved the guy. She had met him once already behind the funeral home— what could one more time hurt?

Strange that he would be at work when there was a maelstrom of criminal difficulties spiraling around him. But Michael was in his office. He had explained to Angie during a phone call that he never went to Pittsburgh because his family members had asked him to stick around town.

"I'm talking to the police and telling them everything," Angie said, embracing her lover, kissing him inside that same back alcove.

"I love you," he said.

"I love you, too, Michael."

They had to be quick. No one could see them together.

"I never felt threatened," Angie later explained,

describing this second meeting with Michael, "when I met him. And if I did, I would have never met him."

Investigators had asked Angie not to tell Michael that she was talking to them. During that second week after Jan Roseboro's murder, Angie and Michael communicated daily, often multiple times. They met, too. Angie never said if she continued to sleep with Michael after learning Jan was murdered. One would guess that sex was the last thing on her mind. But then again, Michael was cut from a different cloth. A narcissist by clinical definition, there's no doubt he would have slept with Angie in a New York minute, had she initiated sex.

Regarding why she continued talking to and meeting with her lover, the only suspect in his wife's murder, after learning Jan had been brutally beaten and drowned, Angie said, "I did not feel that Michael was lying to me, and I did not believe that he did the murder."

What about all those other women? Didn't the fact that Michael Roseboro turned out to be a serial cheater put a damper on future plans?

"I believed," Angie said, "that [the one woman] was stalking Michael. I believed him when he said he was the one being harassed, and I had no reason to fear him. . . . [But] if he did [murder Jan], I *would* be afraid."

Ignorance truly is bliss (and blind).

During one phone call during that second week, after Angie had been told by investigators that Jan and Michael Roseboro had been planning a trip to the Outer Banks, and he had made rather extensive arrangements to renew their marital vows, she confronted Michael. She asked the man whom she thought she would one day marry about this North Carolina trip.

"I canceled it," Roseboro said, meaning the vow-renewal celebration. "The plans were made before we [started our affair]."

Angie was asked if she had ever placed a phone call for Michael to a reverend in the Outer Banks, acting, so

to speak, as the Roseboros' wedding planner, strange as
that might have sounded. They had solid information,
investigators told Angie, that she had called, and they
wanted to know if she knew anyone in North Carolina.
There was a reverend in the Outer Banks who claimed
to have "remembered possibly getting a message from
Angela Funk," Keith Neff explained when he spoke to
Angie about this.

"Well, that freaks me out," she responded to Neff. "I
do not know if I should be worried about this."

No, she had never called anyone in North Carolina,
Angie said. It concerned her, though, that someone had
her name and was saying she had made the call.

The question then became: had Michael Roseboro
had someone else call North Carolina and disguise herself as Angie Funk?

Neff wanted to know why Angie had spoken to Michael
when they had specifically asked her not to do so. It
seemed strange that she would emphatically defy a request by law enforcement.

She never gave him an answer.

Angie explained how Michael reacted when she told
him she was talking to the police. "The police contacted
me," she told him, "and I told them everything. I am
not going to lie, Michael."

Silence for a moment. Michael Roseboro never asked
what she had told the police or how many times she had
spoken to them. It was as if he didn't care. As if he had expected it. Still, he was more upset with her, she said later,
for telling law enforcement about the affair than anything else.

In another conversation, near the same day (Angie
wasn't sure when), she asked Michael about the bruising on Jan, which was reported by investigators. She
wanted to know, again, if he had ever touched Jan. Ever
got physical with her.

He never addressed any of the "bruising" specifically,

Angie later said. Instead, Michael offered: "If that's what police are saying . . . but you have to believe me when I say that I never touched Jan. . . . I love you, Angie."

"I love you, too, Michael."

During another call, Michael said, "I wish you hadn't told police about our affair." He sounded disappointed, desperate. "But you need to cooperate with them."

"I won't lie, Michael."

Angie couldn't remember who brought it up, but they discussed the jewelry again as the second week came to an end. It was near August 1.

"Me and Brian [Binkley] are looking into it" was all Michael said about the jewelry.

There was a familiar tone to Michael's voice as the conversations with Angie carried on during the latter part of that second week. He never expressed "shock," Angie later said, "that this turned out to be a murder and not a drowning, as he had told me."

Michael had given Angie that familiar story about waking up, going to the bathroom, finding the tiki lights still on, seeing Jan in the pool. The fact that police had ruled Jan's death a homicide had not, apparently, had any effect whatsoever on Michael Roseboro's demeanor or his relationship with Angie Funk. According to Angie, Michael never mentioned to her that Jan's death was classified a murder. He said he was going to look for her killer, but he didn't express any anger or sorrow that she had been murdered. What's more, he never displayed any bitterness toward the police that they were accusing him of murder and were not out searching for the "real killer."

Business as usual for Michael Roseboro. Jan's death, if anything, had become a disruption in his plans with Angie. A nuisance. Some sort of hindrance.

A complication.

Yet, as August 1 brought hazy, hot, and humid temperatures, Angie and Michael's lives were about to change once again. Not because he was facing perhaps the rest of his life in prison, if he was tried and found guilty. But Angie had learned—so she claimed—on the morning of August 1 that she was carrying Michael Roseboro's love child, a baby they had made together during one of their many sexual encounters.

How would she tell him? More important, how would she tell the police? If Angie thought the media had been unkind to her thus far—her being the "other woman"—what was going to happen when they got ahold of this piece of salacious information? In addition, what would family members think? Michael Roseboro wouldn't be able to write Angie Funk off as a simple distraction any longer. And Angie's husband, whom she was still living with, what was Randall Funk going to do?

53

There was probably only one way to put it.

"I'm pregnant!" Angie Funk said after calling her lover on August 1.

Was there any other way? Could things get any more complicated?

"Disbelief, shock," Angie later said Michael Roseboro conveyed in those first moments after she broke the news. He had to be baffled, confused, and, almost certainly, a little angry. They had used birth control: condoms. Angie would later talk about a condom malfunctioning, breaking, or coming off; again, she could not recall what exactly happened.

"Well," Michael responded after getting his breath back, "at any other time this would have been, you know, good news. But right now . . . it's not. It's just not the right time."

The timing, actually, could not have been any worse.

They talked about what had happened, Angie said. Then Roseboro mentioned that maybe she should have an abortion.

"I'm against it," he told her, "but, you know, considering what's going on. . . . Well . . . I'm against it . . . but in this case, it might be a good idea."

"No! That's not an option," Angie snapped. There was no changing her mind. She was going to have Michael Roseboro's baby. There was nothing he could say or do to change that. He had better start accepting and dealing with it—because in nine months, Angie Funk was going to give birth to another successor to the Roseboro throne.

Angie said later that she had taken a home pregnancy test that morning. She claimed to have purchased the test at a local Lancaster County CVS with a debit card that had subsequently expired from a bank that had changed names. She was asked about the account number she had used to make the purchase.

"I don't remember," Angie said.

Craig Stedman was with ECTPD detective Kerry Sweigart on Saturday, August 2, 2008. They were sitting in Stedman's downtown Lancaster office, finishing up a search warrant. Larry Martin, Keith Neff, and Jan Walters had nearly finished Michael Roseboro's arrest warrant and were preparing to have a judge sign it.

Sweigart's cell phone buzzed. He looked down.

Angela Funk . . .

The two lawmen looked at each other.

What does she want? It wasn't like Angie to call. If anything, detectives were resigned to have to call *her.*

Sweigart flipped open his cell. "Yeah?"

Stedman stared at the detective, watching his reaction to what Angie was saying. Sweigart was "turning all sorts of shades of red," Stedman recalled. Whatever Angie had to offer, Stedman could tell, was big news.

After a few moments, Sweigart said, "Okay, Angie . . ." and hung up.

Stedman waited.

"Well? . . ."

"I got some news for ya. Angie says she's pregnant with Mike's baby."

"Are you *kidding* me?" Stedman leaned back in his chair.

"I am not kidding you."

They both sat, shaking their heads.

"Yeah, she made a point of saying that she just found out, you know, after everything." Meaning she didn't know she was pregnant when Jan Roseboro was murdered.

"She said," Sweigart continued, "that she had told Mike, and now she wanted to tell us."

Stedman called the ECTPD to let them know.

Michael Roseboro was biding his time. He must have known this. Law enforcement was not going away. If anything, they were closing in. One more piece of the puzzle—which was actually a familiar one, but from a second impartial witness—came in just before Craig Stedman and Kelly Sekula finished writing Roseboro's arrest warrant, which ultimately helped Stedman make the call that they now had enough to arrest the undertaker.

Jill Showalter, a senior educator for the North Museum of Natural History & Science in Lancaster, came forward and explained what she thought was a significant piece of information.

During the summer of 2008, Jill's father, Luke, owned a house about four lots from the Roseboros' home on West Main, heading west, away from Creek Road. Jill often stopped at her parents' house after work to visit with them. She recalled something about the night of July 22, 2008.

Driving to and then leaving her parents' home, Jill had taken the same route for as long as she could remember. West Main Street to Creek Road. Jill had been busy all day at the Northern Lancaster County Fish and Game, conducting what she called "a reptile program for the Youth Conservation School." It had run into the night and Jill didn't arrive at her parents' house until "probably about ten or after ten," she told police.

She stayed about "twenty minutes." Then left. Out of the driveway, a right onto West Main, past the front of the Roseboro home, a right onto Creek Road, and past the side of the Roseboro house where the pool and backyard was. Jill was certain it was dark, pitch dark.

Beyond that, what was more striking to Jill was that the Roseboro home, the inside of the house, "seemed unusually dark that night, the house, the lighting inside the house."

She was talking about the front of the house, the section facing West Main.

The only light she saw that was on—when looking at the house from the front—was in the basement. Odd, she thought, that the basement light would be the only light in the entire house left on.

Turning onto Creek Road, driving south, you cannot really see from the road the pool area because of the grade in the landscaping on that side of the house. The pool sits up on a mound, with shrubbery around it for privacy and the land grade sloping downward from the pool patio. However, it's not hard to see the tiki lights, that black fence, and the pool area itself, which are sort of up on a stage of land.

Driving by the poolside of the house on Creek Road, Jill looked over and saw that there were no lights on: the tiki torches or any other lights.

"I have seen the tiki torches lit at nighttime," she recalled, "on other nights." In addition, she didn't see anybody outside, no one walking around, any strange cars, or anything else that caught her attention.

Just blackness.

When they heard this new information for the first time, it was clear to police now that there were no lights on in the backyard of the Roseboro home. Two separate

witnesses had come forward and relayed this information—
people who had not known each other, had never spoken
to each other, and didn't know that the other was speaking
to the police.

Impartial, corroborating evidence.

54

Craig Stedman and his team were getting nervous that Michael Roseboro might do something to endanger the lives of family and friends—and, maybe worse, take another life. It was time to put the cuffs on, drag him in, see if he wanted to talk, then put him in a cell until his lawyer could figure out what to do.

At 10:31 P.M. on August 2, 2008, ECTPD officers and detectives moved in on the six-foot, two-hundred-pound undertaker as he was inside his parents' house on Walnut Street, down the block from the funeral home, next door to Angie and Randall Funk's house. The bench warrant for Roseboro's arrest stated "criminal homicide" as the complaint. They wanted DNA from Roseboro, too, along with fingerprints. According to the warrant, Michael Roseboro had *intentionally, knowingly, recklessly or negligently* caused *the death of another human being: To wit: the defendant did cause the death of Jan E. Roseboro. . . . The defendant did cause her death by substantial physical contact to include multiple blunt force trauma, strangulation and drowning, thereby causing her death.*

This charge (criminal homicide) carries a no-bail

initiative, which residents voted for in the state of Pennsylvania.

Detective Kerry Sweigart knocked on the door. He explained to Ralph Roseboro that they had come for his son.

Michael Roseboro walked out onto the porch and closed the door behind him.

"What's up?" Michael said. He looked tired and pale, but not in the least bit worried. With all the cops and cars out there in the front of his parents' house, Michael must have known that his time on the street— at least for now—had come to an end.

"You're under arrest . . . ," Sweigart said.

Michael had no reaction.

"Michael Roseboro was arrested without incident," Keith Neff later said. "It was pretty fast. He was cooperative and did not give us any problems. We were in and out, fast."

The hope for Neff was that when they got Roseboro back to the station house, he would open up. Break down. Make this as easy as possible on himself, his kids, and everyone else involved.

Be a man.

After getting him out of the car and allowing him to get comfortable, Michael Roseboro was placed in the interview room at the ECTPD.

Keith Neff and Jan Walters walked in.

"I'm not going to talk to you," he said. "I want to speak to my lawyer."

End of interview.

Roseboro would not spend a long time at the ECTPD. That night, per the law, he was brought before the magisterial justice to be arraigned on charges of criminal homicide and then, right after, locked up in Lancaster County Prison.

On the same day the arrest warrant was served, and Michael Roseboro was being processed, a second search warrant was executed at the Roseboro residence. This time, the warrant asserted that investigators were looking to *examine* [and] *test . . . all electrical switches and controls and circuit breakers at the residence to determine the location and operation of controls and breakers which correspond to any and all outside lighting to include but not limited to dusk-to-dawn lighting.*

The idea was to go into the house and find out how to turn on and off all the lights. Witnesses claimed the lights were off. If an outside attacker had killed Jan—for example, someone who wanted to steal her jewelry—he (or she) would've had to turn on all the lights before leaving the premises. In order to do that, you'd have to know where the switches were (and have a lighter for the tiki torches on you).

The ECTPD thought this to be a ludicrous theory, but yet one that Michael Roseboro would no doubt try to propagate once he and his lawyer got to talking.

What other choice did he have, essentially?

55

On Monday morning, August 4, Craig Stedman sat behind a mahogany conference table in the county commissioner's room, just around the corner from the DA's office, on the fifth floor of 50 North Duke Street, downtown Lancaster. There were several microphones, propped up like *Wizard of Oz* Munchkin lollipops, positioned in front of Stedman's face. Next to him sat Larry Martin, a serious and ominous aura about him. The room was jam-packed with media.

Stedman wore a dark blue suit, gold tie, white shirt. He appeared tired and beaten down, his eyes staring at the paper in front of him. Every once in a while, he looked up at reporters and around the room. He knew most of these people. He had a fairly decent relationship with the press. They were doing their jobs, on hand to get any new details surrounding Michael Roseboro's arrest, which had been the news of the past weekend. The black half-moons under Stedman's eyes were an indication of how taxing the case had been thus far. He and other members of law enforcement had worked around the clock on several nights, putting in twenty-hour days right up until the time Michael was placed in cuffs.

This was it: the fall of Denver's reigning royal family.

Or, as one source later called Michael Roseboro, "The king, so to speak, of the community." Perhaps some liked to see the mighty fall: the poor rob the rich; the rich become destitute; the powerful reduced to mere mortals. If so, this was their day. Many had considered Roseboro infallible, even untouchable. Stedman had seen him as just another murderer who would be found guilty by the evidence.

Craig Stedman liked to deal in facts. He spoke straightforwardly, thought long and hard about what he said, and tried to make sure the community that had appointed him top lawman had as much information as he could give. Here he was, eleven days after Jan Roseboro had been found dead in her pool, announcing that two days prior, on August 2, her husband had been arrested on charges of "one criminal complaint of homicide. . . ."

Fixing his tie every so often, perhaps a nervous tic, Stedman explained the charges in their dramatic, violent detail. The guy had strangled and beaten and drowned his wife. There was no way to put a passive bow on that.

"He's being held in Lancaster County Prison," Stedman added, a ten-minute ride, several blocks southeast of the DA's office, "without bail, pending a preliminary hearing, which has yet to be scheduled."

Trying to head off questions before they came at him like darts, Stedman said, "We have no evidence that there were any other participants in this crime, and no further arrests are expected at this point." This was perhaps a way to put out there—without saying—that charges were not going to be filed against Angie Funk, nor was the DA's office looking into the possibility that she had provoked her lover in any way, or that perhaps Michael Roseboro had hired someone to do his dirty work.

The lanky DA explained that he had not yet looked at the consideration of seeking the death penalty against

Roseboro (which, under Pennsylvania law, was not an option for the DA's office). He was focused, instead, on building his case and working with law enforcement to see that they were ready for the preliminary hearing. There was still a lot of work to do. Information was still filing in.

He thanked everyone. Talked about all the hours his officers and the various departments helping out had put in the entire previous weekend and the one before it. The long nights. The teamwork. It had all paid off. Jan Roseboro's killer was behind bars.

Stedman, who appeared sad and solemn, the weight of such a violent death hanging over him, called the case "very serious." It was "a terrible tragedy," he said. He added that on top of everything—the murder, the dad being arrested, the enormous burden on the community to bear such a tremendous load of shame and disillusionment—there were four children, "three of whom are minors," who had lost their mother. That was the true tragedy here, Stedman vocalized. These kids had no mother "because," Stedman said, "of the choices of their father."

The newspapers and a few of the local websites and chat rooms had not been kind to Angie Funk over the past week. She was being billed as a tramp, whore, home wrecker, and just about every other contentious name one could come up with to describe a woman who had participated in an accelerated, sexual affair with a man who had allegedly murdered his wife. One headline, screaming in bold type across the front page of the paper, said that Angie and Michael had had sex on the afternoon Jan Roseboro was murdered. Words Angie had written to Michael in confidence, those private thoughts and embarrassing emotions of love and lust, had been reprinted and talked about online, with various rumors and innuendo tossed into the mix to make what were scandalous behaviors even more salacious.

This, mind you, while Angie was carrying Rose-boro's baby.

"I want to remind . . . the media," Stedman said, a bit of empathy and mild discontent in his cracking voice, "that she is a real person." He tapped his fingers on the table, looked at his notes, then at everyone around him, knowing that he was reaching out here, maybe stepping over a line to put the brakes, hopefully, on what had turned into, fundamentally, a vitriolic media frenzy, feeding on the conduct of a woman who had simply acted on urges and had had an affair. How many women in the world had had adulterous liaisons and went through life without all this attention? Angie hadn't murdered anyone—she was, one could rightfully argue, another of Michael Roseboro's many victims. "She's going through a very difficult time," Stedman continued, "and you can do what you will, but I would ask you to respect her privacy in this and allow her to continue to cooperate with law enforcement. . . ."

Although the newspapers had splashed it across front pages and on the Internet, Stedman never used Angie's name.

After questions were tossed at Stedman in a mish-mash of words, one reporter asked about the Roseboro family's cooperation in the investigation, and if anything had changed in their behavior.

Stedman took a deep breath. "Umm . . ." He looked straight ahead, at nothing and no one, as if daydreaming, then down at the table. He thought his answer through, and replied with the best politically correct statement he could muster on the spot: "In this case, as I said before, with any murder case, when you have someone murdered in their residence, for us to solve it, it is *vital* that we have access and honesty. . . . We made efforts to communicate with those people in this case, and some were more cooperative than others, and . . .

umm . . . I think I'll—I will defer any further comment on that at this time."

They—reporters and their DA—talked back and forth for a minute or two more about public records and why Stedman had decided to release certain affidavits and warrants, while keeping others under seal, basically sending the message that the public had a right to know.

Then a reporter asked if Angie had an alibi for the night of the murder—that is, other than Randall Funk.

"That's *not* in the public record," Stedman said, "so I cannot comment on it."

Next.

Larry Martin took several questions before the brief press conference ended. Stedman was happy with how it had gone and where his case was headed. Not everyone watching and listening in on the press conference, however, was slapping high fives, jumping for joy, and pleased with what Craig Stedman had to say.

56

Allan Sodomsky must have been stewing as he watched his archenemy, Craig Stedman, because when Sodomsky held his own press conference two days later, it was clear from the first words out of his mouth that he was disappointed in what Stedman had told reporters.

Sodomsky stood, alone, in front of a flashy, gold-lettered (with black outline), embossed sign bearing his name, four bloated microphones pitched on a lectern in front of him. Sodomsky was a good-looking man, esteemed in law circles for the work he did, and known, quite good-naturedly, as a bulldog in the courtroom. His gray-and-black hair, receding profusely in some spots, totally gone in others, suited him well. Sodomsky was a good public speaker. He had done this before, and it was obvious that he and his client were not going to curl up in a ball and cave in because of this prosecutor's charges.

The high-priced defense attorney opened by reading from a prepared statement, saying that because of all the inquiries his office had received from the media, it was high time he spoke up about what was quickly turning into the most high-profile murder case Lancaster County had seen in more years than anyone could remember.

He said his office wanted to make "one statement" to clarify any of the misconceptions floating around about his position on the matter of Michael Roseboro's arrest.

"'Contrary to published reports and widespread speculation,'" the lawyer said, looking down at his notes, stretching certain words for their intended effect, "'Michael Roseboro . . . did . . . *not* . . . kill his wife.'" A quick pause. Slight smile. Then, "'In fact, upon finding her in the family pool, Michael did everything in his power to seek medical assistance and revive his wife. Despite rumors of marital discord, Michael and Jan were married for nineteen years and had four children. It goes without saying that this tragedy has deeply devastated Michael and his children.'"

After a bit more Roseboro family PR, Sodomsky said his client was in the middle of assembling a "team of experts and investigators" to get to the bottom of what happened to Jan Roseboro, perhaps insinuating that there was much more to this soap opera than what had been portrayed in the media and promulgated by the DA's office.

"'It is not our intention to try Michael in the polls of public opinion,'" Sodomsky said matter-of-factly, reading words on the page in front of him as if he were a politician making a speech after a great scandal. "'To do so would belittle our Constitution and the freedom that protects us all.'"

From there, Sodomsky spoke (or warned, actually) about the public not following the lead of the government just because those in power had said it was so. Then he encouraged everyone, sounding a bit like a parent scolding his child, "'Not to churn the rumor mill,'" which had indeed been running at full power, night and day, "'and continue the speculation that begins with an accusation.'"

Such a great turn of phrase: *"the speculation that begins*

with an accusation." Just because someone in the community has been accused of a crime, that accusation did not mean the person was guilty; and it should shed no bias on the individual judging him. Quite true—on paper. Reality, though, was another thing. The moment a perp did that walk, the public began to cast doubt and to judge. Human nature is a fragile feather, easily corrupted and malleable.

After that, Sodomsky explained the rules of law and the government's need to prove its case, and how we, as a people, should give anyone accused of a crime that proverbial benefit of the doubt.

This was all well-intentioned rhetoric. The sincerity Sodomsky tried to project came out preachy, sounding like he was backpedaling. Sodomsky stood tall, doing his best to seem like the be-all and end-all to law, innocence, and what constituted justice. The fact that Sodomsky rattled on about our forefathers and our rights, and how each man deserved a fair shot at justice, didn't help his cause. It came across hackneyed and charged with sarcasm and resentment. Here was the big man, once again, walking on the little guy. Michael Roseboro seemed to be saying from his prison cell: *How dare you accuse* me—*a Roseboro!—of such a heinous crime. . . . You watch, I'll prove all of you wrong.*

"'It is important in an adversarial system that the playing field be leveled,'" Sodomsky said, this after saying it would be premature for him to comment on allegations without a full investigation of his own. "'We believe,'" he added, perhaps beginning an argument for a future appeal, "'that the government's position in all media sources has created the potential for community bias.'" He had an angry look on his face, as though someone had made erroneous accusations against his client without any merit whatsoever. "'As such, we believe this statement'"—his—"'is necessary.'"

For the next few moments, he spoke of his client's

eagerness to answer the government with the *truth* of
what had happened. When it came time for Roseboro
to tell his side, Sodomsky's tone implied, heads were
going to roll, and the community was going to have egg
on its face for doubting such a gracious, respected, innocent man.

What else could Sodomsky say? The charges were not
just accusations. There was not just a trial in the future.
The Roseboro name and its reputation, which the
family had spent a century building, was on the chop-
ping block. Sodomsky was doing his best to begin putting a shine back on the family's respected reputation.

Allan Sodomsky had a cockiness about him, which
was hard to hide. It was part of the nature in defending
murderers, thieves, and criminals of the worst sort. Perhaps it was a raise of the eyebrows when he said something, or maybe a twitch of his right shoulder, the
folding of his hands in front of himself when he
shrugged, possibly a slight smirk or curl of his bottom
lip. Whatever the tic, Sodomsky's confidence was unmistakable. He was certain of himself and his concern that
Craig Stedman had opened up a can of whoopass on his
client and had potentially let loose too many details
about the case, disallowing his client a fair trial. Regarding Stedman's request that reporters leave Angie Funk
alone, Sodomsky chuckled a bit when he repeated himself, smiling off to the corner of his mouth, adding
quite cockily, "Let me say this"—then he reached down,
looked at his buttoned jacket and fidgeted with it, just
stopping short of brushing a piece of lint off his shoulder with a finger flick—"'for the time being, we will
adhere to the district attorney's request to consider Miss
Funk's privacy as she *struggles* to gain credibility with the
people who know her best.'" As he spoke, Sodomsky
went back to his prepared statement, looking down, re-
fraining from speaking off the top of his head. He

wanted to be sure that what he said here was exactly what he meant to say.

A simple question—which deserved a simple answer—was asked by a female reporter: "Can you confirm whether Mr. Roseboro was having an affair with her?"

Sodomsky smiled, bounced on his heels, gently rocked back and forth. He took on the look of a boy who had a secret but felt the time wasn't right to share. "Again, let me reiterate *one* more time," he began, then looked off to the side. "And . . . I . . . appreciate the question. But so we don't have that question predominate this time, I want to once again tell you that 'for the time being'"—and his eyes now returned to that prepared statement on the lectern—"'we will adhere to the district attorney's request to consider Miss Funk's privacy'"—that was *twice* he had said Angie's name and *twice* he had called Randall Funk's wife miss—"'as she *struggles* to gain credibility with the people who know her best.'"

What was Sodomsky saying? Was he implying that Angie was a liar? That she had lied about certain things, and that she had some sort of integrity to protect and rebuild herself? Was he suggesting that Michael Roseboro had some kind of hidden truth about this woman he had been connected to romantically, and was just waiting for the right time to unleash it?

Sodomsky was asked if a change of venue might be in order.

To that, he gave a minute answer which, basically, said nothing more than *Maybe, we'll see. Perhaps. It's up to the judge.*

A reporter tossed out the next question, which begat a becoming rise on his toes once again: "The DA's theory," the reporter asked, ". . . is that nobody else could have done it. Uh . . . could you give us a *hint* as to what your approach or your defense might be?"

Allan Sodomsky dug through his paperwork quickly, smiling, shaking his head, obviously eager to answer.

Judging from the way in which Sodomsky answered questions with his emboldened, overconfident demeanor, one had to consider, had Michael Roseboro lied to him? Had Roseboro told Sodomsky what the attorney wanted to hear before the press conference? You know, loaded the defense attorney with all sorts of denials and claims of *you just wait until my day in court.*

It certainly seemed so.

"That's an interesting question . . . and, um . . . I . . . noted, when the district attorney was having his press conference, that the statement was made that their investigation"—and again, Sodomsky began to smirk and lean forward in an I-know-something-you-don't-know manner, before squinting his eyes—"is not over and has not concluded, which is a tad strange, when you consider that they've already made an *arrest!* . . ."

Any good lawyer worth his weight knew that an arrest was only the beginning; the real work came postarrest, when investigators reinterviewed witnesses, developed new sources, and began to put a legal case together.

Craig Stedman, Kelly Sekula, Keith Neff, Larry Martin, and all those involved in law enforcement knew, while listening to the press conference, it was going to be a war of words and accusations for a few weeks before they got down to brass tacks. The one thing Stedman was clear about was that he was not going to be running to Sodomsky with any deals. Residents of the county deserved better.

To Allan Sodomsky's credit, defense attorneys had no other alternative, truly, but to come out swinging. Sodomsky had started his press conference on a somber note, looking glum and withdrawn, talking about kids and family and poor Michael Roseboro being wrongly accused. But here he was—now halfway through—jumpy and smiling and raising his eyebrows as if to say that the DA's office was out of its mind with these charges.

Near the middle of the press conference, Sodomsky pulled out the probable cause affidavit—the Roseboro arrest document. He had a smile from cheek to cheek. He rocked side to side. "One of the things," he began, referring to a problem he had with the arresting document, turning to the page, reading from it, "is . . . um . . . that she 'was discovered beaten, strangled and drowned in her pool with no signs of forced entry, robbery or sexual assault.'" Here he stopped for a quick pause, smiled, leaned forward. "That is of note—because, as soon as the body was released to the family"—he stopped again, pinched his face, closed his eyes tightly—"it was noted that there was *approximately*," and here he slowed his tone down, speaking in drawn-out syllables and a deliberate inflection, as if speaking to people who did not understand the language, "forty thousand dollars of jewelry missing from Jan's person that she had on! Now, the police *knew* about that before Saturday night, August the second, when they arrested Mr. Roseboro. Yet the affidavit . . . continues to say that there are no signs of robbery!"

For the next eight or more minutes, Sodomsky took questions, many of which he would not answer, understandably so, based on his belief that he wasn't going to try his case in the court of public opinion. One statement he kept repeating was "Michael Roseboro did *not* kill his wife," adding that his team knew what happened that night, but he was not going to be talking about it until the appropriate time and place.

Closer to the end, a question about the jewelry raised Sodomsky's eyebrows somewhat: "So she was wearing them (the jewelry) around the pool?" the reporter wanted to know.

Sodomsky did not hesitate. "That is correct! And anybody who knows Jan knows that she wore them all the time."

"Have you inquired as to where they might be?"

Another one of those sideburn-to-sideburn smiles

from the overly confident lawyer as he said, "Well, we're doing the best we can. . . ."

"Did police ever see any of that stuff on her?"

More serious now, "I don't know that anybody was looking for it at the scene, all I know is what happened when the body was released."

Allan Sodomsky had explained that when a body is taken to the morgue, all of its personal effects go along. He said Jan Roseboro's jewelry should have been with her because she was wearing it that night. And it was clear that this was going to be one of many contentious issues a jury was going to have to make sense of.

"So . . . she was wearing that jewelry earlier that day?"

"I think you'll find that anybody who knows Jan knows she wore those things all the time." He paused. Gave his response some thought. Then: "But yes, Michael says it also. . . ."

He thanked everyone and ended the press conference.

57

To put it mildly, Angie Funk had been walking carefully through a thorny patch of her young life. Her man was in prison. She was pregnant with his baby. The affair and all those e-mails were about to become fodder for the media and Internet, destroying her integrity, calling into question her ethics. Her husband was still at home, supporting her. And yet, one could argue based on her behavior, Angie was still wrapped up in that dream Michael Roseboro had sold her.

Roseboro, on the other hand, realized quickly after being locked up that the pie in the sky he had wanted all along turned out to be miles too high. The guy, apparently, had believed that he could go on cheating on his wife forever, and there would never be a price to pay for it. Well, the father of four (and another on the way) with all the money and social status, the world at his fingertips, was now a number in a system, like every other prisoner around him.

In late August, Keith Neff and Larry Martin brought Angie into the DA's office so they could put on paper all she knew—and had told them over the course of the past few weeks. Craig Stedman and Kelly Sekula were there to advise and participate.

Angie was not happy about talking to the police. Her body language and awkward demeanor while answering questions told that story. She wanted this behind her. She wanted to walk away and believe none of it had ever happened.

The married (pregnant) mother talked about everything: her sex life with Roseboro, how and where they met, the "changes" Roseboro made for her (from rock music to country, a goatee, writing poetry), how often they communicated, how they were planning to get married, how Roseboro was going to leave his wife, and various other subjects the DA asked her about.

Because she understood the depth of her involvement, it seemed Angie was willing to open up. As the interview continued, with Stedman backing him up, Neff said, "There may be a new procedure involving obtaining your blood to test for DNA of your unborn child."

The DA's office needed to have positive proof that Michael Roseboro was the child's father. If they went to trial before the baby was born, the DA was going to have to have DNA. Stedman wanted Angie not to make this a big problem for them. They reiterated the fact that this new test had zero risk of hurting the child or Angie. It was unlike, say, the more popular amniocentesis, a prenatal test doctors used by utilizing an ultrasound as a guide to direct them toward a "safe location" in the pregnant woman's abdomen. Once that was located, a long needle was inserted into the amniotic sac to extract a sample of amniotic fluid through the needle, which could then be tested.

"I would give you consent," Angie said, "to do the test."

With the subject of the baby now out in the open, the interview centered on how Roseboro was feeling about the child. Had Angie talked to him before his arrest about the idea of being a father again.

Angie told them about the conversation she'd had with Michael when he brought up the idea of an abortion.

"Did you talk about the ramifications the pregnancy would have on him?" Neff asked.

"No," Angie said. "We never did."

"What do you think would have happened if Mike was never arrested?" The implication was made regarding the measure of their relationship, and where it would stand if Roseboro had never been suspected and/or arrested in the death of his wife. Would Angie and Roseboro, at some point, ride off into the sunset, as some of those e-mails suggested?

"There's no way I would want to live in *that* house," Angie said, speaking of the Roseboros' home on West Main.

"Have you given any thought to what might have happened to you, given what you now know about this situation?"

"I have thought about that," Angie answered. "It's scary. I would not want to be with someone who is capable of that."

"Have you talked to Mike about providing financial assistance for the unborn baby?" Neff asked.

She thought about it. "I do not plan on pursuing any financial help from him." Then she laid a bombshell on them. "Randy and I will raise this baby," Angie said. "I have no idea what the Roseboro family will do regarding the baby. I haven't even asked Michael if he is willing to admit that the baby is his! And I have *not* yet decided whose name will be on the birth certificate: Michael's or Randy's."

There was silence in the room. That was quite an answer.

Stedman asked Angie about the pool lights—if she could offer anything on that subject.

"I only heard about the lights after he was arrested. I never brought it up with Michael." She explained how he kept telling her that same story about waking up, going to the bathroom, etc.

Keith Neff had an innocence about him that spoke to his comforting nature and soft-spoken tone. He could get people to open up because, simply put, when you're in a room with Neff, he makes you feel like what you have to say is important and he is listening. This was no act on Neff's part. It wasn't some sort of cop veneer he had developed to get suspects and witnesses to talk. It is part of who Keith Neff is as a person. With that same likable pulse, Neff looked at Angie and said, "Do you think Mike did this?"

"I do not know," she answered. "I just *don't* know. In some ways, I don't want to think that he did this—I cannot wrap my brain around it. I feel bad for Jan and the kids. I feel worse for the kids because Jan is dead. Whoever did do this should be in jail for the rest of their life."

"Have you spoken to him lately?"

"Last time I talked with Michael was on August second. It was by phone. I have not spoken to him since his arrest."

Michael Roseboro had hired a private investigator. Stedman asked Angie what, if anything, she had told the guy, adding, "You aware that Mike is denying that he's had a relationship with you?"

"I gave all of the e-mails to the police," she said, meaning that's what she told the PI. "No. I was not aware that Michael is denying our relationship."

Investigators had shown Michael Roseboro's brother-in-law some of the e-mails he and Angie had exchanged, only because, when friends and family were interviewed, all had denied that Roseboro had been in a relationship with Angie. The denials were based on, of course, Roseboro's outcry that the story was being made up to make him look bad. Stedman and his team, in showing the e-mails to Roseboro's brother-in-law, wanted to prove, with Roseboro's own words, that he was a liar. He had been lying to everyone about nearly every aspect of the case and his actions leading up to Jan's murder. Roseboro's brother-in-law told investigators a few days afterward that he had confronted Roseboro with those same e-mails.

"He still denied the affair," Neff explained to Angie, after telling her the story.

"Well, Michael is a liar because an affair *did* take place." She was obviously upset by this betrayal. "I am not protecting Michael in *any* way. . . ."

"Is there anything you're worried about, regarding the investigation, or information that could be taken out of context?" Neff asked.

The insinuation was that perhaps Angie knew more than she was saying and might have played a role in the crime. It was not something the investigation had led them to believe; but they had to play devil's advocate, seeing that Roseboro and his team could perhaps be planning a strategy around this harebrained theory. The idea, if you're a prosecutor, is to ring every bell you can. Surprises will destroy you.

"I was *not* there!" Angie answered angrily. "There would be *no* evidence that I had *anything* to do with what happened to Jan."

They believed her. It was the same sort of reaction one might have expected from Roseboro when he was accused of the crime, but never came.

More than that, Angie had an alibi.

"Do you find it unusual that Mike did not talk to you about what happened to Jan, or the fact that law enforcement were looking at him?"

"He never told me anything. . . . But he did say that his attorney told him not to talk about it to anyone."

Back on the subject of the PI, Angie said she remembered telling the guy, "If Michael did this (murdered Jan), he needs to stop putting her and his kids through this." Then, for no apparent reason, Angie blurted out: "My life is hell because of Michael Roseboro!"

"Angela, I want to ask again," Neff said near the end of the interview—this after they had talked about some of the phone calls she and Michael had exchanged—"did Mr. Roseboro ever talk about a concern for his children, or did he ever mention that he hoped police would catch Jan's killer?"

"No, he never made mention of either—that he hoped the police would catch the killer, or . . . [showed] any concerns for his children's safety." She went on to say that not once did Michael talk about the police searching for Jan's "real" killer. Or show any anger that the police were accusing him. "There is a part of me that wants to think Michael would not do something like this," Angie added, "because it is *unthinkable*. . . . I want justice for Jan."

The interview began at 4:20 P.M. on August 21, 2008. By 5:20 P.M., the interview was over. Ultimately, Angie would be given a copy of the interview to read, and if she agreed with what she had said, she'd sign and date the document.

There was not one interview that she later reviewed on which Angie Funk did not sign off.

58

Craig Stedman had made it public that Michael Roseboro's motive for killing Jan was the affair he'd had and his obsession with Angie Funk, and the two worlds he kept separate were beginning to implode on each other. The outspoken DA was sure that Roseboro had murdered his wife after an argument erupted over this "latest" affair. *Latest,* of course, hinting at the fact that there were others—although no one in the media picked up on that little *wink-wink* immediately. According to various news reports about July 22, Angie had told investigators her lover had promised her he was going to "wait until after his children went to bed that night to tell his wife . . . he was having an affair and was leaving her." In the bench warrant detailing Michael Roseboro's arrest, however, the wording is a bit different: *Funk further stated that she received a phone call from Roseboro at approx. 8:45 P.M. on July 22, 2008, at which time Roseboro stated to Funk that he was going to leave his wife so that he could be with Funk.* There was no mention of Roseboro having said he was going to wait until the kids went to bed before confronting Jan with the end of their marriage.

With that theory now whirling about in public, Stedman looked to back it up with hard evidence. Two additional search warrants were served. One— the third—for the Roseboro house on West Main and the other for Microsoft Online Services. The house warrant was a simple search for any documentation in the form of Jan's will, financial records, and any life insurance papers in Jan Roseboro's and/or Michael Roseboro's name. The idea was to see if a second motive could be tacked on: if Michael had recently taken out a substantial life insurance policy on Jan. Investigators also wanted to see how much money was at stake in the marriage. How much did Michael stand to lose if he walked out on Jan? Maybe more important, how much did Jan stand to gain?

The Microsoft warrant was standard procedure— seeing that people live on their computers, BlackBerrys, mobile devices, and cell phones.

One of the next things on the agenda was to have someone monitor Michael's calls from prison: to sit in a room and listen to the recorded telephone calls he made—a job that would soon yield a few rather interesting discoveries.

A strange dynamic began to play out in the newspapers as Allan Sodomsky talked about Michael Roseboro's demeanor since his incarceration. "He is devastated," Sodomsky said at one point. "The loss of a wife of nineteen years, and now he is separated from his children. His world is all about his children. The sun sets and rises on his children."

As many in the community looked at this statement, and surely those who were close to Michael after Jan's death, it felt contrived and ignorant. During the eleven days that Michael Roseboro was investigated before his arrest, not one friend, distant relative, or close family member reported seeing him busted up over his wife's death, or worried about his children. To say that he was "devastated" was more than a stretch. A devastated man who has lost his wife would not communicate with his lover nearly two hundred times in eleven days after his wife's death.

On September 26, 2008, Michael was presented before Judge Nancy Hamill in courtroom number one, inside the Lancaster County Courthouse on North Duke Street, downtown Lancaster. He had the right to a preliminary hearing.

Craig Stedman was accompanied by Christopher Larsen, Kelly Sekula, and Andrew Gonzalez. Allan Sodomsky, of course, was there to represent Michael Roseboro.

The state brought in seven witnesses—Angela Funk among them. The state was under the burden of proof. Stedman needed to lay out his case with enough gusto to warrant a trial, but at the same time, not show all his cards. There was a fine line here. One of his worst fears was Angie, who had become, essentially, a wild card. By now, Angie had hired her own attorney (suggested by the defense). The relationship she had with the DA's office was tense, to put it mildly. She was pregnant, still in love with Roseboro, and had an incentive for him to be found not guilty: raising the child together and living out that fairy tale.

"I limited my questions to her," Stedman said, "to the absolute minimum. [But] we . . . had to use her to build a circumstantial case."

Stedman's hope was that by the time of trial, Angie's testimony would be far less important. They were working diligently to establish motive without her, building a circumstantial case with hard evidence and other witnesses.

* * *

Confidence in a courtroom is not something you learn in law school; it is an attribute that comes from facing murderers, rapists, and standing two feet away from a guy who liked to touch kids and having the nerve not to allow emotion to control what you need to do to put a scumbag like that away for as long as you can.

Craig Stedman had developed his craft over the years. As a prosecutor, he had never lost a murder trial. Even better, he had always been able to obtain the verdict he sought, without settling for a lesser degree. He had worked on over one hundred homicide cases in various capacities, and still managed to hold on to what is a humble deportment, always quick to point out the obvious: "I must emphasize that any conviction is the result of a team effort with law enforcement, our victim and witness advocates, the secretarial staff here (inside the LCDA's Office), and certainly not just due to me."

The DA continues to sport a marathon runner's body. His style is rather laid-back and conversational when speaking with reporters and those people he encounters throughout his day; but inside a courtroom, standing or sitting in front of a judge, Stedman is all business. He knows what it takes to prosecute and win: guts, grit, integrity to the truth.

His problem in going after Roseboro was that his opponent, Allan Sodomsky, was every bit the trial lawyer he had become, if not more seasoned and schooled in knowing the ins and outs of a courtroom. It was going to be a battle. No two ways about it.

The preliminary hearing the first round.

* * *

At the end of this first day, Craig Stedman and the state came out winners. There was enough evidence to send Michael Roseboro to face a jury of his peers. There were no dramatics or showboating in the courtroom: simple facts presented in a way that spoke to Roseboro's guilt. And in truth, the odds of the case *not* going forward to trial were about the same as Roseboro's intruder theory holding water.

A gazillion to one.

This was not a time to high-five one another and jump for joy inside the LCDA's Office, however. There would be no champagne moments of victory, laughs, or celebration. Stedman was facing trial, which could come as early as the spring or summer of 2009—and he had no forensic evidence.

Allan Sodomsky had said already that the state's prosecution was seriously flawed. "You can't build a case on guesswork," the slick attorney told one reporter, "conjecture and suspicion. . . . And that's all the prosecution has."

Smoke and mirrors.

There was some truth in the statement. Juries want that flashy, *CSI*-on-CBS-inspired, forensic evidence. The type of stuff that will blow their minds and give their conscience the authority and comfort to vote a definite yes required for a conviction. They want science on top of circumstantial evidence. They want DNA. They want experts to explain swabs of this, swabs of that, fibers found here, fibers uncovered there. They want computer graphics akin to *Star Trek*. They want theatrics.

Yet, as of this moment in time, two months after Jan's death, although he could claim victory for the time being, DA Craig Stedman didn't have any forensic/DNA evidence other than a (hopeful) positive result on the test for the child Angie was carrying, a test that had not been completed.

Beyond all that, the DA's office had to hurry: Craig Stedman was concerned that Angie Funk was going to give the baby up and they'd never get a chance to test paternity. Then they'd never be able to prove the baby was Michael Roseboro's.

BOOK FOUR

WHERE I'M CALLING FROM

59

The suggestion that Jan Roseboro had an affair five months before her death was something Michael felt the need to bullhorn from his concrete-walled, steel-barred prison cell as autumn moved into Lancaster County. It was late October, eleven days before Halloween. A time for pumpkin patch rides. Thriller houses. Fairs. Squash. Mums. Purple, orange, red, yellow, and brown leaves falling from trees like drifting kites. Crisp, cool air. And the comforting feeling—for some—that the holiday season was just around the corner, a new year now in sight.

Francis and Karen Tobias had known Jan and Mike Roseboro for about six years. Their boys went to school together and played lacrosse on the same team. The Tobias family lived about a quarter mile down the road from the Roseboros. Francis, who had coached lacrosse with Michael, had stopped by the house during the construction project almost every day, he later said, to check on things, where he frequently saw Jan always doing *something*. Many later called Francis and Michael best friends—and perhaps they were.

Karen saw Jan on the Sunday before she was murdered. It was a normal get-together. They had taken up yoga together and worked out on Sundays. It was Jan's friend Rebecca Donahue who called Karen early in the morning on July 23 and told her that Jan had been found dead. Karen and Francis went to pick up their children, who were staying at a friend's house, then drove straight to the Roseboro home.

With the preliminary hearing behind him and the media frenzy surrounding Roseboro's arrest and upcoming trial now a memory, during the third week of October, Francis and Karen received a letter from Michael. They had written to him in prison many weeks before, but they had not received a response—that is, until now.

In opening his missive, Roseboro apologized for not writing sooner, citing for an excuse that ". . . between eating and sleeping . . ." life for him on the inside was "really busy."

Next, he said he was just being sarcastic. It was "depressing" in prison, he added, without his "daily doses" of Sam and the other children.

Go figure. The guy was facing the rest of his life in prison for murdering his wife and he found it within himself to have a sense of humor.

Roseboro had lost twenty-five pounds, he explained, a consequence of his new life that was "on the bright side," all considering. He had not smoked in three months. Another plus! He said he was constantly thinking about everyone—"the gang," he called them. For the first time in any type of documentation connected to his case, Roseboro brought up God, saying that the Lord "would see" him through it all and "I'll be home. . . ."

He was writing, Roseboro said, mainly because he felt the need to "clarify some things." (Damage control, in other words.) It was important, he added, that Karen and Francis pass along to the rest of "the gang" what he

had to say next. It was time everyone knew the truth.
Friends deserved as much.

Michael claimed he and Jan had endured a marriage
"with its ups and downs. . . ." Like any long-term union,
he said, he and Jan had fought and made up and weath-
ered the storms of being in each other's face every day
for two decades. Theirs was the typical marriage, Roseboro seemed to force on Francis and Karen. And they
might have bought that.

But then came the actual reason behind the letter.

Jan had confided to him in March 2008, Roseboro
said, that "she had an affair [that] November through
February." Michael blamed himself for Jan's affair,
saying he wasn't home much between working on the
house, sitting with Grandpa Louie, on his deathbed,
every night, and holding down the family business.
Roseboro never mentioned, of course, that he was also
running around the county, having sex with Angie Funk
whenever he could, or spending a majority of his time
calling, texting, and e-mailing her.

He left that out.

Quite strikingly, he said that as he and Jan talked
through *her* affair, they decided the best thing to do was
to "end the marriage." Michael insisted that he'd talked
it over with Jan and "convinced her" to wait until their
youngest graduated high school.

And guess what? She agreed!

How 'bout that? *The chances.*

There was that little question of the Outer Banks trip
that Michael Roseboro needed to cover, if convincing his
friends that Jan had instigated adultery, not him. Responding to that, Roseboro said he went ahead with his
plans for renewing their vows because he wouldn't give up
on nineteen years of their lives together. He was going to
fight for his marriage the same way he would fight for
anything else in life he deemed worthy. Regardless of
what Jan had wanted.

It was near the end of May, Roseboro wrote, that he met *this girl, Angie . . . and one thing led to another.* He *let things get out of hand.* His emotions took over from there. He must have assumed those e-mails he wrote would never surface, because next he wrote: *But I had every intention of ending things with Angie . . .* and working *things out with Jan.* He added, perhaps for effect, that his biggest regret was never having the opportunity to apologize to Jan. That "pain and remorse" would be with him, he maintained, for the rest of his life. He asked for forgiveness from his friends, scolding himself for not telling "the gang" about the affair with Angie before the newspapers made it public. He said he loved all of them like brothers and sisters. Speaking specifically about Jan, he wrote, *I miss her so badly. . . .* He added how he couldn't wrap his mind around the notion that *anyone would want to hurt her.* He thanked everyone for their friendship and belief in him. Facing each new day, he added, would not be possible without knowing they were all back home rallying behind him. He wanted Francis and Karen to pass along his thanks to all of those who were at the preliminary hearing, ending with a pledge of sincerity: *I love you all.*

The end result of the letter, or, rather, what Roseboro suggested in his choice of words and phrases, felt as if he was asking his friends to tell everyone they knew Jan had been cheating on *him* for six months before her murder. Jan was the instigator here, Roseboro seemed to suggest. He had gone out and had an affair himself with this Angie person (as he made her sound), only because he was vulnerable and Jan had done it first.

Tit for tat, apparently.

Perhaps he believed no one in his circle of friends knew about all those other women.

"One thing led to another. . . ."

The idea that Jan was having an affair struck Karen and Francis Tobias as a bit overwhelming, if not extraordinary.

It was, for one, impossible to believe, based simply on opportunity alone. Not that Jan was a saint by any means, but she just didn't have that type of unfaithful bone in her body. Jan valued the sanctity of marriage, regardless of how she was being treated. Two wrongs, in Jan's world, never equalized the playing field. Beyond that, Francis Tobias said later in court, "Jan was accountable."

Great point.

"She was a stay-at-home mom," Francis continued, "four kids, different ages, two boys, two girls. They were all involved in a number of activities. She was involved in all of them! She was always with the kids and even volunteered for a lot of activities. She was involved with the church. She had a close relationship with her sister. I know they saw each other all the time. I just cannot believe that, rationally, she would have the *time* and, personally, as I knew Jan, I don't think she could *ever* do that to her kids."

As they thought the entire Jan and Mike Roseboro situation through, Francis and Karen Tobias had to see straight through what was, in essence, a full-blown cock-and-bull story Roseboro was trying to pass off on them. Thinking back to those days after the murder, when they were with Michael, consoling him during what they assumed was the most trying time of his life, what these good people knew now was that even after the ECTPD had instructed Roseboro that his wife had been murdered, he was still telling everyone—"the gang"—it was an accident. Not one of Michael Roseboro's posse would later report that he talked about Jan being murdered. Or was sickened by it. And yet on top of all his nonsense, everyone was now supposed to swallow the notion that Jan had had an affair?

On face value, what Roseboro implied was ludicrous.

What's more, the timing of the letter—October 20, 2008—was viably suspect. Roseboro's preliminary hearing had been only three weeks before (he had held off, in fact, in responding to the letter Francis and Karen had sent, possibly to put a bit of time between him and the facts the hearing had made public). He could no longer deny to anyone that he'd had an affair with Angie, because she had testified to it. He had to play catch-up, so to speak. Backpedal. He needed to put a shine on his terribly tarnished reputation and get all those people back on his side.

Even if you don't want to believe this, and make the claim that this letter was a mere coincidence, you'd still have to ask yourself one *central* question: Why was there no mention by Michael Roseboro to the police at *anytime* of Jan and this alleged affair? He had never said a word about it to anyone before now. One would think this would have been the first statement out of Michael's mouth after learning that his wife had been brutally murdered: *Her angry lover did it!*

The notion that Roseboro was trash-talking his wife from prison was offensive to many who would soon learn about this letter.

"You give no name (of her supposed lover) and you just throw this out there, from nowhere," Keith Neff observed, speaking about the alleged affair Jan had. "It never comes up *before* this letter. There's no evidence of it—we had spoken to all of her friends. On her phone records, we had identified every single number she had ever called between the end of 2007 and the beginning of 2008. There's nothing there. Just one more lie—like the jewelry. 'Drowning's not working, um . . . let's try stolen jewelry. That's not working, okay. . . . Let's toss out there that she's had an affair.'"

Pathetic.

All it did was make Michael Roseboro look guiltier.

60

Tubes of "venous blood" were drawn from Michael Roseboro by court order on November 20, 2008, as Detective Kerry Sweigart looked on. When medic Ross Deck finished, Sweigart watched as the six tubes, 9cc's each, were packaged, sealed, and handed over to Brett Vallicello, a worker for Ravgen Diagnostics. Testing by Ravgen would be completed that same day.

The affidavit accompanying the order revealed the additional evidence the state had uncovered as Thanksgiving 2008 came to pass in Lancaster County. For one, that search warrant for the Roseboro home back on August 2 yielded an important discovery. A walk through the home proved that the only way to turn on or off the dusk-to-dawn light (without simulating darkness) on the small garage outside by the pool was to shut the breaker off downstairs in the basement of the Roseboro home, or unplug the actual light from inside the garage. The point was: would an intruder go to this length, or even know how or where to do it?

That it is reasonable to believe, the affidavit stated, *that Michael Roseboro would be significantly more familiar with the location of the circuit breaker and plug for the dusk-to-dawn light at the residence than other persons.*

Quite true. The guy had overseen just about every detail of the new construction project. He damn well knew where the circuit breaker unit was, because most likely, he had chosen to put it there.

Back on September 5, Larry Martin and Keith Neff interviewed Angie Funk once again. She had *stated that the pregnancy was confirmed through her doctor,* that same affidavit stipulated. The due date given to Angie by her doctor was April 1, 2009. Angie was slated to have Michael Roseboro's illegitimate baby on April Fool's Day.

How appropriate, considering the case Roseboro was trying to build for himself.

Craig Stedman and his staff had one of his investigators consult with Dr. Ravinder Dhallan, of Columbia, Maryland. Dr. Dhallan, a fetal DNA† research expert, who had conducted some groundbreaking work on new ways of testing for birth defects in unborn babies, had told the LCDA's Office about a new test that could determine prenatal paternity as early as five weeks into the pregnancy. Ravgen Diagnostics, a company of which Dr. Dhallan was chairman and CEO, had developed prenatal testing methods that were far less invasive to pregnant mothers and unborn children. Dhallan was well respected and well regarded in his field for his work and research.

Prenatal paternity can be determined because the fetal DNA is present in the plasma of the mother's blood, the affidavit said. Therefore, if investigators retrieved a sample of

---

† They were talking about molecular deoxyribonucleic acid (DNA) in this case: the "blueprint for life." That twisted ladder-like strand of cells that codes everything we are: hair color, height, metabolism. Half of this type of DNA comes from our mother, the other half from our father, which is the reason why each one of us is different. From a scientific standpoint, the best DNA sample for testing comes from one main source, body fluids—including, of course, skin cells.

Angie's blood, the doctor could build a DNA profile of the unborn baby from it. "A sample of blood from the mother and a sample of blood from the [suspected] father can definitely establish or exclude paternity through identifying the sites in the fetal DNA which differ from the mother's DNA but will match the father's DNA," the doctor told investigators.

The best thing about the test turned out to be that it "posed no threat to the fetus," and certainly no threat beyond a common needle stick to the mother or suspected father.

Angie had given blood on the same day as Michael, at Lancaster General Women & Babies Hospital, in front of Detective Sweigart. She didn't look happy about it, but she was there, nonetheless, arm tied in a tourniquet, fist balled up, head turned, offering her DNA.

It was eventually confirmed positively that the child Angie Funk was carrying, now four months into her pregnancy, was Michael Roseboro's baby boy. There was no way Roseboro could deny an affair with Angie.

Science had backed up her claim.

When that bank surveillance tape came in and Keith Neff and the team had a look at it, they were confident that Michael Roseboro's story of Jan wearing $40,000 worth of jewelry was one more piece of manure in what was a growing pile. The video was grainy and a bit out of focus, but there was no doubt about it: there was Jan walking into the Fulton Bank, wearing the same exact sweatshirt she would soon be found dead in.

Neff and his colleagues spent a considerable amount of time looking at and studying the video, pulling out frames (snapshots) to show the jury.

"Clearly," Neff explained, "she is *not* wearing any jewelry."

Not even an everyday gold bracelet.

Nothing.

Instead, Jan Roseboro looked like she was ready for the gym, not, per se, a night walking the red carpet, wearing $40,000 worth of diamonds and gold, which would have made her stand out on that bank video.

"So the assumption is," Neff added, "at least what *they* say—this woman runs errands, hangs out at her pool in the same sweatshirt and clothes, but puts on *forty thousand* dollars' worth of jewelry to go be with the family? It's absurd."

Furthermore, the coroner never found any tear marks on Jan's ears, where someone might have grabbed and ripped earrings from her person. That, or abrasions on her wrists or neck, where an intruder might have done the same.

"She had plenty of trauma," Neff said, "but no visible marks from, like, jewelry being torn off."

The investigation was in a stage of transition: interviews on top of interviews were the main source of information flooding into the ECTPD and the LCDA's Office as the winter of 2008 and 2009 passed. The Roseboro family knew a lot of people. Any one of them had the potential to supply delicate and important information about Jan and Michael's marriage, the ebb and flow of the Roseboros' life, and, of course, their secrets. More than that, who Michael Roseboro was as a father and husband might also come from a careful look into his background. Friends, too, could offer different ideas and insight.

As Keith Neff and Jan Walters spoke to family, friends, more neighbors, and people from Jan and Michael's past, part of their focus was to put out the flame on the intruder theory. It sounded ridiculous, sure. But as a cop, you had better make sure that it wasn't true, or a good defense team would use that lack of investigative experience against you.

How?

The lights, for one. Law enforcement had several witnesses now saying it was pitch black out there all night long.

Only Michael Roseboro had said the lights were on.

"So the intruder turned the lights *on* to make his *escape*?" Keith Neff said, a bit of sarcasm in his inflection.

Part of the puzzle was to get an understanding of the land layout around the Roseboros' property. Richard Pope, the Roseboros' neighbor and tenant, provided the best information to thwart any attempt that might be made regarding an intruder coming from the woods behind the house and sneaking up on Jan Roseboro.

Richard was a good witness. Straitlaced father and husband, hardworking blue-collar guy (pipe layer), who had no beef with the Roseboro family, and actually thought highly of them (Michael, specifically) before July 22.

Regarding the entire stranger theory, Richard had a tough time with it. He lived next door and was often outside at night and early evening, smoking, doing things in the garage, playing with his kid, hanging out with his wife. He also knew most everyone in the neighborhood. A stranger would have stood out like buttons on a snowman. Then there was the presence of Jan's dogs—all the barking and yelping they did.

Richard said the dogs were *always* outside, whenever Jan was. Except on that night. Someone had put the dogs in the basement of the house.

To Richard, that was strange.

But it was the property, he explained, more than anything, that did not present itself as the ideal environment for a potential intruder.

"I would go out in back there," Richard said, "and hit golf balls into the woods. There's pricker bushes and swampland and just real rough shrubbery all along the back of the lot. There's no way anybody could get through it."

Briars, Richard noted, "and, actually, all through[out] . . . it's woods. . . . So just walking through there, you know, walking through the area (surrounding the Roseboro home on two sides), you cannot really get much through these woods. . . . It's pretty much tangled."

There were also two wire fences. "It's just a mess of thorns and bushes and"—he laughed—"hundreds of golf balls, probably."

You'd have to be Rambo. And still, it would be almost impossible.

Where Michael Roseboro, the person, was concerned, Richard was impartial. "Mike never showed me who he was," Richard said. When the house was being remodeled, Michael was there every day, walking the site, picking up garbage, pointing out things to contractors, and checking over his investment. "Everybody in town spoke well about Mike. He was well respected."

The idea that Roseboro was the town mortician didn't creep people out. "He was just that guy in the dark suit who had a family and was working hard to take care of them and get an addition put on his house," Richard remarked.

At least that's what people saw. The suburban mask. The person Michael Roseboro wanted you to see. But there was another side to the man.

"I never saw him smoke before he started with that addition," Richard added. "I'd see him drinking beer and smoking while they worked on the house. I never saw that before. He seemed like he needed to get that addition done as fast as possible."

Like there was something driving him.

A strange addition it is, many who have walked through the house have said. There are sections you cannot get into without walking outside first and then entering from another door. The entire house is not connected via inside hallways and doors. Even the basement is hard to get into without leaving the main house and walking down into it through a separate doorway. You would definitely have to know where you were going to get anywhere in the house. There is no natural flow, like most contemporary homes.

"Yeah," Michael Evanick, Richard's father-in-law, observed, "you'd never get your money back on that house. I don't think they really cared about resale value."

It was, many agreed, as if the addition had been custom built for Michael Roseboro alone.

61

With so many pieces of evidence, "to do" lists on top of "to do" lists written by the DA, along with hundreds of interviews, you are bound as an investigator to send things out for testing to the lab and forget about them. That said, you have confidence in your colleagues to follow through and let you know when the results from a vital piece of forensic evidence are available. This was why Detective Larry Martin became so important to the Roseboro investigation: Martin choreographed the investigation from the ECTPD's standpoint; he made sure no one retraced anyone else's steps, and kept investigators focused on the different aspects of the case they needed to complete.

After what seemed like a long holiday break—investigators still knocking on doors and working the case 24/7 through Christmas and New Year's—the Pennsylvania State Police (PSP) Bureau of Forensic Services, its Harrisburg laboratory, called Keith Neff. It was February 12. The Harrisburg lab was what you'd call a prescreening facility: evidence is sent to Harrisburg from all around the state to see if there is any reason to pass it along to the lab in Greensburg, which conducted more thorough and detailed DNA testing to confirm initial results.

"It's possible that there's some DNA (blood, skin) under Mrs. Roseboro's fingernails," the scientist told Neff.

Nails? DNA? Neff didn't want to jump out of his chair, just yet. These results were, the scientist made clear, preliminary. The possibility, she said, that DNA existed was there, but it would be Greensburg's call whose DNA it was.

"I did not want to get too excited and be let down," Neff said later.

Back during the week when Jan Roseboro was murdered, the pathologist had scraped her fingernails and sent those scrapings to the lab for microscopic study and DNA testing. The lab was now responding to that test.

The theory was that the scratches on Michael Roseboro's face caused a buildup of his skin to form underneath Jan's fingernails. The pathologist was certain that any DNA underneath the nails would have come from a vigorous scratch; it wouldn't have come from superficial scratching or common touching (the chlorine in the water would have washed that type of DNA away). Any DNA still there after Jan had been in that water for an extended period of time would have come from violent or aggressive scratching.

It was going to take some time, the scientist said, for Greensburg to determine the veracity of the tests.

Sit tight, we still have one more hurdle here to jump.

This was a major breakthrough, Neff considered. It looked like they had a match. If that was the case, Michael Roseboro wouldn't be measured as one of a few, or put into a group with what could be ten additional donors. DNA was fail-safe. If they got a hit in Greensburg, it was Roseboro's DNA underneath Jan's fingernails.

Exactly what they needed to bring their case home.

When Greensburg came back with its results, one of the forensic scientists called Neff.

From what Neff could understand, although he said the dynamics of what she had to say were "crazy complicated," the results were positive. That's what Neff heard.

Yes, that was Michael Roseboro's skin underneath Jan's fingernails.

It's a match.

Still, Neff was confused. Larry Martin, who understood DNA perhaps better than your average cop, because his son has a genetic defect, was standing by Neff as he took the call.

"Talk to her, Lar," Neff said, handing his boss the phone. "I think it's good news, but I'm . . . I'm having a hard time, and just not sure."

Neff stood and looked on, watching Martin shake his head yes and ask pertinent questions.

Finished with the call, Martin had a smile on his face.

"Yes," he said. "We got a match!"

"What!"

"Call Craig and Kelly and let them know."

Still, there was work to do. Neff said the next step was to take that evidence to National Medical Services (NMS). NMS has been in business for more than thirty-five years. According to its profile, the lab, well known throughout the medical community, *has been setting the standard for excellence in clinical toxicology and forensic testing—responding to the needs of healthcare providers . . . and other medical researchers, reference labs, hospitals, and the criminal justice system with state-of-the-art tests that other labs don't or can't provide.*

A hired gun, some might call NMS. Yet NMS's reputation is stellar. The work the lab does is some of the most high-tech DNA testing available. Its record is untarnished. You want clean results—either positive or negative (NMS has no stake in the results)—without any muddiness and suspicion of tainting or unreliability, you call on NMS.

"They can do some serious testing," Neff explained, "like linking DNA to a family line."

He's talking about a Y chromosome test. Whereas most DNA tests might come in at, say, 1 in 250 million, 1 in 1 billion, NMS can say, *No, it* had *to come from this family line of donors.* They can exclude everyone else in the world from a sample, but the donor.

"Fresh scratches on Mike's face, his DNA under Jan's nails," Neff said. "Come on, all these little pieces were beginning to line up."

Jan and Michael wrestled. Jan scratched him, perhaps knowing that DNA underneath her nails would convict the guy, had she died.

There was no doubt about it in Neff's mind: Jan had fought for her life, scratching her husband in the face with that hand of hers that had only three fingernails and a thumbnail.

What's more, there was no question about the source of the DNA, which meant that Angie Funk could be completely excluded as a donor.

62

It was near two-thirty in the morning on March 27, 2009. ". . . I think it's time," Angie Funk said over the phone.

Angie's friend was half asleep when she picked up. It was so early in the morning. "Are you kidding?"

"No," Angie said sarcastically, "this is a test run!"

Angie's friend arrived at the house moments later, packed Angie up, and drove her to the hospital.

For support, seeing that Randall Funk obviously wanted no part of this special moment, Angie's mother met her at the hospital. Throughout the early morning, the labor progressed "a little bit." But by one-thirty that afternoon, after "being on Pitocin for maybe ten minutes," Angie said later, "I pushed for three minutes, and it was over."

There he was, a healthy boy, whom Angie promptly named Matthew Francis Alan Rudy. "It didn't take him long," she said later. ". . . It was a nice time. It really was. I was glad that my mom got to see a grandchild born. She's never seen that. . . . It was a very easy labor."

The name Francis was given to Matthew in honor of Francis Tobias, Roseboro's "best friend"; Alan after Michael Roseboro's middle name; Rudy is Angie's maiden name; and Matthew ("a gift from God") was chosen from the Bible.

Not long after the baby was born—two hours, to be exact—a few cc's of blood were drawn from him in front of Detective Larry Martin so they could complete the paternity test full circle. In response to this, to Martin's surprise, Angie was "pleasant," courteous, and more than willing to help any way she could.

As Angie recuperated from her delivery, bonding with her newborn, the dad was in Lancaster County Prison awaiting word on when his trial was going to commence. Michael was becoming antsy and impatient. He wanted out of jail. He had been locked up now for almost eight months and would have to settle for photographs of a child he could not hold, smell, touch, or play with. Word from Allan Sodomsky of what the boy looked like would have to suffice for the moment. Roseboro had called Angie repeatedly from prison. She had picked up the phone once. He heard her answer: "Hello? Hello?" She could not hear him and hung up. At the time, unless you had an account set up with the prison calling system, and had reserve funds in that account, you could not accept calls from an inmate. But then a few weeks after the baby was born, the prison changed its policy. So Roseboro, providing he had money in his commissary account to cover the call, could call anyone on his list.

At some point after the baby was born, the LCDA's Office received a "tip" from someone that Angie and Michael were communicating via their attorneys. Craig Stedman phoned Angie's attorney and asked her about it.

"Letters . . . ," she admitted. Wasn't many. Just one time.

Apparently, according to a stipulation (Roseboro later signed) that outlined the breach of policy, a *member or members* of Allan Sodomsky's law firm had *surreptitiously passed letters between Angela Funk and Michael*

Roseboro during legal visits with Roseboro at the Lancaster County Prison. Someone from Sodomsky's office had taken a letter (or letters) from Michael written to Angie and handed them off to her attorney, who subsequently called Angie and read the letters to her over the phone.

Like so many things that happened between Angie and Michael, Angie had a hard time recalling the content of the letters, when asked about them later. She couldn't even remember if there were "two or three," she said in court. The substance, she added, "mostly was, he didn't do it, and it was basically about my son. That was basically it."

"He didn't do it."

Michael Roseboro had wanted to clarify his innocence with Angie.

Angie sent a response back to Michael through her attorney. A note, she called it, along with a photograph of their son, Matthew.

Please don't call me anymore was all that was in the brief missive, she claimed. *I don't think it's a good idea.*

It wouldn't look good, the two of them communicating. When asked why she thought this, Angie failed to come up with a reason beyond, "I mean, it could hurt me. It could hurt him. It could hurt everybody. I just didn't think it was a good idea. . . . I mean, I am assuming he was told he wasn't supposed to call me, so I just didn't think it was a good idea. I don't know. I cannot really give you a good reason. I just didn't think it was a good idea."

This sort of note passing between inmates and their lovers happens all too often—and granted, both parties think no harm can come in exchanging a few letters that they know will remain private. But prison policy specifies that prison officials have a right to intercede—and read Michael Roseboro's mail, as they did any other inmate's—looking for threats, escape plans, and additional criminal activity.

"Obviously," Craig Stedman said later, "the main concern for us was that Angie was being told what to say (and perhaps not to say) by the defendant."

Michael Roseboro was a manipulator. There was a homicide trial forthcoming. The things Michael told potential witnesses could be important to the prosecution and have an impact on its case. Passing letters was not only in violation of prison policy (which runs on an honor code between the warden and defense attorneys coming in to speak with clients), but could be detrimental to the outcome of the trial.

Which was maybe exactly what Michael Roseboro had intended.

63

It was April 14, 2009, just about two-thirty in the afternoon, not a month after Angie Funk had given birth to Matthew. Falling back into his obsessive nature, Michael Roseboro had made forty-five "attempts" to call Angie since he'd been incarcerated. Each had been met with a dial tone.

Today, however, Michael had solved his communications problems.

"Hey!" Roseboro said. He sounded excited.[‡]

"Hey!" Angie answered, laughing nervously. The call had taken her, Angie said later, "totally off . . . guard."

"Oh, my God, it's good to hear your voice," Roseboro said. There were noises (yelling) echoing in the background. Some shuffling around. Roseboro was calling Angie from prison, but it sounded like a gymnasium.

"It's good to hear yours, too," she said. Angie had an anxious giddiness in her tone. There was a subtle sarcasm in her voice that seemed to say it was her duty to accept the call, not that her heart was into it.

"Ah, how you doin,' baby?" Roseboro said next.

[‡]You can go online and hear these calls. Conduct a simple search on any reputable search engine.

"I'm doing good. How 'bout you?"

"I've been a lot better. But it's a lot better now."

"Good. Good."

"How's everything goin'?"

"It's goin' all right. It's tough, but it's goin' okay." Seemed like Angie didn't know what to say. They knew the conversation was being recorded.

"How's Matthew doin'?"

"He's doin' wonderful. He's a great baby."

"I can't believe you didn't name him 'Zebulon,'" Roseboro said, then let out a breathy laugh.

That comment sparked an animated giggle from Angie. "Really?"

"I'm serious!"

Laughing loudly now, she answered, "No. . . ."

Zebulon was a name they had clearly talked or joked about at some point.

"Aw, come on," Roseboro said, "he was one of the strongest tribes of Israel."

"Yeah . . . but, you know . . ."

"I'm teasin' with you," Roseboro admitted, talking over Angie's laughter. "I like the name, but 'Matthew' is much better."

Avoiding what mattered in the arena of their relationship seemed to dominate the first minute of the conversation. Listening to this banter and laughter between them, you'd never know one was facing a murder rap, and the other had just given birth to his love child and was about to become the center of a scandalous, high-profile homicide trial. They had this bond between them now that would be there forever. There was no way for Angie of breaking completely away. She was tied to this man now by the hip, which was—some sources claimed—what she had wanted from day one.

After they discussed the child's name, Roseboro said, "I wish I could have been there."

"My mom was there," Angie said. She sounded comforted by the thought.

"Was she?"

"Yeah."

"How's your family doing with everything?" Roseboro asked, finally getting into the context of the storm swirling around them.

"Um . . . ," Angie said slowly, thinking about her answer, "they're handling it. Um, um, it's not necessarily all with what happened. It's—it's what people are saying about me and stuff. So—"

"I know," Roseboro chimed in, cutting her off.

"Yeah, so. I hope to *God* you don't believe a lot of that stuff that's said."

"I feel the same way."

"There are some really awful people out there."

"I know . . . and I know what Allan's been telling me what Stedman's been feeding you," Roseboro said. "And it's just, I don't—I don't believe anything I have heard, so it's just . . ." Roseboro stopped himself, took a deep breath.

This comment was puzzling to the LCDA's Office when they later sat and listened to the recording. At the time of the call, the ECTPD and Stedman's office had no substantive contact with Angie, and hadn't for months. In fact, they had limited contact with Angie after the preliminary hearing; and all of those meetings took place with Angie's attorney present. Why was Roseboro suggesting that they were "feeding" Angie anything, when they weren't even talking to her?

Angie made no comment on the subject, but picked up the dialogue along the same lines, saying, "Well, you know, it's people who's claiming that . . . well, it's people that's—quote, unquote—*family,* that I really don't even know that somehow just turned really ugly."

"I know."

Angie was perhaps referring to two locally run Internet

sites that had been publishing some not so nice things about her, on top of a few rumors and speculative pieces of information, supplied by, Angie insinuated, a family member or two. Beyond the sometimes disparaging content on the sites (in fact, some of the reporting turned out later to be accurate), it was the comments that browsers were leaving, calling Angie any number of insulting and gross indignities. Readers could leave any type of comments they chose, sometimes defaming Angie's character and reputation without explanation or proof. It exposed one of the problems of the Internet: there's no buffer zone, no editor, no legal read (vetting), before things are slapped up on a site for the world to read. Angie had her lawyer send a letter to one of the sites and an e-mail to the other—and the letter and e-mail, of course, were promptly published in their entirety online. Part of the letter said that the site had *been spreading untrue and malicious information both verbally and over the Internet about* Angie. And if the "activity" wasn't immediately stopped, *legal action may be taken against you.*

It continued, however.

"Well, I gave them a good reason to hate me, though," Angie said to Roseboro, talking about that "family member" who had turned on her and the malicious things being spread via the Internet, "because I had my attorney . . . telling them to shut up."

Roseboro changed the subject and asked Angie about her girls.

"The girls absolutely love him," she said of baby Matthew.

"Good."

She said she had given her lawyer some photographs for Roseboro to see, adding that the child was a "spitting image" of his father.

They chitchatted some more about how good it was to hear each other's voices; and how Roseboro was able to call her now without any complications from the phone company or prison, finishing one statement with a question, "Is it a problem if I call you?"

"No," Angie said, "but you know it's recorded, and I don't want anybody to—"

"Oh, no. . . ."

"You know?"

"No. I understand."

"But I don't want them to," Angie said, and it sounded as though she meant it, "you know, have anything."

"Oh, no. . . ."

Roseboro talked again about how he wished he could have been there for the birth. To which, Angie started to say, "I wish you could have, too. . . ."

Then Roseboro said, "I just don't want you to give up on us." Over the loudspeaker in the background, a guard gave instructions or called out to someone. It was loud and overpowering.

"Don't be what?" Angie asked, maybe startled by this statement, confused by it, or unable to hear it.

"I don't want you to give up on us."

"Oh! I haven't." It came out sounding nonplussed.

"Because I won't." It seemed that Roseboro's voice had changed. He sounded serious.

"Good . . . ," Angie said.

"Because I totally plan on being out of here in August."

To this, Angie laughed at first; then, "Let's hope so."

August was about the time his trial would be over. It was slated to begin in July.

"I know."

"Let's hope so" was about all Angie could say.

Roseboro explained that his lawyer always made him feel good about himself and his chances for acquittal, adding that his attorney's assistant had been there for him. She's an "expert on jury selection," Roseboro bragged.

This gave Angie an avenue to talk about her attorney and how she had become more of a friend than someone she had simply hired.

They discussed how relieved Roseboro was to hear that Angie had lawyered-up. She said she didn't want to get one, but, "um, but it got to the point where every time I left there (the DA's office), I felt like they were accusing me more and more. I just got tired of it." There was not one piece of documentation available to back up Angie on this point. The ECTPD, if she was referring to its investigators, or the LCDA's Office, had definitely put her under close scrutiny during the early part of the investigation, but had not once pointed a finger in her face and made a direct accusation against her.

Roseboro said "they" had just come for more of his blood.

"Yeah, I know," Angie responded. "They took another blood test from him, too. I was furious! Two hours after he was born, they were in the hospital. It infuriated me."

Regarding that moment when blood was taken from the child, Detective Larry Martin, who was there, said, "Angie was pleasant when the warrant was served. I found that curious, considering she told Mike on the prison phone call that she was furious about the warrant being served."

Conflicting stories from the same mouth.

". . . I'm so proud of you," Roseboro said, "for the way you're handling things. I mean, I'm getting everything from [my attorney]. He always keeps me informed. I am so proud of you and the way you're handling yourself."

Makes you wonder if Roseboro would have patted Angie on the head while saying this, if she was there in front of him, the way it came out.

"Thank you," Angie said to that.

They discussed how Angie, Roseboro's family, and his children were being treated by "the papers." He didn't like it. No, *not* what was being reported about *him,* but everyone else. And as he talked, he broke off from that and said, "Oh, my goodness. Just great to hear your voice. . . . Oh—"

"Well, I almost didn't answer," Angie said, because she had to go pick up one of the kids.

Roseboro asked if he could call again.

"Yeah."

Then he wondered when his child had been born. He didn't know the date. His lawyer, he said, had told him April 1.

Angie cleared up the confusion.

"He was eager to get out of there, huh?"

A laugh and another explanation of how great it was to give birth to Matthew.

The talk then focused on how supportive their families and friends had been during what was a time of mostly downs, very few ups. The baby had changed that for the time being and had brought a bit of hope into Angie's world. Maybe for both of them. Roseboro mentioned how good a friend Francis Tobias had been, and how the police "confiscated" that letter Roseboro had sent him.

"Yeah?" Angie said.

"Which it was just writing to say," Roseboro answered, now lying about the letter he had written to Francis and Karen Tobias, "'Hey, how are ya?' So it just—it just, I don't know."

"It's a shame," Angie said.

Then it was back to talking about family. Roseboro mentioned Jan's sister and brother. Angie asked, "I didn't know how they would be treating you at all."

"Of course," he said, "there's going to be some animosity, but they're—"

Angie cut him off: "I know you and [Jan's brother] were very close."

Animosity? The guy was accused of killing their sister! Roseboro here made it sound as if they would get over it and be his pal again.

Roseboro mentioned his oldest son, Sam, and how great the boy had been, coming in to see him and stepping up to take on a mature role in the other children's lives and helping out Michael's parents. Suzie Van Zant was living at the Roseboro house still, taking care of the minor children. Sam lived with his grandparents.

After a few more statements about Sam and his parents, Roseboro said, "Well, it's—oh, my goodness . . . I *will* call again."

"Okay," Angie answered.

"It was so good talking to you."

"It was good talking to *you*."

"I love you," Roseboro said seriously.

Angie laughed, embarrassed. Then, quickly, almost under her breath, "I love you, too."

They said good-bye a few times and hung up.

64

The relationship between Jan's family and Michael Roseboro was becoming volatile as the month of April came to pass. In the weeks that followed, things would happen to shape a different type of association between the two families. That aside for the moment, investigators learned many things while listening to that call between Roseboro and Angie Funk. Number one, in his letter to Francis Tobias, Michael had said he was working things out with Jan. That his affair with Angie was finished. Now they had Michael (and Angie), a consummate impostor if there ever was one, on tape saying they loved each other. Was Angie going to end up being a hostile witness for the prosecution, out there fighting for her man, perhaps protecting him when she sat in the witness stand?

It seemed so.

Judged from the way she acted during that call, her presence in court would be ambiguous at best, supporting the rival team at worst. The prosecution knew Angie needed to stay somewhere in the middle to have an impact.

Michael was still standing on two different sides of the fence himself, depending on whom he spoke to. His wife was dead and here he was still chasing Angie Funk and proclaiming his love for her.

"Oh, my God, it's good to hear your voice . . . baby."

It was astonishing to some that Michael's infatuation with the woman had not been tampered by the charges against him. He was still holding out hope that he would be released, and somehow he, Angie, and their child were all going to be together.

Two days after that first call, Michael was not able to get through to Angie. Guess what? He called her back.

Again, he chose the afternoon hour, mainly because Randall Funk—the man who was living with, supporting, and caring for Michael's child—was at work.

Opening this call, Roseboro said the last time they spoke he'd forgotten to "congratulate" Angie on a recent Philadelphia Phillies (2008) World Series victory.

Angie laughed her guarded, schoolgirl giggle, which came across as phony and contrived, saying, "Oh—and the Steelers!"

"Well, that goes without saying," Roseboro offered. He, too, was a Steelers fan, and had, in fact, dedicated his entire rec room in the basement of the new addition to a Steelers theme. (The team had won the Super Bowl in 2008.)

"It was a good sport year," Angie added.

They carried on about sports for a brief time. Roseboro told Angie how sick and tired he was of watching basketball inside the prison, adding, "I mean, they get to the point where they even put professional women's basketball on—" (He didn't say who he meant by "they.")

"I'm not a basketball fan," Angie said, interrupting.

Concluding his earlier thought, Roseboro gave a little hint as to who he had meant by "they," saying, ". . . that and, ah, Black Entertainment Television."

"Really?" Angie asked, feigning surprise.

"Yeah, it's a . . . We got one officer to put on Country

Music Television. I thought there was going to be a riot in here."

That comment cracked up Angie.

"We just did it for a joke," Roseboro added.

"That's funny!"

From there, Roseboro changed the subject. "No, actually, there's a date that I plan on being home in August . . . 'cause I, when I came in here, I was, I . . . was furious."

"I'm sure you were." That comment had put the brakes on Angie's laughing spell. There were sounds in the background—those echoes again, from the long prison hallways and guards talking over the loudspeakers, slamming and locking doors—reminding the two of them where this man was calling from. They could joke all they wanted, but it didn't change the fact that Roseboro was in prison, facing the rest of his life behind bars.

More serious, Roseboro said he had given his entire situation "up to God's hands." Being in jail, locked up like he was, had given him a "lot of good prayer time . . . and, ah, I just feel really good."

"Good, good," Angie responded quickly.

He said it bummed him out "that people would, someone would even think I would do something like that—that bums me out."

"Yeah, well, you know," Angie said. "There's people that think that I had something to do with it, too."

"I know," Roseboro said.

"That I manipulated you and all that stuff, and that's not who I am and never was like that. . . ."

"I know. . . . I know. . . ."

"And it hurts, it really hurts . . . that people can hate so badly."

In this discussion, there was no mention of the notion that Jan had lost her life. The suffering was on the children's shoulders now and for those who knew Jan best—her family. This talk between Angie and Roseboro centered on themselves. No remorse. No empathy. No simple compassion for a woman who was murdered in a brutal rage. It was as if Jan had never existed.

Angie went on to talk about a friend of hers who had "been there" for her. She mentioned how Jesus had become a central part of their lives and how Christ had taught them all to deal with the situation of being cast out, essentially, of the community and looked down on by anyone they came into contact with.

To that, Roseboro said: "Well, that's what I've been saying to my parents. I gotta forgive them, because how am I supposed to be forgiven, if I can't forgive them?"

The world they lived in—Denver/Reinholds and the other surrounding towns—was a God-fearing region of Lancaster County. People here are believers. They embrace the word of God, and church attendance is high in this area. On Sundays, you can watch as horse and buggies carrying the Amish and Mennonites travel along the road in processions of what appears to be hundreds on their way to meeting houses. The Lutheran and other denominational churches, as well, are full. And yet Roseboro was not one of those devout, pious people, leaning on God, living a life under God's commandments, but here he was now, backed into a corner, beginning to speak as though he had been an altar boy and devoted churchgoer.

Angie talked more about her friends and the support she was getting and how grateful she was for it. But there was no way to get away from the lashing Angie said she was getting from "people."

Roseboro said he felt fortunate for being the one locked up, and not being on the receiving end of that collective, societal hostility.

"I pray for you every day," he told Angie at one point, "for what you're going through. Like I said, I am so proud of you for the way you're handling yourself."

As Angie thanked her man, she let out two short

laughs (nerves). As she did that, Roseboro broke off into a different subject: the inmates he had become "real good friends" with inside the prison. There was one guy Roseboro mentioned by name.

"Oh, cool," Angie said, almost as if she didn't want to hear, "what's he in for?"

Roseboro started to say, "Ra . . ."—perhaps *rape* or *robbery*?—but then stopped himself abruptly, opting instead for, "Breaking and entering." This "good guy," as Roseboro described him, had been sentenced for his crimes recently: "They gave him twenty to forty [years]. . . . I could have cried for him."

This man Roseboro had nearly shed tears for (the "good guy"), according to witness testimony during his case, had targeted Amish women in two separate home invasions, and even had touched one woman as she slept. Two of the victims had chased the man from their home.

Angie gasped in a quick breath. Then, "Are you serious?"

"Well, and that's what I said to my mom. . . ." Because of this man and others he had met on the inside, Roseboro felt compelled to "do something" when he got out, he explained. "Get these guys some sort of a job. Do something to help them get into a workplace. Because they don't have an option. They get out of here—no one wants to hire them."

Angie understood.

"Then they go right back to what they came in for."

They talked about being strong themselves for the kids. Roseboro was happy to hear from his mother, he said, that there were people on the outside who still believed in him.

"I must have gotten about five hundred letters and cards so far," Roseboro said.

"That's awesome."

Angie asked Roseboro about having a temper at lacrosse

games, which had been reported, and Roseboro brushed it off, saying, "That wasn't a temper. I just got wrapped up in the game."

Angie said, "Yeah, I know. . . . I have a temper."

"I know," Roseboro said.

"I'm stubborn," Angie responded. "You know, that doesn't mean I'm gonna go out and kill somebody." She was laughing, adding that just because someone has a "temper," it doesn't mean they're prone to violence.

"You got a worse temper than I do," Roseboro said, totally bypassing that "kill somebody" remark.

"Oh, I do not."

"I'm kiddin' ya!"

For a few moments, they discussed the baby. Angie talked about the delivery. How she had "no morning sickness," and that she was afraid Matthew would be colicky because mothers who undergo stress during pregnancy—so she had heard—end up with colicky babies. "I've been dying to know what kind of baby you were," she asked Roseboro, "just so—"

"I was perfect!" he said. "What do you mean, 'what kind of baby' was I?"

There was a peculiar nature to the conversation at this point. Not even a year before, Jan was alive, and Angie Funk and Michael Roseboro's affair had not yet begun. Now, here they were—Roseboro behind bars, Angie raising their love child with *her* husband—talking about it all as though they were discussing a soap opera they had both watched. There was a certain surrealism to the conversation as it carried on.

Angie brought the conversation back to a serious timbre, saying that Roseboro's mother was having a hard time with the baby.

"She's just really torn."

"I understand that," Angie said. She mentioned how Roseboro's mother passed by her house but "wouldn't look in."

"She really wants to talk to you and see the baby, but she's just . . . I don't know. She's in a hard place, and she won't talk to me, and I don't want to talk to her about it over the phone."

"Yeah," Angie said.

"But . . . she'll—she'll be okay."

Angie said someone from Roseboro's attorney's office suggested that she write Ann Roseboro a letter. Angie had sat down and wanted to do it "so many times," she admitted, telling them all how sorry she was "that things . . . happened the way that they did. . . . You know, sorry that you and I had an affair and caused this for their family." But then someone in Sodomsky's office told her it wouldn't be a good idea to send a letter to Michael's mother. Not now, anyway.

Roseboro offered, "I understand."

For another minute—with that lovely prison computer voice interrupting, letting them know that their call would be disconnected in three minutes—they talked about Matthew and how well he was getting along with Angie's children. Roseboro said how much he adored the name, Matthew Francis.

"Oh, man," Roseboro said with some frustration near the end of the call, feeling the pressure of the line going dead at any moment. "All right, well, I'll call you next week."

"Okay."

"Okay. I won't call you on weekends or nights," Roseboro clarified.

"Okay."

"But, um . . ."

"Take care of yourself," Angie said, as though it would be the last time they spoke for a while.

"I—I am. You, too, do the same."

"All right. Hang in there."

"I am. I am. Yeah," Roseboro replied.

"Okay."

"I love you, Angela," Roseboro said.

Angie ignored the remark entirely, not responding to it. Instead, "I'll keep you in my thoughts and prayers," she said.

"I know."

"Okay."

"Yeah," Roseboro answered.

"All right."

"I'll see you."

"All right," Angie said. "See you."

65

Detective Keith Neff called Suzie Van Zant on May 19, 2009. Neff wanted to give the family the results from the PSP's forensic lab that the outside lab, unaffiliated with the PSP or LCDA's Office, had confirmed. Neff told Suzie he wanted to do this in person. These good people, Neff surmised, deserved nothing less than a face-to-face.

Larry Martin and Keith Neff met with Suzie and other family members, including Sam, while Jan's brother, Brian Binkley, listened on speakerphone.

Neff explained that DNA found underneath Jan Roseboro's fingernails had been confirmed to be Michael's. More significantly, both labs insisted the DNA—skin and blood cells—underneath Jan's fingernails was not from "casual contact," say, scratching someone's back, a handshake, or any other routine touch. The only way that this particular amount of DNA found could have accumulated underneath Jan's nails was under violent or aggressive conditions.

Suzie became "quite upset" and left the room when she heard this. It was disturbing information, certainly. It made a strong case against any doubt Suzie or the family might have had up until then that Michael was being railroaded by the state. Here was forensic proof, or so it seemed, that Jan and Michael were involved in a struggle on the night Jan died.

After sitting with the family for a time, Neff and Martin said they'd be in touch, then left.

Later that same day, Sam Roseboro took a call from his dad. Sam was living at his grandparents' house on Walnut Street and helping out at the funeral home. Roseboro was calling the house as much as he could. Some later said Sam was being groomed to take over the family business, where his father had left off; others, however, said Sam had no interest in making the handling of dead bodies and consoling grieving families his vocation.

After some small talk about how everyone was doing, the conversation shifted. "Yeah, they talked," Sam said. "They came down then and talked." (They were Martin and Neff.)

The fuzz.

"Yeah," Michael Roseboro told his son. "Yup. . . . Yup. . . ." He wanted off this subject. Fast.

"So I was glad," Sam continued, not picking up on his father's wish to stifle the conversation, "'cause that's what I was thinking this morning, just something like that . . . but then [the private investigator] said—" It was almost as if they were speaking in code about an earlier agreement.

Michael cut his son off abruptly, speaking over him, skipping his voice like a stone on water: "Ah . . . bup-bup-bup-bup-bup . . . okay?"

"What?" Sam asked.

"Nothing!"

"O-o-o-kay."

"Um . . . um . . ."—Roseboro changed the subject entirely—"did you get the Jeep taken care of?"

They talked about other inconsequential things for a few more minutes and then hung up.

Nine days after that call, on May 28, the private investigator hired by Michael Roseboro interviewed Sam as part of this "new investigation" that the defense had promised. Just so happened that this interview took place after the results of the DNA had come back from both labs. If one was to view this with the eye of a skeptic, Roseboro needed to explain two things: the DNA found underneath Jan's nails and the scratches on his face.

The private investigator asked Sam about the scratches on his dad's face. Did he know anything about that?

"My dad told me that he was scratched [by my sister in the pool while playing basketball earlier that day], but I didn't see it happen."

Sam later said he was there, poolside, his back turned to them as they played in the water, but that he had *heard* them horsing around.

Turned out, though, that the child who had supposedly scratched her father on the face was a chronic nail biter. She had no fingernails. Just nubs. Those scratches were deep. So profound, in fact, they were oozing on the night of Jan's murder.

During this interview with the private investigator, Sam mentioned how he thought he knew where the DNA underneath his mother's fingernails might have come from. He had recalled (for the first time) that he saw his mother scratching his father's back as he was leaving the pool patio area with his friend that night. He had just remembered this.

The problem investigators had with this sudden revelation was that Sam, who had been questioned by the police extensively about that night and his father's life in general, had never mentioned this back-scratching incident. Moreover, Sam had gone to visit his father on that Monday after Neff and Martin had told the family about the DNA. As an aside, Sam and his father had spoken, according to prison phone records, almost every day since Michael's arrest. Literally, hundreds of conversations.

"I—I was . . . I was told not to tell anybody," Sam said in court later, referring to the notion of keeping this information to himself all that time, "because . . . I thought I was told not to tell anybody outside of, like, my grandmother."

When asked who had told him not to talk about the back-scratching incident, Sam responded, "My grand-mother."

Keith Neff and office manager Heather Smith were going through Jan's phone records in preparation for trial, which was now slated to begin in mid-to-late July. In looking at the calls made to and from Jan's cell phone, they realized a call had been made to Jan's voice mail on July 22, 2008, at 10:36 P.M., close to what police believed was the time of her death. This meant some-one was checking Jan's voice mail messages. And there was another call made a minute later at 10:37 P.M. from Jan's cell phone to her mother-in-law, Ann Roseboro, who Jan knew was not at home.

Both calls seemed out of place when compared to the behavior Jan elicited with her cell phone. For one, Jan hardly ever called her mother-in-law. In the three months leading up to the murder, Jan's phone had com-municated three times with Ann Roseboro's: one incom-ing call and two outgoing calls, including that one at ten thirty-seven on the night Jan was murdered. Number two, Jan's best friend, Rebecca Donahue, had "a prob-lem" with the idea of Jan having her cell phone out at the pool. It was so unlike Jan that it grated on Rebecca's conscience postmurder. After thinking about it for a few days, Rebecca confronted Michael Roseboro about it, asking him, "Why was Jan's cell phone out there?"

Michael shrugged. "I don't know."

Rebecca called Michael some days later, just before his arrest. She asked him again. ("It bothered me," she recalled later.)

"I don't know," Michael said. He paused. Then: "She was checking her messages. She was checking her messages when I went to bed."

"Who was the last person Jan spoke to?" Rebecca asked.

"I don't know," Michael answered.

"You can go in right now and pull it up on the computer, the billing information," Rebecca explained.

Michael changed the subject. ("He never answered me.")

The last time Jan had checked her voice mail before that night (if it was indeed her) was a week prior. She could have cared less who called her—especially at 10:37 P.M., while supposedly sitting poolside by herself.

More important: how could Roseboro, law enforcement wondered, see his wife checking her cell phone messages at 10:37 P.M., which Jan's cell phone records proved, if he was in bed, as he had originally told them? (Roseboro's story was that he did not find his wife until 10:58 P.M.)

"You cannot know that Jan checked her messages at that time," one investigator told me, "*unless* you were up and you did it yourself."

BOOK FIVE

ANGIE AND THE ROCK STAR

66

The dream team, as clichéd as it might sound today, was what Michael Roseboro's defense resembled as they wheeled their briefcases and boxes of documents along the sidewalk toward 50 North Duke Street, downtown Lancaster, heading for courtroom 12 on July 8, 2009. The ephemeral presence of such a serious-looking group of lawyers aptly set the stage. Accusations from both sides had been hurled like insults for months. The local news media was primed, ready for a spectacle; a packed courtroom buzzed with anticipation, everyone geared up to hear testimony in the *Commonwealth of Pennsylvania* v. *Michael Alan Roseboro,* the Honorable Judge James Cullen overseeing the drama. Allan Sodomsky, flanked by his group of assistants, legal experts and co-counsel, walked with the guarded sense of gravity his role in this tragedy carried. District Attorney Craig Stedman, representing the state with ADAs Kelly Sekula and Christopher Larsen, had only to saunter a few short steps out of his office to the elevator and head down to the fourth floor.

This much activity, centered around such a high-profile family, was certainly not a sight Lancaster County, Denver and Reinholds in particular, was used to. One newspaper estimated that its online version of a public forum had produced 150,000 words of comments about the case since Jan's death. Denver residents could not get enough of a case that seemed to have all the earmarks of a Lifetime Television movie of the week: sex, drugs, booze, wealthy people, rumor and gossip driving the ship, adultery and—of course—a sympathetic victim, adored by her community, viciously murdered. To top it off, not much beyond the obvious was known about the defendant, other than his family members were icons in this small, tight-knit Amish community known more for its rolling hills and simple living, strawberry and peach preserves, pepper jellies, breads and antiques. The promise had been made long ago that Michael Roseboro needed only his day in court to prove he was no murderer.

Well, that time was upon him.

The state had subpoenaed 164 witnesses (an unprecedented number); while Allan Sodomsky had sent word to sixty-four that their testimony could be needed.

Neither would come close to utilizing all of these people.

In the packed gallery sat producers from the CBS magazine show *48 Hours.* They took notes, made contact with the players, hoping to see if there was fodder here for one of the network's salacious, over-the-top, hour-long Saturday-night crime shows.

Sodomsky had motioned for a change of venue.

It was denied.

His concern—very much warranted, to be fair—was that too many rumors had been spread. Picking an untainted jury among a community of peers so flushed by the rancorous outpouring of speculation circling the case was going to be difficult. With the World Wide Web (www) came a host of new problems for attorneys, a few of which would ultimately play out in this trial. Early on, the fear Sodomsky had, it's safe to say, was that all of those comments being made by anonymous, faceless people sitting in front of keyboards, screen names hiding who they were, would somehow trickle down into the minds of jurors and poison their judgment. Heck, a few of the potential jurors could have made remarks themselves. Not to mention all the talk about town, in the newspapers and on local television. The guy had every reason to voice concern for his client.

By the end of the day, July 8, 2009, ten of twelve jurors had been chosen, however. Word was that testimony would begin as soon as Friday, July 10.

The following day, July 9, had brought one more juror.

The next day, the final juror was selected, with testimony now slated to begin on Monday morning, July 13, nine o'clock.

Ann Roseboro, one of the local newspapers reported, caught a glimpse of her son from a courtroom door's tiny window—she watched as the star of the show, Michael Roseboro himself, shackled and in handcuffs, was walked into the courtroom by guards. It was a surreal moment for the Roseboro matriarch: to see her son presented to the public as the accused felon he was. Ann looked to be almost in tears as she watched her boy sit at the table that would become his home for, some predicted, the next three weeks. Craig Stedman had given Ann and Ralph Roseboro the option of sitting in on proceedings, even though they were slated to testify. But both chose not to sit behind their golden child. Michael would have to brave this impasse himself, with only his legal team and a few others to lean on, one of whom was the Reverend William Cluley, a Lutheran pastor chosen by the family to be its ears and eyes in the courtroom. Cluley was there, keeping tabs on every moment, no doubt reporting back to the family.

Michael Roseboro had a grim look to him that many presumed was his natural state—the glum deportment of an undertaker: dark, cold, baleful. Yet beyond those beady eyes (one that appeared larger than the other), there had to be a serious sense of dread and fear weighing on the forty-two-year-old, whispering in his ear ever so softly that his life could be lost in a matrix of steel doors, concrete walls, lonely hallways, and the obedience that had become his daily routine for almost the past year while residing in Lancaster County Prison.

67

Michael Roseboro was a man who had to look a certain way before he left the house. Everything—clothes, hair, nails, anything outwardly trendy or stylish that the public would see—had to be just right. One might picture Roseboro standing in front of a mirror, straightening his cuffs, brushing a piece of lint off his suit shoulder, wetting a finger to fix a stray, out-of-place hair, flattening his eyebrows, pushing the knot of his tie up tightly. Then he would stop for a long moment to check himself out before departure. Indeed, if he wore black shoes, Michael insisted on a black belt and matching sunglasses. Regarding that sort of attention to detail, "Michael," said one Roseboro family member, "took this to the extreme."

On Monday, July 13, Michael Roseboro would *not* have the advantage of a dressing room and his array of ostentatious suits, chic colognes, and vanity at his disposal. Instead, he would have to rely on the suit his attorney had sent over to the prison (black, of course).

After the judge gave about an hour and a half's worth of directives to the jury, Craig Stedman stood. He looked at Michael, who was—incredibly—wearing his wedding ring, sitting next to his attorneys with a look that said he was going to walk away from this trial unscathed, right back into that life he had left behind.

It was 10:38 A.M. when Judge James Cullen turned the courtroom over to Craig Stedman. The opening was something Stedman had been working on until the wee hours of the morning on most nights leading up to trial. There in the basement of his home, little notes he had written and collected throughout the case spread around him as though he had been writing a Ph.D. dissertation, the prosecutor had scribed what would be one of the most extensive openings he had ever given.

One of the main "themes" (his word) Stedman had to get across to the jury—as senseless as pointing this out to the jury seemed—was that Jan Roseboro had been murdered.

"If I can get the jury to internalize that Jan was murdered," Stedman recalled, "then the only reasonable conclusion, based on all of this evidence, is that *Mike* did it."

And yet, most trial attorneys knew from experience that juries recalled the opening lines, the last few, and just some of the more dramatic elements in the middle of an opening argument. The key was to keep the flow moving toward a revealing, thunderous conclusion.

Equally important to consider was the idea that Michael Roseboro did not look like your average killer, with his superficial charm, tears turned on and off when he believed he needed them, and an overall good standing in the community. Another impediment Stedman would have to overcome: the pretense that your next-door neighbor—in this case, a mild-mannered, perhaps even docile man with a laconic, seemingly nonthreatening way about him, smiling to you every morning and consoling you when your loved one died—was a violent and vicious murderer who had beaten and strangled his wife.

"By the time of trial, Mike had lost about thirty to forty pounds," Stedman said. "He was pretty thin. He looks a little effeminate, too. We had an image problem to contend with. But I kept thinking, 'If I can get the jury to accept that Jan was murdered, they're going to convict him.'"

There was a time when the DA's office seriously looked into the idea that Michael Roseboro was a closeted homosexual. Some men double up on women and sex more than the average guy in order to prove to themselves that they can live a straight life. This breeds a suppressed, aggressive storm within a fraction of these men—one that can sometimes emerge later in life as violence against females.

"The theory (of Roseboro being a homosexual) was discussed by us," Stedman said. "But there was no direct evidence, so we did not pursue it."

The first few lines of Stedman's opening put Jan's murder into context: "This case is about lies. It's about betrayal. It's about some greed, of course. It's about murder. But more than anything else, it's about *obsession*."

The prosecutor allowed the words to hang in the room for a brief moment.

Roaming back and forth in front of the jury, wound up and passionate about what he was saying, Stedman introduced the affair, then talked about how often Michael Roseboro had called Angie Funk, no doubt the witness everyone was waiting to hear from more than any other. "Sometimes thirty, forty, even *fifty* (calls) every day. . . . And, of course, that doesn't even count the times they would get together and have sex and see each other."

There was not a single sound—beyond Stedman's tired-sounding voice—echoing throughout that courtroom after he said those words. The speculation around town, the rumor mill, the Internet gossip, conversations over coffee counters, at gas stations, and at watercoolers all came down to cold, hard facts now. Craig Stedman was there to present evidence; Allan Sodomsky waiting patiently to pounce on any contravention he saw.

Stedman mentioned motive, the cost of divorce, losing the family business, that obsession he had focused on, Michael's social status, and how much he lied to everyone around him before and after the murder. He went into Jan Roseboro's bio, her friends, how she was well revered around town. How much Jan will be missed. How people "know each other's business" in Denver, and how evil can sometimes penetrate the veneer of good and come across in many different forms.

Yes, even as a mild-mannered undertaker who seemed to have it all.

Then the DA focused on Angie Funk. Poor Angie was going to take a tremendous hit from all sides during this trial. Neighbors had reported that Angie, unabashed by the accusations and determined not to crawl into a shell and disappear, had been spotted at times pushing the little Roseboro love child in a stroller around Denver, past the funeral home and Roseboro's parents' house. This woman was not going away. Scared, and yet unafraid to speak her truth, she was prepared to testify.

"Basically," Stedman said about Angie and her feelings toward Michael Roseboro before the affair started, "he was a rock star to her."

She had sought him out. Set her fiery eyes upon this man and—lo and behold—caught him.

Stedman talked about all those e-mails.

The phone calls.

The text messages.

The sexual trysts inside the vacant apartment.

The supposed wedding vow renewal ceremony that never was.

Niagara Falls.

Then, of course, the pregnancy—Roseboro and Funk's child.

And for the next two hours, Stedman spoke to every possible piece of evidence the state had uncovered, leaving nothing left unsaid. He covered all the bases, as if no one piece of evidence was more crucial than the next, but all together created a carefully planned out picture of murder that each witness would reinforce.

"We're going to show you through the evidence," Craig Stedman concluded near the end, ". . . that the defendant murdered his wife because he was obsessed with his girlfriend and he needed to do what he needed to do to be with his girlfriend—so he could *have* it all."

Allan Sodomsky, looking on, listening intently, was ready. It was his turn now to put on the best argument he could for his client.

68

After a break for lunch, Allan Sodomsky got right to work. In the opening few lines of his argument, Sodomsky boiled Michael Roseboro's case down to what he described as, smartly, one crucial piece of evidence missing from the DA's two-hour-plus condemnation of his client. "The only thing you *don't* have to guess or speculate about when it comes to what the evidence will show is that Mike Roseboro went in to go to sleep around ten P.M. on July 22, 2008." And it was that "fact" alone, Sodomsky insisted, that jurors should hold close to their vests all the way through the trial: Roseboro was sound asleep when his wife was killed.

From that point, Sodomsky turned to the lights being *on*, not off, as several neighbors had reported; the children watching TV in the Roseboro bedroom; and how Roseboro "saw his wife floating in the pool, head underwater," a fact that had not been disclosed until this moment. The ongoing belief by just about everyone (including the description Michael gave police) was that Jan had been found somewhere near the bottom of the pool.

Then the defense attorney—who came across as believable and knowledgeable about the law, maybe even sincere—talked about how Michael had pulled his wife from the pool near eleven o'clock, calling all of what he had to say thus far "direct evidence . . . and there will be *no* direct evidence to contradict that!"

Then he mentioned Sam and the other kids. How well everyone got along. How distressed Michael Roseboro was when Sam and his friend returned to find chaos abounding, and his mother on her way to the hospital, presumably fighting for her life or even dead.

He said Jan had made calls that night—at ten thirty-six and ten thirty-seven—from her cell phone. And Michael Roseboro spoke to the police without question. There was no evidence found to indicate a murder had taken place, and that their medical experts would contradict the state's on that front.

Sodomsky admitted there was an affair, which seemed to be the first time Roseboro had indicated and submitted to this fact in public. How could he deny it, with so much evidence to the contrary?

From there, Sodomsky bit into Angie Funk, saying, "It began over a cup of coffee at a Turkey Hill." He said this unabashedly, as if it was nothing more than a mere happenstance meeting of two souls destined to fall in love. "And on June thirteenth . . . exactly sixteen days later, that affair became sexual."

Sodomsky kept saying that the "evidence time frame" would play a role in proving his client's innocence, but he made no mention of exactly how it would play out. Money could not have been the motive here, he said, explaining that "1.63 million" was the half that Michael Roseboro would have received in a divorce settlement, which was a lot of money to walk away with "*without* killing anybody."

In listening to this, one was jostled into hearkening back to Craig Stedman's point that greed would be central to the state's case. A greedy man knows no bounds. When is enough, enough? How much is enough? It's not about the

money, one could argue, when speaking to greed as
motive—it's about all or nothing.

Moving on to the DNA, Sodomsky downplayed it.
"The experts will say that DNA absolutely could have
come from scratching of the back. . . . There was no
evidence of her head hitting the ground. It is much more
likely, so the medical evidence will show, that she was hit
with a blunt object, presumably a fist or two or three or
four. She was beaten, strangled, and drowned. And the
injuries on her head and body are significant. . . . Mr.
Stedman said the evidence will show that Jan died in
hand-to-hand combat. With whom?" Sodomsky asked
rhetorically. "And the evidence will show it wasn't with
Mike Roseboro."

Quite elegantly, Allan Sodomsky made a great point as
he finished his hour-long opening, relaying to the jury
one major hurdle Craig Stedman's team was going to
have to make it over at some point: "Ladies and gentlemen, based on the evidence you will hear . . . you will
have to guess or speculate as to what happened between
that ten and eleven P.M. hour on July 22, 2008—and
that, ladies and gentlemen, is something your oath just
will *not* let you do."

69

Ending the previous day, Craig Stedman had called Michael Firestone, the first cop to respond to the scene, and another, Officer Brian Dilliplaine, putting jurors right in the center of what had happened on the night of July 22, 2008. Each witness, beyond giving a detailed account of how Jan Roseboro had been worked on at the scene and taken away quickly after being found unresponsive, made a point to say that Michael had not once asked about the status of his wife's condition, or jumped at the opportunity to ride with Jan in the ambulance. To their shock, Michael Roseboro had stayed behind.

Proceedings on Tuesday, July 14, got under way at 9:04 A.M. ADA Kelly Sekula had been waiting on this day for some time. One of Sekula's interests throughout the year had been the 911 call. She had focused a lot of attention on it, studying it ten ways to Sunday. Sekula, who had even argued with her father about the veracity of the call at one point, believed—same as just about everyone else in law enforcement—that the 911 call, by itself, spoke to Michael Roseboro's guilt.

"The first thing he says on the 911 tape," Sekula later explained, "is 'I believe my wife just drowned. . . .' He doesn't know what happened to Jan. He could say he found her in the pool. But he shouldn't know that she is dead. For all he knew, she had a heart attack, or tripped and fell. Why doesn't he say, 'Get over here now and save her!' And then he begins stalling and stalling and stalling about doing CPR. Why?

"Because he knows she's dead."

The flat demeanor on the tape depicts a man calling 911 to report a dead woman in his pool—not a man who has just found his wife unconscious in his pool.

"He's not the least bit winded," Sekula added. "This, after supposedly dragging his wife out from the deep end, the bottom of the pool, and finding her unresponsive."

Before any of the day's witnesses were questioned— witnesses who would soon describe what had happened after Roseboro made the call—the DA's office played the 911 tape to put into context what they would be talking about.

The unfolding of that night continued throughout much of the morning as those professionals (paramedics and police) on hand the night Jan died came in and told different versions of the same truth. All of them mentioned how Roseboro seemed too damn composed for a man who had just pulled his listless, breathless wife from their pool. Several of the witnesses described what Roseboro was wearing—no shirt, swimming trunks, no shoes—and how he started to tell that scripted story he would soon vocalize to anybody and everyone.

With witnesses, Craig Stedman and Kelly Sekula were able to establish that every one of these people had a hard time opening the gate into the pool area. If you didn't know how to unlatch the gate, you needed help. (This was more testimony that spoke to how difficult it would have been for an intruder to simply wander onto the property without Jan noticing and calling 911 from the cell phone she supposedly had with her.)

Then Sam's friend Mike Texter, an extremely nervous, tense, and, some might contend, hostile witness, came in and explained what he saw that night. Texter mentioned nothing about seeing Jan scratching her husband's back as he left with Sam. Protocol for examining witnesses was that the attorneys remained seated, unless they needed to point out something on an exhibit or show a piece of evidence. Witnesses faced the prosecution table, but it was easy to turn and face Michael Roseboro, who, as Texter talked about being one of the last people outside the family to see Jan alive, wept openly, dabbing his crocodile tears with tissues.

At one point, Stedman asked Texter, "You don't want him (Roseboro) to be convicted of murder, do you?" There was some obvious animosity between the two of them. Texter had raised his voice a few times. Stedman too.

"Of course not! No one would who knew him. He's a nice guy."

"Oh, well, please," Stedman said, his voice increasing with disgust. "Do you want to tell us more great things about Mr. Roseboro right now? And keep going! I'm more than happy to sit here and listen to you tell us how *great* Mr. Roseboro is!"

There was a pause.

"All right, counsel," the judge said, "let's dial down the sarcasm."

Craig Stedman was flushed.

After lunch, Detective Keith Neff sat in the witness stand and raised his right hand. Neff had come close a few times, but he had never testified in a trial. This, like investigating the murder of Jan Roseboro, was a first for the ECTPD investigator. Neff was anxious, he later admitted, but he had taken some rather sage advice from his colleagues, who had told him not to sweat it. Tell the truth. Let the facts hang out there by themselves for the jury to contemplate, feel, understand. What else *can* you do? You explained what you knew without expanding on it or coloring in the gray areas. A lot of times the truth was more powerful than anything you could come up with, anyway. As dissident and Nobel laureate Aleksandr Solzhenitsyn, the acclaimed Russian author, speaking words that epitomized what Lady Justice would say to those sitting in a courtroom, once observed, "Everything you add to the truth subtracts from the truth."

Tell it like it is, and let the chips fall.

Neff was a keeper of excellent records. He was well organized and on top of his game. All of which was going to help. He sat and told the jury how he had become part of the case and how the investigation quickly became his full-time (at times night and day) job. He read the jury a note-for-note account of the first statement Michael Roseboro gave to him and Larry Martin on the night of Jan's death. Neff said that Roseboro read the statement and signed it, initialing every question.

He next talked the jury through the lighting on the Roseboro property, setting up the state's contention that it would be nearly impossible for an intruder to turn out every light after cleaning up a crime scene. He also talked Craig Stedman through a series of photographs depicting the inside and outside of the Roseboro home.

After a break, Stedman had Neff describe the content of that second interview he conducted with Michael Roseboro, the one out by the pool Jan Walters had participated in. Roseboro was asked to give them more details about how he had found Jan.

Near the end of his direct examination, Stedman had Neff talk about the scratches on Roseboro's face, telling the court that the detective would have to be recalled "for some other things later."

Deferring the witness to Allan Sodomsky, the defense attorney tried getting out of the detective anything he could use to cause doubt. They went back and forth for a time, talking about *how* Michael Roseboro said he had pulled Jan from the pool. Then Sodomsky keyed on the idea that Roseboro didn't know Larry Martin, who had sat in on the interview that night at the station house, was a police officer. The implication was that Larry Martin and Keith Neff intimidated Roseboro, shined a light in his face, and pushed him into talking.

"And during that first interview, you were just trying to find out what happened, right?"

"Correct," Neff answered.

"You thought it was a drowning, right?"

"It was a *possibility* that it was a drowning," Neff answered. "We weren't sure what happened, and that's why we asked him to come back—to try to get some answers and figure out what happened."

But Michael Roseboro seemed evasive and unhelpful, not to mention unemotional and not upset by the loss of his wife. All indicators to Neff and Martin that he was hiding something.

The witness and attorney discussed the interviews that Neff and Martin had done with Roseboro. Sodomsky couldn't draw much of anything out of Neff that was going to help him. This sort of cross-examination rarely worked: questioning someone about the minutia of an event or events. It came across, as it did here, like bullying; beating an issue to the ground. Sodomsky was searching for something, hoping to catch Neff off guard, but there was nothing there. The detective had done his job by the book. If Neff wasn't sure of something, he asked someone more experienced.

By 4:59 P.M., the judge recessed until the following day.

Craig Stedman had taken over as Lancaster County DA nearly seven months before the Michael Roseboro case had come across his desk. Heading into trial, the ambitious, hardworking DA was feeling the weight of the case getting to him.

"We didn't have an eyewitness. We didn't have a confession. We had very little forensic evidence—that is, until that DNA underneath Jan's nails came into play."

Stedman respected Allan Sodomsky. He had known him for "many, many years," but he had never met up with Sodomsky on the opposing sides of a courtroom. From Stedman's view, the trial was "battle royal." Roseboro was sparing no expense on experts, doctors, private investigators, and, of course, a high-powered, high-profile attorney who knew his way around a courtroom. "He's not going to hold back," Stedman added, meaning Sodomsky. "He's a fighter."

Still, Craig Stedman was convinced of Michael Roseboro's guilt *and* the evidence his staff and team of law enforcement had prepared for trial. The DA had created lists, very long lists, for Keith Neff and others to check off as they went through and made sure nothing was left undone. But one of the biggest obstacles Stedman now faced wasn't overlooking an important piece of evidence. Or forgetting to prepare a witness. It was Angie Funk. She was a reluctant witness. Not that she was going to protect Michael Roseboro, but Angie had made it clear to the DA's office through her attorney that yes, she'd show up for court. Yes, she'd testify truthfully to what she recalled. But several months before trial, Angie had decided not to help the DA by giving additional interviews or participating in meetings before trial to prepare. So it was on the shoulders of the DA whether to use Angie.

Yet how could he not? The commonwealth's entire case centered around the affair. Angie was one of Roseboro's motives for killing his wife.

Stedman kept going back to those calls between Angie and Roseboro in April. She was giddy and laughing and talking to Roseboro as if she still loved him. She had even expressed her love to him during the first call.

"It was clear her feelings had not gone away," Stedman said. "So we had to ask ourselves, 'What were we going to get out of Angie during trial?'"

Because of the ambiguity swirling around Angie, Stedman and Kelly Sekula prepared for whichever Angie Funk showed up: hostile or cooperative. It was the only way to be completely ready. But Stedman wasn't convinced that Angie was the right witness to call early on, or at all, just yet. So on July 15, 2009, he stuck to the flow of the investigation in calling Dr. Steven Zebert, the ER doctor from Ephrata Community Hospital. Angie could wait.

Dr. Zebert described the scene at the hospital on the night Jan Roseboro was brought in. He said it was his decision to stop CPR near midnight. There just wasn't any use.

Jan was dead.

The other key piece of information Dr. Steven Zebert offered was his surprise and shock that no one had called the hospital to check in on Jan to see how she was doing. Nor had Michael Roseboro shown up to see his wife and hear from the doctor firsthand what had happened.

* * *

Allan Sodomsky's cross-examination produced nothing that could be even remotely construed as doubt.

With Dr. Zebert out of the way, Keith Neff was recalled for the conclusion of his cross-examination. For the most part, Sodomsky hammered Neff on one point: when did law enforcement decide it was a murder and not a drowning?

Neff explained himself thoroughly, honestly, pointedly, never backing down from his reports. The facts spoke for themselves.

The remainder of the morning was consumed by Jan Roseboro's family: Suzie Van Zant, Brian Binkley, Alex and Melissa Van Zant (Suzie's son and daughter-in-law), and Allison Van Zant (another of Jan's nieces).

Most talked about Michael's demeanor post–Jan's death. Level. Unaffected. Unworried. Eerily tolerable of Jan not being alive anymore. Nor had Michael seemed bothered by the fact that someone had murdered his wife.

Strange—but true.

"In your presence," Craig Stedman asked Allison Van Zant, "did [Mr. Roseboro] ever even say that Jan Roseboro had actually been murdered?"

"Never."

"Did he ever make any statements about anything being stolen or missing from the home?" (This was a reference to that mysterious missing $40,000 worth of jewelry.)

"Not to me directly."

Allan Sodomsky did not have much for Jan's family members. They had spoken their truth, repeated what they had heard, and that was it. There was no sense in badgering people who had lost someone dear to them. It would serve no purpose but to alienate jurors.

* * *

Detective Scott Eelman, coordinator for the Lancaster County Forensic Unit, talked about his fourteen years of experience before telling jurors that he and others inspected the crime scene, which had been washed out by that crash-and-boom, soaking thunderstorm on the night of the murder.

Eelman helped introduce photographs of the crime scene. He had sprayed down several areas with luminol, he testified, looking for any trace of blood, but he could not find one droplet. Yet, through what seemed to be a disappointing investigation of a crime scene, Eelman was able to give the jury a proper explanation as to why there might *not* have been any blood on the scene, despite all the rain.

"Are there any substances," Craig Stedman asked, "that you're aware of, from your training or experiences, that can, in addition to, obviously, rain . . . get rid of blood?"

"A common substance would be hydrogen peroxide."

Which every household medicine cabinet had—and funeral homes likely purchased in five-gallon buckets.

It would also make blood "nondetectable," Stedman pointed out in his next question.

"Hydrogen peroxide will make blood nondetectable if significant amounts are used. . . ."

Surprisingly, Stedman was done with his direct examination after just a few more questions regarding photographs.

One of Allan Sodomsky's co-counsels, Jay Nigrini, asked Scott Eelman if he had attended Jan Roseboro's autopsy.

He said yes.

Nigrini asked about the injury behind Jan's ear, if Eelman was aware of it.

He said he was.

Then Nigrini probed the notion that the pathologist had "removed" that section of skin, like a patch, containing the injury, for "tool mark" analysis so it could be checked against anything found at the Roseboro house.

Eelman said he had heard that, but he couldn't recall if the doctor "removed it or not."

The impression was made that inside or outside the house, the "blunt object" that had supposedly made an L-shaped gash in the skull of Jan's head could not be located.

Eelman said they had not found anything with blood on it to match up to the wound.

Sodomsky's intruder theory was beckoning.

By the time Nigrini was finished with Eelman, it was close to 4:41 P.M.

"Counsel," Judge Cullen said, looking at both sides, "we will resume at nine."

70

Keith Neff was recalled on July 16, when court resumed at 9:04 A.M. Neff talked Craig Stedman through one of the many charts—photographs of the neighborhood where the Roseboro family lived. For the few minutes he was on the stand, Neff's purpose was to explain what the jury would be looking at that morning, setting up the next several witnesses.

Jan Roseboro's neighbors.

And so in and out they came, ten of Michael and Jan Roseboro's neighbors, describing for the jury that not one of them had seen a prowler that night lurking in the shadows of the dark; and also that the neighborhood was not known for burglaries or strangers walking about. It was a quiet suburban Amish township. Peaceful. The same activity, day after day, night after night—the kind of redundant monotony that small-town life breeds. Nothing ever really happened out of the norm. Many of these people had dogs, they said, that would have barked if an outsider had been roaming through yards, hanging around the streets.

The last of the neighbors, a teenager who lived just down the street from the Roseboro house on Creek Road, said he actually saw Michael Roseboro the morning after the murder. It was near six-thirty. He had walked by the Roseboro house, poolside, down to the end of Creek Road, adding, "Well, I was walking by and I saw Michael Roseboro. He was around the side, and he was pacing up and down alongside the pool. It looked like he was *cleaning* the pool."

The witness said he didn't have the slightest idea of what had happened the previous night. He didn't know the Roseboro family that well.

Craig Stedman had him point to a map and describe exactly where he was walking that morning, and where he saw Roseboro.

After a few more questions, Stedman said he had nothing further.

Allan Sodomsky pointed out for the jury that they were not hearing the testimony of a man, as such, but a seventeen-year-old kid. With his questioning, Sodomsky seemed to suggest, by ending his cross with the question of the witness's age, that perhaps because of his age, what the witness had to say shouldn't be taken all that seriously.

Richard Pope came in next and gave a description of the landscape around the Roseboros' yard as if he were both a land surveyor and host of *Man vs. Wild*. Richard spared no detail. There was an organic sincerity about Richard Pope, a community native's viewpoint. It stood out. He was funny. At ease. Entirely believable. The way Richard saw it, there was not a chance someone had roamed onto the Roseboros' property that night through the woods.

After that, he talked about Jan Roseboro, calling her his landlord and his friend, noting how homey and unassuming she was.

"She struck me [as] a casual dresser. . . . I never noticed any jewelry. I'm not saying she never wore jewelry, but it seemed the way she dressed, she normally looked like she was a down dresser to me when she was home."

Sweats. T-shirts. Sneakers. Flip-flops. Bare feet.

Without realizing it, Richard humanized Jan Rose-boro, describing anyone, and everyone. She was the woman next door. Laid-back. Humble. Friendly. A kind-hearted person.

Allan Sodomsky questioned Richard about the jungle-like terrain around the Roseboros' house in the back. Not much came of it, other than Pope's rehashing and reaffirmation of what he had said already. You'd have to be wearing a bomb squad Kevlar suit to get through the brush and pricker bushes unscathed, Richard made clear.

Cassandra Evanick Pope was next. Cassie talked about that scream she heard, giving the trial its first real taste of high drama, with perhaps a vision of violence. Cassie came across as cute and cuddly, warm and innocent. She spoke with a slight country twang, same as her hus-band, and was there to tell the jury what she saw and heard, nothing more.

The payoff statement from Cassie came a few minutes into Craig Stedman's direct: "I heard a female scream from the back area," she said, "the pool area of the Roseboros."

There was a good chance everyone in that courtroom was picturing Michael Roseboro with his hands around his wife's neck.

"Was it loud?" Stedman pressed.

Cassie came back with the perfect response: "Loud enough for me to hear it in my living room."

"Were your windows open?"

"No."

Another collective gasp.

"Was it long?"

"No."

After that, was there really much more Cassie could offer?

Craig Stedman didn't think so.

It took Allan Sodomsky some time, but he eased his way into talking about the scream, at one point asking, "Am I correct, Mrs. Pope, that you told the police that you heard a scream, but you did not know where the scream came from, [that] it was very short, and it was a female's scream? Did you say that?"

"I don't recall saying that."

"Now, four days later, you had a chance to speak to the police again—is that correct?"

"Yes."

". . . And that time, *four* days later, did you know where the scream came from? Do you remember that?"

"Yes."

"Now, you didn't read the newspapers in those four days, did you, ma'am?"

"I don't believe so, no."

Sodomsky suggested with his next line of questioning that Jan Roseboro's death was a media event in Lancaster County. That many in the neighborhood were talking about it—some of them enjoying their "fifteen minutes" while being interviewed by local news stations. And this may have influenced what Cassie Pope had heard.

They talked about the interviews Cassie had given to police.

Concluding, Sodomsky made the inference that Cassie had no idea where the scream had come from *until* that second interview, four days later, *after* she had spoken to neighbors and saw various news reports of Jan's death.

Cassie disagreed. Never backing down from her testimony.

It would be up to the jury to decide if Cassie was

remembering things correctly, because Sodomsky let it go there.

Corporal James Strosser, an eighteen-year PSP veteran, now a computer forensic specialist for the state police, testified about Angie Funk's and Michael Roseboro's computers, and how the PSP was able to locate all the e-mails. Strosser was no novice to the profession of computer forensics; he had been on the job for eleven years. In total, his team took a look at four computers.

Strosser explained how he had taken a duplicate image—an electronic photocopy, essentially—of the hard drives on each computer. An important fact Strosser made clear was the sheer volume of e-mails he had uncovered in Angie's deleted box that were *not* between her and Michael Roseboro.

"Two hundred and fifteen that were deleted between June 3 and August 4, 2008," Strosser told Kelly Sekula. None of these were from Michael Roseboro. None to Michael from Angie. In effect, Angie had "double deleted" all the e-mails between her and Michael. But left the others alone.

On the surface, this seemed sketchy. It was evidence of Angie hiding evidence of the relationship.

Or maybe evidence of something else.

Strosser said he was able to recover them, anyway, along with fragments of additional e-mails between the lovers.

Strosser was here to read a selection of those e-mails in their entirety. Sekula submitted over two hundred e-mails, a stack of paper about two inches thick. Nearly the entire correspondence between Angie Funk and Michael Roseboro, throughout the time of their affair. It was now in the hands of the jury. Every syrupy promise and electric line of purple prose. Every wish for marriage and desire to touch and feel and rub oil on each other. Every word of lust and obsession on Michael Roseboro's part.

All there in black and white.

While many of the more sexy and revealing e-mails were read into the record, the gallery flinching and embarrassed, whispering and cringing, Michael Roseboro seemed unaffected. It was like Strosser was talking about someone else. Keith Neff was sitting behind Craig Stedman and Kelly Sekula's table during proceedings (the lead detective in any murder case is allowed to sit in on the trial even though he is testifying). With stacked crates of documents towering above him, he watched the jury as Strosser read. Neff was looking for "glaring jurors," those who had an emotional response to the words Strosser read into the record.

And just about all did at some point.

"I was amazed that Mike could continue the charade of innocence after these were read," one person in the courtroom said later.

Not only did Michael Roseboro continue to act as though nothing was amiss as Corporal James Strosser read, but he tried to sell himself as the most industrious defendant ever. He flipped papers around, making it look as though he was busy and interested in something that was said. He kept whispering to Allan Sodomsky, shifting in his seat, giving the impression that he did not want to hear the content of the e-mails and perhaps disagreed with some of what was being said.

It was all an act.

Strosser had finished only with the month of June, and the hour had come for recess until the following day. There was still the month of July left to read.

The judge warned the jury not to discuss the case.

Courtroom 12 closed its July 16, 2009, session at 4:47 P.M.

71

James Strosser concluded his testimony after reading another broad selection of e-mails from the month of July, leading jurors up to Jan Roseboro's murder. It was almost painful for some to sit and listen to this e-chat back and forth between Michael and Angie as the date of Jan's death grew closer with each e-mail that the state cop read. Jan was staring down the barrel of death, and her husband was writing to his lover that he never believed for a moment he would "ever, ever want to go horseback riding." Or how passionately one kiss from Angie could "arouse" him so much. Walking hand in hand along the beach. Not being able to live without her. And yet, in all of the correspondence Strosser read, not once did Michael Roseboro suggest that he had a plan to divorce his wife.

Why was this? the state had intoned.

Because his plan was to kill her, instead.

It was a pathetic display of a man's obsessive emotions—one that jurors would find all at once appalling and cold. Sitting, watching jurors, anyone in the courtroom could see that the men and women chosen to decide Roseboro's fate were nauseated by how he so blatantly had disgraced his nineteen-year marriage.

The defense's cross of Corporal James Strosser was brief. The idea was to ask Strosser a few questions about his craft and shift the focus of the testimony *away* from the content of those now-devastating e-mails. Better to lick your wounds on this one and allow the state to move on.

It was near two o'clock on the afternoon of July 17, 2009, when the jury got to hear from the state's next witness, Peter Savage Jr., a county detective working for Craig Stedman's office, who had helped Keith Neff, Larry Martin, and Jan Walters at various stages of the investigation and, in addition, inspect the computers. Savage had almost thirty years of law enforcement experience. A true pro.

Throughout the afternoon, Kelly Sekula had Savage reiterate what James Strosser had testified to earlier. Savage explained, however, how they also conducted searches on the four computers for "key words," such as "drowning," "pool," "Clorox," "strangle," "murder," "suffocation," and other words relating to Michael Roseboro and Angie Funk possibly talking about Jan's murder and/or Michael and/or Angie searching the Internet for any of these terms.

"And am I correct, based upon your forensic examination of . . . those computers, nothing of any value was a result of those [search] terms?" Allan Sodomsky's co-counsel, Jay Nigrini, asked Savage near the end of his cross-examination.

"Nothing of any value came up with those," Savage admitted.

The next five witnesses—all friends and neighbors of Mike and Jan's—came in one after the other and explained four important (albeit opinionated) factors for the state: One, Jan Roseboro had no enemies. Two, Michael Roseboro, during those days immediately following his wife's tragic, untimely death, was not overcome with grief, sorrow, or sadness. Three, Michael Roseboro either never mentioned Angie Funk or had lied about her and the role she played in his life, when faced with evidence of a connection to her. And four, Michael Roseboro never made a move to secure his house and showed no concern for himself or his children, which one could deduce a man whose wife had been murdered by a random killer probably would have done. In addition to all that, most of these witnesses made the claim that Roseboro had never said *anything* about jewelry being stolen from Jan's person or missing from the house.

Why, the jury members had to ask themselves as each witness testified, wasn't this man running around in a manic state of fear and confusion, crazy worried, crying over Jan's death? Why wasn't he asking himself and his friends, *Who could have killed my wife? Who could have done this to our family? Why haven't they caught her killer?*

The state's contention, in putting all of these witnesses on, was that Roseboro wasn't concerned or frightened, because *he* knew who had killed his wife.

The highlight of the following day's testimony, Monday, July 20, was when Francis Tobias, once said to be Michael Roseboro's best friend, took the stand.

Tobias had a wan look of concern about his face. He knew the information he was bringing into the trial had the potential to hurt his friend, and yet, at the same time, Tobias wanted nothing more than to tell the truth. He wasn't there to protect anyone. If anything, he was there to honor his friend Jan Roseboro and her memory by sharing the information. The previous Friday, Karen Tobias had talked about that letter Michael Roseboro had written to her and her husband in October 2008. The one in which Roseboro, pissing on the grave of his wife, accused Jan of having an affair.

The surprise Francis Tobias dropped, however, was how Michael Roseboro, after the police had told him Jan was murdered in a violent fashion, told the Tobiases that Jan had died accidentally. This was a slip on Michael's part, the state maintained. Michael didn't want friends to know Jan was murdered because they might point a finger at him.

Allan Sodomsky didn't have much, other than having Tobias disagree that he said, "Mike was in shock all night" after Jan's death. What Francis Tobias had said, he clarified, was ". . . Mike appeared to be in a state of shock and drained."

The next major witness—whose testimony would draw gasps from the otherwise hushed gallery—was Karen Wagner, a research nurse from the Regional Gastroenterology Associates of Lancaster.

Wagner said she had been asked to look at records her office kept for July 22, 2008, the day of Jan Roseboro's murder, which also happened to be the day Michael and Angie met and had sex inside that Mount Joy apartment. Roseboro had told police (and all of his friends and family) he was at a doctor's appointment all afternoon taking a medical test.

The research nurse explained that Roseboro's appointment was scheduled for 1:30 P.M. He was there to participate in a study the office had been conducting. Roseboro signed the office consent form for the study at 1:07 P.M. At 1:20 P.M., according to her notes, Wagner drew a tube of his blood.

"By one-thirty," she concluded, "he should have been finished."

"Okay. Thank you," Stedman said.

Michael Roseboro was not at the doctor's office all afternoon, as he had explained to police (covering up that time he spent having sex with Angie). He was at the doctor's office for about twenty minutes.

The remainder of the day was filled with testimony from Larry Martin, who discussed the phone records and how the ECTPD was able to obtain warrants for all the phone numbers connected to the case and what they had uncovered; Keith Neff, who once again introduced several exhibits; and Larry Miller, a forensic officer with the ECTPD. Miller had taken many of the photos that Craig Stedman and Kelly Sekula introduced: the tiki torches, the dusk-to-dawn light and wiring; Jan's cell phone on the bottom of the pool, next to her glasses.

As Larry Miller finished testifying, the day ended.

As the gallery left the courtroom, word buzzing in the halls was that the state's next witness would be explosive.

No, not Angie Funk. She was still waiting in the wings—in hiding, more like it. But her husband, Randall, was up next.

What would the other man at the center of this affair have to say? Would he trash his wife and her lover? Did Randall know anything about the crime?

72

Randall Funk had an amorphous way about him. He was everyman: that guy you passed ten times a day and did not notice. Simple. Sincere. Friendly. Very much likable. The hell this man had been through over the past year was something no one could deny him. He was a victim, too—one more on Michael Roseboro's growing list. His wife's name and moral character had been attacked from all sides, perhaps rightly so. He, himself, had been viewed as a pushover, having stayed with her, helping her to raise her bastard child. The comment sections on the local public Internet forums had been brutal on Randall Funk.

Entirely merciless.

Angie Funk's husband took the stand and stared at Roseboro, who sat diagonally across from him. Randall was not happy to be where the state had placed him. This was clear in his tense gaze. Randall, a project manager for a building supply company, had a straitlaced, professional look about him. In one photo, he sports a spotty salt-and-pepper beard, which had not fully come in, eyeglasses, a smile.

Everyman.

Craig Stedman called in Randall Funk to alibi Angie.

As much as Stedman needed to prove that Michael Roseboro committed the murder, he had to demonstrate to the jury that everyone else had been eliminated, especially Angie.

The slim, owlish man first told the jury who his wife was and how many kids they had together—a six- and four-year-old—which made his role in the saga seem all the more tragic and heartbreaking.

"And am I also correct," Stedman asked after talking Randall through his vitals, "that you were unaware that your wife was having any type of affair prior to the murder of Jan Roseboro?"

"That's correct."

From there, Stedman had Randall tell the jury that his wife was at home on the night of July 22, 2008, but that he had gone to bed at nine, read for a half hour, watched his wife come into the bedroom, change into her pajamas, then retreat back down the stairs.

"And did she come up to bed at some point?"

"Yes, sir, she did."

"About what time would that have been?"

"Between ten and eleven."

Stedman made a point to have Randall Funk say that he had witnessed no injuries or scratches on his wife in the days following Jan Roseboro's murder. And cleared up any confusion the defense might bring into the record regarding Angie having any relatives or siblings involved in wedding planning or wedding vow renewal.

Allan Sodomsky, not moving from where he sat, said, "Good morning, Mr. Funk," after Stedman finished his questioning. "I have nothing further, Your Honor."

Smart move. Beating up on the mistress's husband was not going to get Sodomsky anywhere.

Randall Funk walked out of the courtroom, literally passing his wife in the hallway, as Angie Funk, arguably the star of the show, made her way toward the witness stand.

* * *

Michael Roseboro's son was nearly four months old as the boy's mother sauntered with the excitement and cockiness of a peacock into the courtroom—her head held high, some said, a look of resolve on her face—and took her seat in the witness stand. Angie was thirty-nine years old. She still had that short, boyish haircut, embarrassed smile, and prideful manner about her. She was attractive in a subtle, girl-next-door sort of way—a librarian without her glasses. You could see the Mennonite influence on Angie in the way she dressed, carried herself, and the accent she spoke with.

After asking Angie to tell the jury where she worked, for how long, and how old her two children with Randall were, Stedman asked Angie about "the other child."

"Matthew," she said.

"What's his full name?"

"Matthew Francis Alan Rudy."

A mouthful.

Being prompted by Craig Stedman, Angie talked about where she lived in relation to the Roseboro Funeral Home, how long ("five years") she had known Roseboro before the affair, and how she and her girlfriend would "make jokes" about Michael Roseboro and getting together with him, as if he were some sort of wizard who could make all her dreams come true.

The tension between prosecutor and witness was taut and obvious. There was an air of a showdown in the room. Sarcasm on both sides. Angie talked about when they met, how they met, and how Roseboro made that call on May 29, 2008, asking her to lunch.

The beginning of the end.

After that, she said, they met up just about every workday at the Turkey Hill convenience store for morning coffee.

As Stedman pried into the relationship and how it

progressed, Angie became that same person he and his investigators had pulled out their hair over while interviewing. Getting her to extrapolate on anything, or add to the information presented, was impossible. *I don't remember* and *I don't recall* became Angie's favorite phrases to lean on when she didn't want to go any further into a subject. As in, "How many times," Stedman asked, "would you say you stopped at the funeral home between June and July?"

"Oh," Angie stated, "I couldn't tell you. I don't know."

Stedman pressed, almost trying to walk her through a response, his voice getting louder as his patience waned. "The best estimate you can give. Are we talking about *two* times? Are we talking about *twenty* times?"

"I don't know," Angie said. Then she paused. Thought about it: "Maybe five. I don't know."

They discussed the first time she and Roseboro said they loved each other. Angie admitted Michael said it ("probably") right before they had sex for the first time. The way she made it sound, he said it right before entering her.

After that, Angie talked about Roseboro bringing up the notion of marriage. She said at the time of all this matrimony talk and the hot sex they were having, her marriage to Randall Funk was "very poor."

Of course, it was.

As the afternoon progressed, Craig Stedman carefully coached Angie Funk down into the pipe dream that had become her extramarital relationship with Michael Roseboro. During her time on the stand, Angie rarely looked at her former lover. She stayed focused on Stedman and the questions, often staring down at her lap, even though she did her best to dodge the subjects that made her most uncomfortable. From all indications, Angie told the truth, as she saw it. She wasn't there to support the prosecution and she wasn't there to help Michael. Mainly, Angie Funk wanted to clarify what had happened between her and Michael Roseboro and, at the risk of using a cliché, set the record straight. (According to several law enforcement sources, in their shared opinion, Angie Funk was holding back. She knew more.)

Stedman had his witness talk through several phone calls, most of which Angie said she could not recall. The prosecutor introduced charts and graphs to show the jury how many times the two lovebirds communicated, the results of which were staggering to look at on paper: between thirty and forty—sometimes more, almost never less—calls per day between them, not counting the e-mails and text messages. Most of the calls were generated by Roseboro, who appeared to be entirely absorbed by and obsessed with this woman and could not speak to her enough.

One intense exchange between the DA and the mistress centered on the day of the murder. Stedman, in having Angie talk the jury through that day, was able to paint a picture of Michael's mind-set in the hours leading up to Jan Roseboro's murder. He had not spent the afternoon at the doctor's, that was one lie he told police. Instead, Stedman wanted to point out, Roseboro had spent the afternoon with Angie.

"You had sex with him on the afternoon of the murder, right?"

"Yes."

"Did you see any scratches on his face?"

"No."

"What did he [ultimately] say about the scratches on his face?" Stedman questioned.

"He said his youngest daughter did it while they were playing in the pool."

"That night?"

"Yes."

"And that came up because you asked him about it?" the attorney asked.

"Right."

"What other things do you remember talking to him about this case?"

Angie thought about the question. "If he had prior affairs," she answered.

"Did you ask him about that?"

"Yes."

"And what did he say?"

"He said no."

Stedman had already submitted several stipulations, which Roseboro had signed, proving these additional affairs.

In turn, Angie said, Roseboro had lied to her. One of many, apparently.

Angie told the jury that Roseboro never mentioned jewelry missing until a week *after* the murder, when he suddenly realized that $40,000 worth of necklaces and bracelets and rings had vanished.

She said he never expressed any "shock" that Jan had been murdered.

She said Roseboro told her women were stalking him and his family.

She said he mentioned how he wished she had never told the police about their affair.

She said Roseboro kissed her in the parking lot of the funeral home *after* the murder.

She said, between the time Jan was murdered and he was arrested, she didn't remember how many calls and text messages they exchanged.

So Stedman clarified those numbers: fifty-nine phone calls, 165 texts.

In just over a week.

Ouch.

There was some talk about the fragmentary e-mails that forensic computer investigators had pulled from their computers, but Angie could not recall any additional information other than what was found.

Shocking!

Not even in a fragment e-mail with the subject line "Our future."

Nothing.

Throughout the afternoon Stedman and Angie talked through the amount of lies Roseboro had told her and how (through the police) she found out he was lying. They discussed the baby. The promises Roseboro had made. Their dreams of marrying on a remote beach, with their children present. And the idea that Roseboro was concerned about losing everything to Jan, but had not once mentioned a plan for divorcing her. Only the cost of the end of the relationship.

Then they moved on to the phone calls from prison in April, just over three months ago.

Before he asked about the phone calls, Stedman tried to get Angie to admit that she still had feelings for Roseboro. "You don't—you don't really want to say anything up there that is going to help convict Mike Roseboro of murder, right?"

Stunning the packed courtroom, Angie said: "I'm not . . ." Then she stopped. Regrouped. Continued: "If he's guilty, then he's *guilty*. But if he's not, he's *not*. I'm not going to alter my conversation or testimony to benefit *anybody*."

"You loved him in July '08?"

"Yes."

"You loved him"—Stedman looked down at a yellow legal pad in front of him—"you *clearly* loved him in April '09, right?"

"Yeah. I'll always love him. But that doesn't mean I'm going to protect him in any way."

Angie Funk had found her groove.

"You love him right now, right?" Stedman asked, pushing harder.

"I'll always love him. He's the father of my son."

Michael Roseboro looked on, without emotion or reaction.

"And if he's found not guilty, you're going to be with him, right?"

"No."

"He's not in your future anymore?"

"No."

"You're in a loveless marriage right now, right?"

Sucker punch.

"For lack of a better word . . . *yeah!*"

"And I'm sorry to get into that, but we've got to get into it. And you love Mr. Roseboro, right?"

"Yes!"

They had been talking back and forth, getting louder with each question. Cutting each other off. The judge looked dismayed, about to lose his patience. At one point, a few questions later, Judge Cullen interrupted, saying, "This yelling back and forth makes it impossible for the jury to understand what anyone is saying. This is not a track meet. There is no benefit to speed. I want you to clearly understand that." He explained how he wanted the questioning to continue: wait until the other finishes.

They both answered, "Yes, sir."

Stedman was able to get Angie to admit that she and Roseboro had talked about a reunion (if he was acquitted) during those April prison calls. "You guys, I mean, you're saying you want him found not guilty because you're not giving up on 'us,' on you and him, right?"

"I have now."

"But not in April?"

"No."

"What changed?" Stedman wondered.

"I don't know. Change of heart." Angie looked down. Then up, directly at Stedman. "I don't *know.*"

Three or four questions later, "Have you truthfully told us all you know about the murder of Jan Roseboro?"

Angie did not hesitate: "Absolutely."

The jury heard tapes of the prison calls. The transcripts were ready for them to study. Stedman was stuck on those calls. He wasn't sure, simply because Angie sounded so unsure of herself, that Angie felt the way she insisted. He believed there were feelings between them, and a verdict of not guilty could spell a new beginning for the beleaguered couple. He referred to Angie's statement on the tape of her not wanting the prosecution to have anything on Michael Roseboro. It sounded so final, so unwavering, as if she'd never give up on her man.

Angie said what she had meant by that was how she didn't want Roseboro to say something on the phone he'd later regret.

"Like what?" Stedman pried.

"Just like—" She stopped, and looked down again at her hands.

"Just like what, Mrs. Funk?" the DA pressed.

"Just like 'I haven't given up on us.'"

"How would he regret *that*?"

"Because that's what you're using as a *motive*."

Tears might have begun to form in the ducts of Angie's eyes. The conversation was taking a turn toward an end—not in the testimony, but of the fairy tale.

Stedman asked again about the two of them being together *if* Roseboro was found not guilty.

Angie repeated that it wasn't an option any longer.

He asked again.

"No! I'm still married," she said.

"If you'd get a divorce, you could be together with him, right?"

Tears. "I could."

"I mean, your marriage is terrible, and you said that, right?"

"Yes."

"It's not like you're giving up something that's wonderful. You're living in a house with a husband you cheated on, and every day you [and Randall] have to see the baby of the man who you cheated with, right?"

More tears. Angie wasn't looking anywhere but down. That comment hurt like a burn. "Right . . . ," she finally admitted.

"I mean, you guys [Randall and Angie] aren't speaking to each other, other than about the children, right?"

"Pretty much," she said, collecting her composure.

"And you stayed with [Randall] for insurance purposes for the baby, right?"

"No!"

"That's not true?"

"No."

It was near 3:30 P.M. Stedman asked Angie a few more questions about the content of an e-mail (dated the day of Jan's death), in which she had said she and Roseboro weren't going to have to wait too much longer to be together. Angie said the statement was a mere coincidence and had nothing whatsoever to do with Jan's murder. She didn't know anything about the murder prior to it happening.

Craig Stedman asked if she was certain about that.

"Yes," Angie Funk answered.

The prosecutor said he had nothing further.

Allan Sodomsky shifted in his chair. The question one had to ask as Angie took a sip of water and prepared herself for Sodomsky: how was the defense attorney going to handle the state's motive for his client's guilt—with kid gloves or a jackhammer?

73

Allan Sodomsky had about an hour left to the day. Sixty minutes, the seasoned defense attorney knew, was more than enough time to get jurors thinking about Angie Funk's intentions for scoring herself a catch like Mr. Michael Roseboro—not to mention the role she had played in this horribly tragic drama.

Sodomsky made it clear from his first questions that he had not spoken to Angie in almost a year, besides questioning her at the preliminary hearing the previous fall. He told Angie how important it was for her to tell the truth, as if saying this implied she had good reason to lie.

They established off the bat that Michael had not once indicated to her in any form or fashion that he was planning (or going) to kill Jan Roseboro. He had never given Angie any indication, as a matter of fact, that Jan was going to become a problem he had to dispose of. And through this line of questioning, Sodomsky's point was well taken: although Angie and Michael had talked and e-mailed about getting married and being together for the rest of their lives, Roseboro had never referred to killing his wife as a means to that end.

Sodomsky asked Angie about her home life.

"I told my husband I would try to work it out with him," she said. Then, referring to the contrast of this statement outlined in that April phone call, Angie responded, "Well, I mean, I wasn't at *that* point of working it out with my husband *yet*, no."

"But now you *are* at point?"

"Yes." Angie started to cry again. Sodomsky offered tissues to her. "No," she said defiantly. "I'm okay."

Get this over. The sooner, the better.

"I believe you said on direct examination—I don't want to put words in your mouth—but you said 'he is not my future anymore,' when you were talking about Mr. Roseboro. Were those your words?"

"No, that was Mr. Stedman's words."

"Mr. Roseboro is *not* your future anymore in terms of a husband. Is that a fair statement?"

"Yes."

Sodomsky did his best to minimize the phone calls, trying to sell the jury, in the form of a question, that 1,400 calls over a seven-week period really weren't that numerous when one took into account how many hang-ups there would have been, how many times they said "hi" and "bye" quickly, or left messages on each other's voice mail.

Angie agreed.

Some in the courtroom wondered what in the world this guy was talking about. Fourteen hundred calls in forty-nine days was more than what most teenagers made, an exorbitant amount. Trying to downplay it—well, it simply made the calls stand out all that much more.

". . . Did you tell the police," Sodomsky asked Angie, "on July twenty-fourth, that a week or two before that date, Mike Roseboro said to you that he would be willing to give up the funeral home for you, if it came to that?"

"Yes."

"Is that the truth?"

"Yes."

"Is that what he said to you?"

"Yes."

Several questions later, "The two of you got fairly deeply sexually involved in thirty-nine days—fair statement?"

"Yes."

As the questioning went on throughout the latter part of the afternoon, the jury was already exhausted from a day's worth of testimony. Mostly, it was a "yes/no" back-and-forth tennis match that didn't shed too much light on anything that could help or hurt Roseboro. Angie verified that she loved Michael. She said she didn't know he was going to kill Jan—if he indeed did. She talked about their relationship being in a "dream stage" most of the time, as if it weren't real.

Craig Stedman objected a few times, asking the court if the questions were relevant. The judge told Sodomsky to continue, but to move things forward.

The jury looked tired, bored.

"Mrs. Funk, at any time, did you ever tell anyone, including the police, that Mr. Roseboro told you that July 22, 2008, was going to be significant because he was going to tell his wife about you?"

This was probably the most emphatic question of Sodomsky's entire cross-exam.

"No," Angie stated, clearly sick of answering questions.

From there, Sodomsky had Angie discuss how she and Roseboro had talked about leaving their spouses. Most of this had been covered already to a great degree. It was beyond redundant.

"Look," one legal professional in the courtroom told me later, "Sodomsky had his hands tied. What did he really have to work with?"

"Sodomsky is an excellent lawyer and has a tremendous courtroom presence, but had very little to work with in this case," Stedman explained. "The defendant was guilty, and the evidence was overwhelming."

True, Stedman had all but quashed the intruder theory with several of the neighbor witnesses, along with lengthy testimony about the lights being off and then Michael Roseboro claiming they were on. The only real defense Roseboro had left was to get up on the stand himself and claim he snapped—that it was an accident. Clinical narcissists, however, rarely cave and admit any culpability simply because they believe they're smarter than everyone else. It's all or nothing. In addition, Sodomsky had indicated in his voir dire questioning of potential jurors that Roseboro was not going to take the stand, somewhat showing his cards, when the lawyer asked potential jurors if they would be biased against a defendant who chose *not* to testify.

Sodomsky ended by going through several of the e-mails. Angie once more agreed that she had written them, making the point that she had never discussed (and neither had her lover) killing Jan in any of the e-mails.

The day was over.

Finally.

Wednesday, July 22, 2009, a year to the day that Jan Roseboro was murdered, began with a blast of hot and humid weather. Proceedings began promptly at 9:00 A.M. as Angie Funk was reminded that she was under oath.

As if she could forget.

The tone was different this morning. Allan Sodomsky started by having Angie talk about how ambivalent Michael Roseboro was regarding their affair being made public. He didn't care one way or the other, Angie suggested. He didn't express concern.

That was a reach. Angie had told police he did care.

Craig Stedman was eager to get another crack at Angie. The only thing that mattered, from where the prosecutor sat, was the content of those e-mails, not what Angie *thought* about Roseboro's demeanor or his *feelings* about telling Jan. Those e-mails portrayed a man who was fixated on a woman and would have done anything—including murder—to be with her. He had made that clear in just about every e-mail. This talk about *not* getting divorce attorneys and *not* taking real steps to end their marriages was significant: Roseboro was going to fix all that, Stedman wanted to clarify, by strangling and drowning his wife.

After a half hour or so, Sodomsky concluded.

Craig Stedman had that stack of e-mails sitting on the table in front of him. "Mr. Sodomsky," he said with passion, "asked you some questions yesterday about your communications with the defendant . . . and I think you ended up saying to him and agreeing with him . . . that they were 'lustful banter,' is that right?"

"Yeah."

Stedman held up the stack of e-mails. He told Angie Funk she could see them if she needed to refresh her memory.

"No!" Angie said, looking away.

"There's actually not a lot about sex in there. There's a few comments here and there, but there's not much in there about just lust and sex, is there?"

"I—I—I," Angie said, stumbling now, tired and dazed by all these questions, "I wanted it clean for work, so I didn't—yeah, there's not a whole lot about sex, no."

Stedman pointed out that Angie and Roseboro had made *specific* wedding plans.

"They were not specific," she said. "I mean, those were dreaming. . . ."

As Stedman's redirect continued, he sounded like he

was beating up on Angie by continually raising his voice
and calling her on many of the vague responses she had
given Allan Sodomsky.

Angie appeared to be ready to break down. She was
kept on the stand until 10:30 A.M., an hour and a half,
answering more questions from Sodomsky on recross,
before being cut loose. Sodomsky, in concluding his recross, apologized to Angie for having to put her through
such a taxing experience.

Craig Stedman brought in a few more neighbors to
expand on his "the lights were off" argument. Then
Sabine Panzer-Kaelin came in and schooled the jury
on DNA. It was time to get into that whole skin-under-
the-fingernails/scratches-on-Roseboro's-face part of
the saga.

Panzer-Kaelin clarified that the DNA found underneath Jan's three fingernails was, indeed, from her husband. All the technical mumbo jumbo she talked
about—explaining in detail the minutia involved in
DNA collecting and testing—led to one conclusion that
the jury was certain to grasp. In Panzer-Kaelin's per-
fectly crafted layman's way of talking about such complicated matters, it became obvious that Michael
Roseboro "donated" that DNA under the fingernails,
but there was no test available that would tell how it
got there.

That was a piece of the puzzle left up to Gary Frees to
explain.

Frees, a senior planner for a local concrete company,
had known Jan and Michael Roseboro about a year, he
said. Frees had driven Michael to the ECTPD on that
night of Jan's death. When they got to the station
house, Frees testified, he noticed something about his
friend.

"He was wiping his upper lip. Just . . . there was

oozing [of blood and pus] coming out of his upper lip. He was wiping that."

As Frees left the stand after cross, redirect, and recross, Judge James Cullen banged his gavel. It was 5:02 P.M.

Another day in the books.

74

It is, in the end, those subtle pieces of evidence that ultimately put the proverbial nail in the lying killer's coffin. You know, those "things" most killers never think of. It's generally not DNA, eyewitness testimony, or phone records that put a person away. No. Some of that helps, sure. But if killing is an art, then every brush-stroke one ponders and labors over must add to the picture, not contort it, or toss confusion into the psychology behind its meaning.

For example, on July 23, 2009, Craig Stedman brought in several witnesses to talk about what Michael Roseboro was wearing on the night he "found" his wife in the family pool. It was thought that Roseboro had been wearing the same swimming trunks he had said he swam in earlier that night.

If that was the case, Roseboro had gone to bed wearing wet swimming trunks.

No one would do that.

But this was something he probably overlooked when planning a way out of killing his wife.

Then, at one point, witnesses talked about Jan Roseboro's dogs. Jan loved her dogs, maybe even more than her philandering husband. Wherever Jan went outside on the Roseboro property, she generally had those dogs by her side, especially if she was out at the pool at night by herself.

Just so happened on the night of her murder, Jan's dogs had been caged in the basement of the house.

One had to ask, why? Or, better yet, by whom?

Then there were the kids. Besides Sam, who had left to go swimming with friends, the three other children—a thirteen-year-old among them—were in bed sleeping by 9:30 to 9:45 P.M. A thirteen-year-old during summer break sleeping by 9:45 P.M.? It seemed impossible. Neighbors had said the kids were awake—on most nights—until eleven or twelve. The family had just opened this new pool. More than that, the kids—all of them—slept through the entire episode until late the following morning. Dozens of people inside the house. The cops walking into their rooms at one point, and they were all out.

Cold.

Without saying it, or providing evidence, it was clear that the prosecution believed Roseboro had maybe slipped a few milliliters of Benadryl into the kids' late-night snacks.

Subtle evidence. It is part of every murder case. Here, Craig Stedman was convinced that the jury could come to only one conclusion based on all of this evidence.

Like the dawn-to-dusk light. How could anyone besides Michael Roseboro turn that light on or off?

It would be absurd to think anyone else killed Jan Roseboro.

And so that is how the next few days, save for the weekend in between, went in the *Commonwealth of Pennsylvania* v. *Michael Alan Roseboro:* for those sitting, day in and day out, watching the proceedings, it seemed as though the state won every round. Not one witness or statement had gone against them. Not one piece of evidence disputed or was out of place.

Ending the state's case on July 27, 2009, Stedman had

Dr. Wayne Ross talk about how Jan Roseboro died. Ross told his tale of pathology as Craig Stedman introduced graphic photographs, showing clearly how deep and brutal that gouge was on the back of Jan's shaved head. It was no accidental tap. Whatever caused that injury to the back of Jan's head had struck her with force and anger and violence.

Intruders, the insinuation was made clear, do not kill in this manner.

Ross brought a sense of authenticity to the trial, a true realization that Jan had been murdered in a fit of aggression and rage. This trial was no longer about an affair. It was now focused on murder—the victim no longer a headline in the newspapers, but a homicide victim on a slab of steel being dissected like an eighth-grade biology experiment.

At one point, Ross talked about drowning, saying, "It is a *good* way to hide murder."

Then, in a dramatic turn of events, Dr. Ross stood in front of the jury box as Detective Keith Neff got up from his seat and walked toward him. Ross then put Neff into a choke hold like the one he believed Jan's killer had used in order to demonstrate how, "like a vise, or nutcracker," Jan's killer squeezed her unconscious. Neff knew this hold from his jiujitsu experience. There were two or three jurors, Neff said, whom he looked at while under the choke hold, who became emotional watching the display.

"I was not aware we were going to do the demo," Neff recalled. "So it caught me by surprise. The choke hold is common in jiujitsu, and I have been put in it many times. I never thought I would end up on the receiving end of this choke in open court, in front of a jury."

After a long morning of medical testimony, wrapped around that one striking moment of Dr. Wayne Ross and Keith Neff acting out the murder, and Allan Sodomsky then trying to trip the doctor up on anything he could manage (to no avail), Stedman introduced a litany of photographs and additional pieces of evidence.

Then the DA stood.

"Judge," Craig Stedman said, "with that, the commonwealth rests."

75

Jay Nigrini, Allan Sodomsky's co-counsel, called Dr. Neil Allan Hoffman first. Hoffman was there to dispute how Jan Roseboro had died, and certainly had the credentials to argue an alternative theory. Hoffman had acquired his medical degree in 1967, the year Michael Roseboro was born. He was a pathologist at Reading Hospital. He had conducted over three thousand autopsies.

Hoffman had done a second autopsy on Jan Roseboro's body. In doing so, he had come to, basically, the same conclusion (strangulation and drowning), agreeing with Dr. Wayne Ross on the cause, but disagreeing on how Jan had gotten her injuries.

Jan's injuries, he said, "were caused by blunt impact to the head. By that, I mean either the head hit a blunt object or a blunt object hit the head, and there were multiple impacts"—and here came the major difference in opinions—"not necessarily all from the same source, or at the same time."

The point was then made that Jan could have fallen or been pushed into the water. Hoffman mentioned that some of the injuries could have been "preexisting."

Nigrini's direct was brief. No need to bore the jury, or

tire them any more than necessary; the trial was beginning to get long and tedious.

Craig Stedman had the doctor talk about who hired him (Allan Sodomsky) and how much his services had cost the defendant.

"Twenty-five hundred, I believe," Dr. Hoffman said.

"And are you getting three hundred and fifty dollars an hour today?"

"Yes."

Stedman thought about that a moment. After calculating, he said, "So you've made over two thousand dollars sitting here today?"

"Perhaps, yes."

"And I guess the longer I keep talking, the more you keep making. Is that right?"

The doctor didn't answer.

Stedman, having made his point, moved on.

He ripped apart, medical report by medical report, every possible aspect of Dr. Neil Hoffman's argument, leaving the jury to draw one conclusion: This guy was being paid to have a different opinion, which, when the facts were further explained, wasn't all that much different from what the state's medical examiner had uncovered. Jan Roseboro was murdered violently and died in that water, still breathing.

Allan Sodomsky called Zach Martin, one of Sam Roseboro's friends, who was with Sam on July 22, 2008.

Zach testified that nothing seemed out of whack when he saw Mr. and Mrs. Roseboro by the pool. They seemed happy. They seemed at ease. Just an old married couple enjoying a night out at the pool.

Craig Stedman smartly focused on one item during

his cross-examination, asking Zach, "You didn't see any scratches on the face of Mr. Roseboro during the period of time that you were there, did you, sir?"

"No."

A few more questions and Zach Martin was excused.

Jay Nigrini called Scott Eelman, the state's forensic examiner. Nigrini was concerned about two hairs found by the pool that the state police's forensic lab had refused to test.

Eelman explained that the hairs were found on the coping of the pool, and the lab refused to test them.

On cross, Eelman explained why.

There were no roots in the hairs. Testing them would be fruitless, a waste of taxpayer money.

Talk inside the courthouse as Michael Roseboro's defense put on witnesses the following day, July 28, 2009, a Tuesday, was *When is this thing going to end?* There was not a chance Roseboro would be acquitted. Save for a stranger, walking into the courtroom, who proclaimed his guilt, Roseboro was finished.

Allan Sodomsky called Brandi Walls. She was as nervous as a child sitting outside the principal's office. Sodomsky told Brandi to take a deep breath and relax.

Brandi had been a fire hall volunteer at the time Jan Roseboro was murdered. She was on the Roseboro property that night. Not yet eighteen years old, she was in training, and knew the Roseboro family.

The young woman told the jury that all the lights were on when she arrived, including the tiki torches. She said the time was 11:05 P.M. when she got there, just minutes after Michael Roseboro had phoned 911. She said Roseboro was "slightly calm," and became much more stable after Sam arrived.

At one point, Brandi said she believed Michael was wearing "boxer length–type shorts." And so, with that, Brandi's presence had been established: she was there to toss out the claim that Roseboro was wearing his swimsuit, as nearly everyone else had testified.

When Craig Stedman questioned Brandi, she admitted she wasn't sure if Roseboro was wearing boxers, shorts, or a swimsuit. She just didn't know.

If this was all Roseboro had up his sleeve, he had better hope for that stranger to show up right about now; because a wet swimsuit was the least of his problems heading into the homestretch of this trial.

LCDA's Office detective David Odenwalt took a seat in the witness stand next. Allan Sodomsky tried to get Odenwalt to admit he screwed up a report detailing that scream Cassandra Pope said she heard on the night Jan Roseboro was murdered. Odenwalt never backed down from what he reported. He had created a facsimile of what Cassie had told him.

Craig Stedman had Odenwalt reiterate this point.

Michael Roseboro's defense called three more witnesses, then rested. It wasn't even three o'clock yet. Still plenty of time left in the day.

The judge recessed until the following morning.

On Wednesday, July 29, 2009, court resumed. The judge announced that closing arguments were about to begin.

Allan Sodomsky went first.

Within the first two minutes, Sodomsky said "reasonable doubt" eight times, hammering home his point that if jurors had *one* qualm of uncertainty, they would have to acquit.

"Let's talk a minute about the *lie*," Sodomsky said. "Let's talk for a moment about the *big* lie. And I do not mean that facetiously. . . . Mr. Roseboro, Michael Roseboro, lied, and he cheated. But . . . he only lied about cheating."

Craig Stedman smiled.

"I'm not asking you to go over there and pat him on the back and say, 'It's okay, don't worry about it,'" Sodomsky continued. "Because it's a disgrace. It's a disgrace when you lie. It's a disgrace when you lie, and, of course, when you lie about cheating—it's even worse. But it isn't cheating and lying, I guess, unless you lie about the cheating. And that's what you have."

Sodomsky toned down the swimsuit angle, arguing plaid versus patterns of colors that witnesses had described, asking if they were truly certain about what they had seen?

He said Michael's daughter most certainly scratched his face in the pool that afternoon while they were playing basketball—only problem with this was that everyone else had disagreed, and Michael Roseboro was having sex all afternoon with Angie. He was not swimming with his kids.

He talked about how Michael was comforting and consoling everyone during those first few days after Jan's death, which was why he never had a chance to grieve himself. He was in work mode, being the skilled undertaker even when it was his wife lying in the morgue awaiting preparation for cremation.

"Ladies and gentlemen, Michael Roseboro is a funeral director. Guess what he does for a living? He comforts and consoles others."

The worst thing a defense attorney can do is carry on and on during his closing when the trial that jurors

have witnessed is leaning the way of the prosecution.
There's a pleading, begging quality to the argument,
turning jurors away. Not to say Sodomsky could not
fight for his client—and, boy, did he ever; the outcome
here would not be a reflection on the quality of defense
or the expert trial lawyer Sodomsky was and will always
be—and a jury needed to understand that and be patient. But there comes a time when an attorney must
consider that less is more. Sodomsky kept referring
back to the state not proving motive. He did this,
mainly, by mentioning Angie Funk as little as possible.
(That lust Roseboro had for this woman. It overpowered
him. Overtook his emotions. He was going to do anything to make it work and not lose all he had worked
for. This had been clear throughout the trial. Not addressing the subject was an insult to the intelligence
of jurors.)

When he finally did talk about Angie, Sodomsky said
he couldn't make sense out of a dream and lust turning
a guy into a murderer.

"Six sexual rendezvous, thirty-nine days, ladies and
gentlemen, and for *that*"—he raised his voice and then
paused—"you orphan your children?"

No mention of the baby. Or that beach wedding with
flowing gowns and the sun and surf and wind in their
hair. Or of the fact that Roseboro was communicating
with Angie, on some days, hundreds of times.

Sodomsky finished his closing where he started:
reasonable doubt. It was stamped, he suggested, all over
this case. Anywhere you looked. Questions unan-
swered. Evidence missing. A lot of he said/she said,
lights on/lights off nonsense. None of it amounted to a
man killing his wife as their children slept mere feet
away inside the house. There is only *speculation* as to
what occurred between that witching hour, ten to eleven,
Sodomsky asserted.

"There is no *reason*, ladies and gentlemen. There is no *reason*. That's your reasonable doubt."

Allan Sodomsky's closing had eaten up most of the morning session.

Court would resume, the judge said, at one o'clock.

76

Craig Stedman had listened open-mindedly to Allan Sodomsky's closing. The DA had even agreed with Sodomsky on one major point. Sodomsky had told the jury during his closing that it made little sense for a killer to "stop the carotid neck hold" once he had gotten his victim into it. That theory, proven by both doctors, flew in the face of common sense. Reasonably speaking, a random killer would have grabbed Jan by the neck and choked her to death, tossing her limp (dead) body into the pool, before stealing that jewelry Michael Roseboro had claimed went missing.

Thus, in effect, Stedman believed, Sodomsky had argued for the state's case in bringing up this idea. Addressing the jury early into his closing, Stedman said, "It makes no sense for a random killer to stop the carotid neck hold once you've got your victim in that. It makes absolutely *no* sense!"

Then the prosecutor sketched out the scene for jurors.

"You're a random killer. You're there to kill her. You do kill her. You've got her in a position where she's unconscious . . . keeping [the choke hold] going until she is dead. Absolutely. [Mr. Sodomsky] is *absolutely* right! It makes no sense for a random killer to *stop* once he's got her in that position."

Then the drumroll and cymbal crash. . . . "But it *does* make sense," Stedman said, raising his voice, "for *one* person to stop the carotid neck hold. *This* person," he said thunderously, pointing to Roseboro. "You know why? Because he wants to make it *look* like an accident. You've got to stop the . . . neck hold before she dies so you can get her in the pool so she can gulp in water. If you kill her before—if you kill her *before* you put her in the pool . . . there's no water in her lungs. There's no drowning. There's no accident." He paused and lowered his voice. "You don't get away with murder."

Stedman went on to explain how Roseboro had gone to great lengths to make the murder appear to be an accident—but failed.

Then Stedman laid out his case, point by point, noting that Roseboro's DNA underneath his wife's fingernails and the scratches on Roseboro's face told a story all by itself.

Whatever you want to call it, Stedman said, the writing was not on the wall. It was written all over Michael Roseboro's demeanor and behavior, beginning with the 911 call, and following into those ten days after Jan Roseboro's murder as he told one lie after the next, then had the audacity to write a letter saying Jan had had an affair.

This was all nothing more than a desperate man grasping for a lifeline.

One important factor Stedman brought up was that Roseboro had been expecting a phone bill days after Jan was murdered. The bill was $688 and some change. Jan did the household finances. She was going to see that bill and know her husband had been stepping out on her once again. Thus, the phone bill, that talk of marrying Angie and being with her all the time, along with his compulsive desire for the woman, had backed him into a corner. The time had come. He was going to lose everything, or so he feared. Sprinkle a bit of mania and a bastard child on that situation and you have a recipe for murder.

Stedman spent two hours outlining his case. In the end, he told jurors, "You've got a *mountain* of evidence. . . . Find him guilty of murder in the first degree, not because *I* say so," he said, pointing at himself, "but because the *evidence* says so."

It was 3:26 P.M.

The judge released the jury for the day. He wanted everyone back first thing in the morning, when deliberations were set to begin.

The following day, July 30, 2009, Judge James Cullen gave instructions to the eight women and four men of the jury.

By 9:53 A.M., Michael Roseboro's fate was in their hands.

77

"There's nothing else I could have done," Craig Stedman recalled. He was addressing co-counsel Kelly Sekula as they waited for the jury. "No matter what the verdict is, we gave it all."

Sekula agreed.

"I felt like we were going to win," Stedman said, adding later, "Despite all Angie did . . . she did one fundamentally huge thing Mr. Roseboro did not. She admitted the affair right from the start." He paused. "While [Roseboro] lied to everyone."

Stedman retreated to his office. He wanted to be alone.

An hour into deliberations, the jury asked to hear the 911 tape.

When Stedman heard about the request, he felt a sense of relief. That 911 tape was a crucial piece of evidence. So important to Stedman, he had planned on playing it during his closing; but at the last minute, he decided not to, for fear of running too long.

The jury got to hear it again, anyway.

Yes!

So everyone piled back into the courtroom. As the tape was played for the jury this second time, Stedman and Sekula could see some of the jurors counting along with the compressions the 911 operator had instructed Roseboro to perform on Jan's chest. Thirty was the number the operator had told Roseboro.

"One, two, three . . ." Some jurors were counting along under their breath.

Michael Roseboro whipped up some "faux tears," said one person in the courtroom, and got louder and more animated, shuffling papers around and sniffling, when he felt the jury wasn't watching him. It was so strange that Roseboro had cried in court listening to the tape, and yet had not shed one tear during the call itself.

But when the compression count (by jurors) stopped at about ten, and some jurors realized Roseboro had come nowhere near thirty (but had told the 911 operator he had), there were sighs and raised eyebrows by those jurors. Roseboro had never done the compressions— it was obvious when listening to the tape that he was lying to the 911 operator.

Unstated evidence once again poking its head back into proceedings.

Lunch hour came, and the jury hadn't indicated it was ready.

Patience.

Detective Keith Neff was upstairs in the DA's office, sitting around, fidgeting, wondering when the jury was going to come back. At one point, he got up and walked down the corridor to Detective Jan Walters's office, which is in the same building, on the same floor, as the DA's office.

Near 2:30 P.M., Larry Martin poked his head into Walters's office doorway as Neff and Walters were yapping.

"The jury's back."

Neff recalled later that a "jolt of adrenaline" shot through him. "I had gone over to talk with Jan several times during the trial," Neff remembered. "Jan is such a calm presence and talking to him always seemed to get me on point." There were others, Neff said respectfully, who were mere balls of stress, and Neff didn't want to absorb any of it. So he stayed away from them. "After being told the verdict was in, I felt like we all had to rush down to the courtroom, when we really had plenty of time."

During the elevator ride downstairs, there was no conversation. Everyone was numb. All that work had come down to this: a human decision. Most law enforcement can tell you that juries can go either way. It's when you think you have one in the bag that you're slapped with a dose of reality and the jury acquits. Strange things happen during deliberations. One holdout and a verdict is in jeopardy.

The courtroom was filled more than usual. Standing room only. And many took advantage of any empty space.

The jury walked in and the foreman handed the verdict to the bailiff, who then walked it over to the judge.

Judge James Cullen read the verdict to himself, nodded, then folded the piece of paper back in half.

The bailiff took the verdict slip and returned it to the jury.

The jury forewoman stood and read the verdict at 2:47 P.M.

"'Guilty.'"

Everyone let out a deep breath.

Jurors were polled individually and each stated that one word Michael Roseboro did not want to hear.

The convicted murderer showed no reaction.

"I really believe it took me weeks to totally recover," Keith Neff later said. "My wife told me she felt the same way. Afterward, she told me I had been preoccupied that entire year. She understood why, but there was no one more glad it was over than her. I'm sure I was hard to live with. My wife was very supportive of me and took care of the home front. I was so glad to be back with my family."

"There was no way," Craig Stedman concluded, "I expected to hear *not* guilty at the time the jury came back. They came back so fast. Going into the case, I thought the worst we could do would have been a hung jury."

Michael Roseboro did not, at any time, respond to the verdict, but his mother, Ann Roseboro, had "an extreme reaction," said one trial watcher, obviously swept away with dread and fear for a son whom she still believed in.

78

Michael Roseboro was in lockup. A report claimed he was on "suicide watch," but that was an overstatement, taken out of context. Like anyone else convicted of murder, Roseboro was in the facility's medical housing unit undergoing observation and evaluation to see how he was handling the jury's verdict. Lancaster County Prison warden Vincent Guarini confirmed to the local press that Roseboro was "moved to the unit" on Friday, July 31, but he called the move what it was: "a precaution."

Guarini told one reporter, "There's been no behavioral change. When someone gets a life or murder conviction, we'll look at the prisoner and make sure he's okay."

When he got out of the psych unit and was placed into the general population, trolling around Lancaster County Prison one afternoon, waiting for his sentencing date, Roseboro was approached by an inmate.

"Why you in here?" the guy asked.

"I killed my wife," Roseboro said in jest, as if the guy didn't know who he was. Heck, Roseboro's face had been plastered all over the front pages of the local papers, guilty written across it. He was a quasi celebrity.

Acting shocked by the statement, the guy repeated, "You killed your wife, man?" He said it more as a question.

He was likely referring to Roseboro's unwavering determination all throughout the trial that he was innocent.

"What do you think?" Roseboro asked.

The guy thought about it. "I think you did it."

Roseboro shook his head. Nodded yes. And, according to multiple sources, Michael Roseboro then said, "Yeah, I did it," finally admitting to murdering his wife.

79

Michael Roseboro might have thought he caught a break a week after the verdict. A local newspaper broke a story that had the potential to turn things around for the embattled murderer. There was light, hope on Roseboro's part for a second wind.

The *Intelligencer Journal/Lancaster New Era* reported shortly after the verdict that two jurors, Nick Keene and Michael Hecker, did not necessarily enjoy the time they spent on the jury during Roseboro's murder trial. They had often been vocal about it on Facebook.

Before, during, and after the trial, the newspaper uncovered, both jurors had "facebooked" friends regarding their feelings. They had complained to Facebook friends that they were, for one, picked for the jury; and two, the trial had dragged along.

Yea, it blows, nineteen-year-old Nick Keene wrote in one Facebook post that June, before jury selection concluded. **Three [f-ing] weeks.** If the trial went that long, Keene continued, he'd have all of **two weeks until school starts.**

Then on July 27, the start of what turned out to be the final week of the trial, Michael Hecker, somewhat older than Keene, wrote that he was **hoping this will be the last week of court.**

That comment, posted at 7:24 A.M., close to two hours before court started, wasn't so bad. It was the answers the comment elicited that stunned many later, and perhaps raised some concern that Keene and Hecker had stepped over the line and failed to follow the judge's order not to talk about the case.

Ha, one friend posted in reaction to Hecker's line.

Fry him, another friend answered.

Why were you in court? asked another.

I'm a juror on a 1st degree murder trial, Hecker responded to his friends that night, well after court had ended for the day. He then explained how he had been on the jury for the last three weeks, saying how unfortunate it was and how he couldn't wait till I can share my thoughts on it.

A friend encouraged Hecker to stop in at work sometime and share. . . .

There was no indication if Hecker ever did.

On the day Stedman rested the state's case, at 5:53 P.M., Hecker posted this gem: THANK GOD, before explaining how the case had been dragging on and on.

The ethical question about all this banter wasn't if these jurors had done anything wrong. They did not discuss the content of the case, evidence, witnesses, or Michael Roseboro himself. Basically, they were venting, same as you might at the local diner or post office, about being a juror.

Still, did these jurors disregard the judge's instructions? Did they maintain their integrity as jurists?

Allan Sodomsky didn't think they had. In fact, he believed Michael Roseboro deserved a new trial based on this revelation.

On August 3, 2009, Judge James Cullen asked for a conference call with both attorneys to discuss what had been brought to light.

"In our opinion," Craig Stedman told reporters, "there's nothing there." The DA explained that while the jurors in question talked about their feelings, they did not talk about facts. "A person on Facebook, that's their way of coming home and blowing off steam," he added. "Whereas, before you would do it at the dinner table and talking to people."

After the conference call, Stedman was confident the issue had been resolved, saying, "The judge had the power to schedule a hearing if he felt he needed to, in this case. He didn't do that. You can draw your own conclusion."

It wouldn't end there, however.

But first, regardless of what was going on with the Facebook allegations, the judge needed to impose a sentence on Michael Roseboro.

The sentencing was a mere formality. On September 25, 2009, Roseboro received a mandatory life sentence without parole. He could appeal, of course, which Allan Sodomsky was actually working on already. But for now, Roseboro was slated to spend the rest of his life in a maximum-security facility upstate, far away from family and friends.

"What stands out to me is the selfishness and senselessness of this crime," Craig Stedman told the court. ". . . This murder should *not* have happened. We should not be here. . . . Mr. Roseboro had opportunities most people do not have and can only dream of. But he wanted it all."

Sodomsky asked the judge if Roseboro could be held at Lancaster County Prison for the next ten days so he could work with him on the appeal.

Judge James Cullen said he would allow it. Then he ordered Roseboro to pay $25,000 in restitution for what the judge called "necessary counseling for your children," none of whom attended the sentencing.

In early October, after Allan Sodomsky had a chance to review all of the Facebook comments, he filed a motion in Lancaster County court claiming "juror misconduct."

The judge ordered Craig Stedman's office to respond.

"This motion is yet another attempt by this murderer," Stedman said, lashing out at Roseboro, as he talked to the press, "to try and avoid responsibility for cowardly killing his wife."

Sodomsky ignored the comments and decided to dig into the law. He demanded a hearing on the matter. He wanted to see both jurors brought into court and placed under oath, so they could answer questions about what Sodomsky referred to as "unauthorized communications." The law, Sodomsky wrote, entitles Michael Roseboro to a hearing to *determine whether there were communications between jurors and outsiders about the trial, and whether they prejudiced the verdict.*

A fact-finding mission was all Sodomsky was after.

In that same motion, Sodomsky pointed out: *The juror, Hecker, who was clearly disgruntled, bored, and eager to see a speedy end to the trial and to jury deliberations, was advised by a "friend"—who had reason to know the details of the prosecution's case due to media coverage of the trial—that Hecker "should just vote guilty and get it over with" and that he should "fry him."*

Perhaps the defense lawyer had a point?

This was a gray area, predominantly. Social networking was not something courts had had to deal with all that much in the past. Yet, the future was looking to be something different.

Sodomsky wrote in his motion that he wanted to examine cell phones, computers, hard drives, Facebook accounts, e-mail, and Internet accounts of the two jurors.

A clear invasion of privacy.

Stedman countered by saying that "nothing in the alleged Facebook communications," from what he had read, "remotely approaches grounds for relief. . . . In the copies of the alleged communications we were provided with," the DA continued, "no juror discusses the facts of the case." To the contrary, one juror, Hecker, had even noted that he could not wait for the case to end so he could finally discuss it.

Obviously, the judge would have to take some time and decide if Michael Roseboro deserved a new trial or, at the least, a hearing.

80

The Amish are not immune to the attraction of American culture and its pull. On December 8, 2009, the PSP arrested an Amish man on charges of drunk driving after he was found "asleep in his moving buggy." The twenty-two-year-old was slumped over and passed out, horses pulling him and the slow-moving buggy along the road. *An off-duty officer from nearby,* one report stated, noticed the horse *pulling the buggy at a walking pace as it straddled the center line.* Ultimately, the Amish man blew a Breathalyzer test of 0.18, which is more than twice the 0.08 legal limit. This incident, perhaps, proved that rural Pennsylvania, with its rolling hills and plush green landscapes, a nod to life one hundred years ago, was not immune to modernism. In the same way that the Roseboro case had proven that a violent murderer can reside next door—a man disguised as a mild-mannered husband and father, smiling and waving to you as you go about your day—an Amish man arrested and charged with drunk driving (a horse and buggy) was a clear indication that times had changed. In that respect, a court had to consider that jurors would forever be attached to their electronics. Unless you sequestered them and stripped them of all their gadgets, you ran the risk of a juror "tweeting" or "facebooking" his or her feelings.

On Friday, January 29, 2010, Michael Roseboro's chances for a new trial or hearing based on juror misconduct were wiped clear. Judge James Cullen had taken his time, almost three months. In the end, Cullen denied the convicted killer's request for a new trial, and said a hearing was unnecessary.

Cullen's opinion was twenty-one pages long. Part of it spoke directly to the heart of the matter: *While regrettable and contrary to the Court's instructions, and the unsolicited comments of others, [the comments] are woefully insufficient to taint the unanimous verdict of the jury,* adding that the jury had *heard testimony from sixty-five witnesses and viewed over 700 exhibits over the course of twelve days of testimony. . . . The Court concludes that there is no reasonable possibility that any of the status updates or comments resulted in any prejudice to the Defendant.* The motion for appeal itself, Judge Cullen maintained, slapping Roseboro personally, *failed to show that there is any reason to believe, beyond his hopes or imagination, that there is anything more to this issue than what appears on the available Facebook webpages.*

In making his practical, candid opinion clearly heard, Judge Cullen compared the remarks the jurors made on Facebook to a person standing "outside the courthouse." Those direct comments, Cullen wrote, *such as "fry him" or "vote guilty,"* were nothing more than protesters standing around the steps of the courthouse shouting at jurors as they entered and exited the building.

Although Judge Cullen didn't agree those Facebook remarks made a difference in the scope of Roseboro's case, courts all over the country were beginning to recognize that technology was going to be a problem for judges in the future if the issue wasn't addressed. On January 28, 2010, a day before Cullen issued his opinion, the Judicial Conference of the United States, the policy-making body

of the federal courts, released a memo, offering a new
juror instruction model for federal courts across the country, asking federal judges to explain to jurors, in part: *You
may not communicate with anyone about the case on your cell-
phone, through e-mail, Blackberry, iPhone, text messaging, or on
Twitter, through any blog or website, through any Internet chat
room, or by way of any other social networking websites, including
Facebook, MySpace, LinkedIn and YouTube.*

State courts were a different matter, however. There
have been no nationwide instructions issued for state
courts, simply because each state assumes and asserts its
own set of jury instructions to the courts in its counties.

Michael Roseboro could take his appeal all the way
to the Supreme Court, if he chose to. The Constitution
gave him that right. But the fact of the matter remained:
Michael Roseboro was going to serve the rest of his life
in the State Correctional Institution (SCI)-Mahanoy in
Frackville, Schuylkill County, Pennsylvania, for murdering his wife, as he himself had admitted in front of a few
of his fellow inmates after the verdict. He took a mother
away from her four children because he didn't want to
face up to his responsibilities and admit he was a coward
and cheater, afraid he would lose everything.

A self-proclaimed God-fearing man, Roseboro had allowed two of the Seven Deadly Sins to control his life: greed
and lust. From there, he broke several of the Ten Commandments, the foremost being "thou shall not murder."

All because he didn't want to give up his luxurious life.

In the end, though, Michael Roseboro lost all of it,
anyway—including the woman (and their child) he had
supposedly killed for.

EPILOGUE

The Roseboro family, just before Michael's appeal was denied, sold the funeral home to Stradling Funeral Homes, a competitor and larger business based in Ephrata, Pennsylvania. Then Ann and Ralph Roseboro sold the house on Walnut Street, just down the block from their new grandchild and the Roseboro Funeral Home, and purchased a spacious lot in the same neighborhood as their daughter and her husband.

The former Roseboro Funeral Home will now be called Roseboro Stradling Funeral and Cremation Services.

A Roseboro family legacy has come to an end.

At the time of this writing, Angie and Randall Funk are still married. Angie is seen walking Roseboro's baby around town.

Jan Roseboro's minor children live with her sister, Suzie, in the same home they grew up in. Sam lives with his paternal grandmother and grandfather.

I am told by good sources that Michael Roseboro has been asked to give up on his fight for retrial, save that money, and provide for his children and their caretaker. As of this writing, I have not heard of any monetary agreement Roseboro has made that would support his children. He continues, instead, a cry of innocence and will, one assumes, exhaust any money he has ever made to more appeals, leaving his kids nothing.

I reached out to Angie Funk (twice), Michael Roseboro (twice), the Roseboro family members (several times), and Allan Sodomsky (three times), but none of these people decided to speak to me for whatever reason. All of them did, however, speak to *48 Hours*.

In truth, though, what could they have said that might have changed the *facts* of this case?

ACKNOWLEDGMENTS

It takes a lot of people to produce a book. For me, I need to have the cooperation of key players in any case before I commit. In the Roseboro case, I had some reservations early on that there was not a big enough story for me to explore. My editor, Michaela Hamilton, was excited about this case from the get-go, and I appreciated her encouragement. The locals I spoke to early in the process informed me that there was a much larger story here, that I shouldn't be fooled by the narrowness of some of the media's coverage. And sure enough, the more that I looked into the matter, the more I realized that Jan Roseboro's murder and the affair Michael Roseboro had with Angie Funk were the results of a deeper, more serious criminal mind.

Michael Roseboro comes across as a husband and father, the kind of neighborhood guy you'd think was the last person on earth to be a murderer. That, however, is what makes him more dangerous than a guy waving a gun around and threatening people.

Of course, I had at least a dozen sources who chose to remain anonymous. I applaud each and every one of them for coming forward and standing up to Roseboro and Funk and speaking their truth. They changed the outcome of this book.

I appreciate that Craig Stedman was always honest and open with me about the case. I appreciate all of his and Kelly Sekula's help. I can become quite the pest and bother people about the tiniest detail—the smallest, seemingly inconsequential fact—and I know multiple e-mails per day become burdensome. But in the end, all those small facts help me to produce a book that my readers expect. Thus, I cannot thank Stedman and his investigators enough for taking the time (and having the patience) to put up with me.

I despise lists of any kind. But I can think of no other way to thank those who should be acknowledged for their hard work in this case, some of whom helped me out considerably: First ADA Christopher Larsen, ADA Andrew Gonzalez, Melissa Kurtz, Deanna Weaver, Tammy Weeks, Chief County Detective Michael Landis, Jan Walters, Dean Miller, David Odenwalt, Joe Geesey, William Chalfant, Dennis Arnold, Joanne Resh, Joseph Hockley, Heather Smith, Sergeant Larry Martin, Larry Miller, Lynn Martin, Brian Dilliplaine, Gail Sizer, Michael Firestone, David Fisher, Steve Savage, Darrick Keppley, Kerry Sweigart, and, of course, Detective Keith Neff, who went far above and beyond what I ever expected to make sure I got most of it right. Other law enforcement who participated in the investigation should be recognized: John Schofield, Brad Ortenzi, Graeme Quinn, Lieutenant Edward Tobin, Eric Zimmerman, Jonathan Heisse, Matthew Hinkle, and Corporal Robert Courtright and Trooper Chadwick Roberts. Also, PSP corporal James Strosser, Pete Savage, Scott Eelman, Preston Gentzler, Sergeant Eric Schmidt, Steve Tori, and Steve Gochenaur. There were also a few law enforcement departments involved: Ocean City, New Jersey, Police Department, ECTPD, and PSP, and all three should be recognized.

The crew behind the Phelps machine: my business manager, Peter Miller, Adrianne Rosado, and Natalie Horbachevsky, all of whom reside at PMA Literary & Film Management, Inc. Without their constant help and encouragement, I could not continue to do what I do. They mean the world to me.

Michaela Hamilton, Richard Ember, Laurie Perkin, and Doug Mendini, from Kensington Publishing, have been behind me for a long time. They deserve my gratitude and thanks.

My readers . . . God bless all of you. Thank you for returning, book after book. I hope I never disappoint. I am grateful for your continued support.

My family.

I also want to thank Elena Siviero, who runs the M. William Phelps Fan Club on FaceBook. I know it takes time to do those things and I greatly appreciate Elena volunteering on my behalf. Please sign up on the fan club, if you have not done so already: *www.facebook.com/!/group.php?gid=527520016144.*

Enjoy this exclusive preview of M. William Phelps's next exciting true-crime release!

Too Young to Kill

They befriended her . . . then strangled, burned, and dismembered her. . . .

M. William Phelps

Coming next from Pinnacle . . .
Turn the page now and prepare for
Too Young to Kill !

1

Joanne Reynolds pulled into her driveway on Seventh Street in East Moline, Illinois, near 4:00 P.M., on January 21, 2005. As she did every late afternoon after arriving home from her shift at the local Hy-Vee supermarket, Joanne got out of her car, checked the mail, then headed into the house. Inside, she tossed her keys on the kitchen counter and started down the hallway toward the bathroom to freshen up. Joanne's husband, Tony, had just gotten home himself, right behind her. Joanne and Tony had a good life here in the QC, Quad Cities. Located in the Mid-Mississippi Valley, the towns of Moline, East Moline, and Rock Island, Illinois, along with Bettendorf and Davenport, Iowa, housed some four hundred thousand residents making up the QC, an imaginary state line through the Mississippi River that split the east and west sides of the quad in half. We're talking Middle America here. Small-town. John Deere's world headquarters is located in Moline.

Pure Americana.

Tony and Joanne were high-school friends who lost touch for twenty years and met again later in life. Theirs was a rough road to love. Tony had done some time in prison, been married once. Joanne was divorced, too.

Her two adult boys—twins—lived with her and Tony, along with their wives and a baby, and Tony's adopted daughter, Adrienne. No, not the perfect, textbook family, scripted on the pages of *Functional Life* magazine. But they loved one another and got along. When the statistics said it shouldn't, the Reynolds' blended family, like so many in America today, worked.

From the late-afternoon twilight, as the sun did its lazy dance over Mark Twain's Mississippi, located approximately three miles north of Joanne and Tony's modest, ranch-style home, Joanne had been thinking about Adrienne, Tony's sixteen-year-old daughter. "Lil' Bit" was what they called Adrienne. She was the pride and joy of Tony Reynolds, a man Adrienne had called "Dad" all her life. Adrienne had moved in with Tony and Joanne in October 2004. This, after a spell of living in the Reynolds' East Moline home a year prior. That first time Adrienne had come to live with Joanne and Tony did not go so well. Adrienne and Joanne disagreed. Fought like cats. Stopped talking for days at a clip. Tony was constantly stressed, he said. A truck driver, he was always on the road, leaving Joanne to deal with the bulk of teen angst that Adrienne threw at them.

"I want her out," Joanne had said probably more times than she wanted to recall, back when Adrienne lived in the house the first time. Later, Joanne admitted that she was scared for her two boys. Adrienne had made an "accusation" against her stepfather in Texas, recanted, then made the accusation again. Joanne was concerned that she might do the same with one of her boys.

But ever since Adrienne had been back, she and Joanne—although not skipping stones together, or taking sunset walks along the mighty Mississippi—had reached an impasse and decided to get along. Joanne and Adrienne had a scheduled session with a therapist on that Friday afternoon, January 21, a follow up to a session the previous Friday, which, according to Joanne, "went very well."

In truth, they had reconciled.

When Joanne walked past Adrienne's room on her way to the bathroom, she noticed Adrienne's work garments laid out.

Odd, Joanne thought, stopping, staring. *She should be at work.*

From there, Joanne took a quick peek around the house. Nothing had been touched. She had asked Adrienne to empty the dishwasher and do a few additional chores. Adrienne had always done what she was told to, as far as her chores went. But Joanne was quickly succumbing to the *opposite* of one of those feelings you get when you know someone has been inside your house. In fact, she felt no one had been home all day long. Which was strange.

"Tony?" Joanne yelled. Tony was glad to be home— a Friday night, especially—from his truck-driving shift. Ten hours on the road wreaked havoc on his back. Tony needed some rest.

"Yeah?" Tony answered.

Joanne knew Adrienne had to work that night. "I woke her up this morning," she told Tony. "She told me she had to be in at five."

"Ain't dat right," Tony said in a heavy drawl.

They both peered into Adrienne's room. There, on the floor in front of them, was Adrienne's work uniform. The room was a mess—as most teenagers feel that cleaning is one of those "things" that can wait until later on in life.

"Yeah, she said five." Joanne was certain.

"She done went to work without her uniform?" Tony asked, more to himself than Joanne. He looked at his watch. It was close to five. Adrienne should have been home to get dressed and head out to work, maybe one of them for a ride.

Joanne spotted Adrienne's work shoes on the floor. She'd never go to work without them. Moreover, Adrienne Reynolds was not a teen who blew off her shift. She loved the job at Checkers, a nearby fast-food joint. It was easy. Very little stress. Plus, it put a little pocket money in her purse. She generally got home from school at noon. Adrienne was in a special GED program at the Blackhawk College Outreach Center nearby, on the Avenue of the Cities. High school had been something Adrienne, to put it mildly, despised. So much so, she had not accumulated any credits to graduate—heading toward the end of her sophomore year—and would need to step it up in order to get her GED. The outreach center program fit Adrienne's school work ethic, her attitude toward education in general. No homework. Everything you did, you completed at school. You got out by noon. This allowed a people person, like Adrienne, lots of time for socializing, which was something the young girl had put at the top of her "to do" list every morning.

"Adrienne," an old friend said, "wanted to be liked. She loved to have friends."

Slightly concerned, Joanne called a few family members and friends, while Tony went about his daily routine, undeterred by Adrienne's uniform lying there on the floor. Who knew—maybe she had two uniforms? Perhaps she didn't have to work, after all.

"I was not the least bit worried," Tony later said. "Not then."

Adrienne had been making lots of friends since moving into town. She was always hanging out with someone. One of her favorite places these days was the teen center at the YMCA. And, of course, the local mall.

Ten minutes went by. Joanne made several additional calls. "No one's heard from her," Joanne told Tony. Joanne didn't like the feeling she had in saying those words. Something was wrong. She could sense it.

Gut instinct.

"Let's take a ride to Checkers," Tony suggested.

It would be a journey opening up a mystery that would end with the most gruesome, sinister set of circumstances and murder that East Moline has ever experienced—with a group of teens, their leader a young girl no one seemed to know much about, at the center.

ABOUT THE AUTHOR

Crime expert, television personality, lecturer, and investigative journalist M. William Phelps is the national best-selling, award-winning author of fifteen nonfiction books, all of which are still in print. Winner of the 2008 New England Book Festival Award for *I'll Be Watching You,* Phelps has appeared on CBS's *Early Show,* truTV, the Discovery Channel, Fox News Channel, ABC's *Good Morning America,* The Learning Channel, Biography Channel, History Channel, *Montel Williams,* Investigative Discovery, *Geraldo At Large,* USA Radio Network, Catholic Radio, ABC News Radio, and Radio America, which calls him "the nation's leading authority on the mind of the female murderer." Phelps has been profiled in such noted publications as *Writer's Digest, New York Daily News, Newsday, Albany Times-Union, Hartford Courant, Forensic Nursing,* and *New York Post.* He has also consulted for the Showtime cable-television series *Dexter.* And has been a recurrent, featured guest on ID's hit show *Deadly Women.* Phelps lives in a small Connecticut farming community and can be reached at his author website, www.mwilliamphelps.com.